Michael Logue and the Catholic Church in Ireland, 1879–1925

Manchester University Press

Michael Logue and the Catholic Church in Ireland, 1879–1925

JOHN PRIVILEGE

Manchester
University Press

Manchester and New York

distributed in the United States exclusively by Palgrave Macmillan

Published by Manchester University Press
Oxford Road, Manchester M13 9NR, UK
and Room 400, 175 Fifth Avenue, New York, NY 10010, USA
www.manchesteruniversitypress.co.uk

Distributed in the United States exclusively by
Palgrave Macmillan, 175 Fifth Avenue, New York,
NY 10010, USA

Distributed in Canada exclusively by
UBC Press, University of British Columbia, 2029 West Mall,
Vancouver, BC, Canada V6T 1Z2

British Library Cataloguing-in-Publication Data
A catalogue record for this book is available from the British Library

Library of Congress Cataloging-in-Publication Data applied for

ISBN   978 0 7190 7735 7   *hardback*

First published 2009

18 17 16 15 14 13 12 11 10 09   10 9 8 7 6 5 4 3 2 1

Typeset in Minion
by Servis Filmsetting Ltd, Stockport, Cheshire
Printed in Great Britain
by the MPG Books Group

This book is dedicated to the memory of my mother, Eileen Privilege, an extraordinary woman who always said I should.

Contents

Preface

Michael Logue remains Ireland's longest-serving Catholic primate. He joined the hierarchy as Bishop of Raphoe in 1879 and was appointed Primate of All Ireland and Archbishop of Armagh in 1887. In 1893 Pope Leo XIII elevated him to the Sacred College of Cardinals, the first Primate of All Ireland to receive the honour. His tenure spanned a period of intense political and social change. He was a bishop during the Land War and primate during the Plan of Campaign. He presided over the Irish hierarchy during the Parnell crisis and the failure of two home rule bills. Away from national politics, he played a prominent and integral part in the Church's long-running campaign for a university for Catholics in Ireland and also faced the challenges posed by the scientific revolution of the nineteenth century. Logue officiated through the reunification of the Irish party at the turn of the century, its eventual collapse and the rise of militant nationalism. He steered the Irish Church through the First World War and Ireland's descent into violent conflict from 1916 and witnessed the creation of two separate Irish states.

Historians, however, have rather ignored Logue and he has consistently failed to figure prominently in the histories of the period. To a certain extent he has been eclipsed as a subject for study by the other great ecclesiastical figures of Thomas William Croke and William Walsh. Logue was not as confrontational or politically adventurous as Croke. He did not, as Walsh did, bequeath a voluminous catalogue of books and pamphlets on the political and social questions of the day. Nevertheless, Michael Logue was the spiritual leader of a generation of Irish men and women. His was a powerful and constant voice; and this book will consider his role, and that of the Catholic Church, in the political and social changes of the period.

Acknowledgements

Historical research is often a solitary business but no one ever completes a piece of work alone. I am indebted, once again, to Professor Keith Jeffery, for his seemingly endless patience, attention to detail and infectious passion for history. Sincere thanks also to Professor Greta Jones for her invaluable wisdom and guidance. Thanks are also due to Professor Vincent Comerford of St Patrick's NUI, Maynooth.

This work would not have been completed without the archivists and custodians of the various Catholic archives I have visited. I would therefore like to gratefully acknowledge the unselfish cooperation of the following: Crónán Ó Doibhlin, Joe and all the staff at the Ó Fiaich Library in Armagh; David Sheehy, late of the Dublin Diocesan Archive; Monsignor Albert McDonnell, Vice-Rector, and all the staff at the Irish College in Rome; Matthew Tobin at the Limerick Diocesan Archive and John Silke PhD at the Raphoe Diocesan Archive. I would also like to offer my thanks to the staff at the National Library of Ireland, PRONI, The National Archives at Kew, the library of the University of Ulster, and the library of Queen's University, Belfast; to Elaine Pordes and the staff at the British Library, and to Maria Castrillo and the staff at the National Library of Scotland. Thank you also to Alison Welsby and Emma Brennan at Manchester University Press.

Sincere thanks go also to Dr Robert Jordan for the invaluable Latin refresher course at QUB and to the Very Rev. Daniel Whyte PP, VF for some translations. I am indebted to the Department of Employment and Learning and to the University of Ulster for financial assistance. I am also indebted to Dr Allan Blackstock of the Academy for Irish Cultural Heritages for all his help; and to Dr Sean O'Connell, Dr Fearghal McGarry and Professor David Hayton at QUB. Thank you also to my colleagues at UU, Catherine Switzer, Chris Manson, Susan Kelly, Terry Daly and Colin Cousins; and to my good and constant friends, Lesley-Anne Black and

Claire Peterson. Thanks also to Paul Burns and Madelaine Murray at belfastbookshop.com and to my Dad, James Privilege. Lastly I owe a huge debt of gratitude to my wife, Clare, whom I love very much, for never losing faith that what I was doing was the right thing.

Abbreviations

Abbreviations used in the text

AOH	Ancient Order of Hibernians
BAAS	British Association for the Advancement of Science
BEF	British Expeditionary Force
DORA	Defence of the Realm Act
GHQ	General Headquarters
GOC	General Officer Commanding
GOIA	Government of Ireland Act
INL	Irish Nation League
IRA	Irish Republican Army
IRB	Irish Republican Brotherhood
RIC	Royal Irish Constabulary
ROIA	Restoration of Order in Ireland Act
RUC	Royal Ulster Constabulary
UIL	United Irish League
UVF	Ulster Volunteer Force

Abbreviations used in footnotes

ADA	Armagh Diocesan Archive
AICR	Archives of the Irish College, Rome
BL	British Library
CAB	Cabinet
DDA	Dublin Diocesan Archive
ICD	*Irish Catholic Directory*
IER	*Irish Ecclesiastical Record*
LDA	Limerick Diocesan Archive
NLI	National Library of Ireland

NLS   National Library of Scotland
RDA   Raphoe Diocesan Archive
TNA   The National Archives, Kew
WC   War Cabinet

1

Bright as an angel

Much of what we know about Logue's early life and career can be found in the loose-leaf typed and handwritten pages of an unpublished biography compiled by Patrick Toner, former Professor of Theology at Maynooth and co-founder of the *Irish Theological Quarterly*. The work was commissioned by Logue's successor as Archbishop of Armagh, Patrick O'Donnell, and was intended to provide a hagiography of the late cardinal, though it was never completed. Most of the information is apocryphal, the result of a public appeal by Toner for letters, anecdotes and stories regarding Logue, and thus much of it remains unverifiable. Despite its brevity and the nature of the material, nevertheless, Toner's work does shed some light on the early life and career of Michael Logue. There is little in it to suggest the kind of man he would become or the stellar career he would, in Logue's own opinion, rather endure than enjoy. However, Toner's biography, written as it is in the slightly lachrymose and elegising fashion of a work intended for popular consumption by the faithful, represents a useful starting point to examine the life of Ireland's longest-serving primate.

Michael Logue was born on 1 October 1840 in Kilmacrenan, County Donegal. His father, a smallholder and innkeeper was originally from Carrigart and it was there that he would spend some of his early years. Logue was enrolled in the local school under the tutelage of Charles Carr where he excelled in his studies, particularly mathematics. But his parents were dissatisfied with the standard of education there and he was transferred to a private school in Kilmacrenan. The Robertson Academy was nominally a Protestant school but it accepted Catholics. It also taught the classics which Logue's parents thought essential if, as they seemed determined to ensure, their boy was to become a priest.[1] He maintained a high academic performance and was transferred to a boarding school in Buncrana in preparation for the Maynooth entrance exam in 1857. Logue took the test a year early at the age of seventeen. Despite being the youngest candidate, he achieved first place and was accepted into the seminary. The result was by no means certain as parents of other boys argued that he should be disqualified because of his age. However, the priest in charge of the panel, Daniel McGettigan, intervened on Logue's behalf and the result was allowed to stand.[2] The encounter was fortuitous. McGettigan had just been named as Bishop of Raphoe and he saw great potential in Logue who, as time went by, became something of a protégé.

Logue's ecclesiastical career got off to a shaky start. He returned a poor academic performance in his first year at Maynooth and was reprimanded before the Seminary Council for fighting.[3] His performance improved and he began to excel in the fields of dogmatic theology and scripture to the extent that he was given classes in theology to teach. In 1865, Logue enrolled early in the Dunboyne course, a series of postgraduate classes requiring the submission of a treatise in theology in competition for a prize. In addition to this he was studying for ordination and had begun to feel under pressure. He told McGettigan in April 1865, 'I feel my health rapidly giving way under the continued strain, being obliged to overwork myself during the day and in consequence passing [a] great part of the night sleepless'.[4] The relationship between Logue and his bishop had developed into a close one. McGettigan received regular reports on all his students at Maynooth but paid particular attention to Logue. The bishop remarked, not unkindly, that 'young Logue is as ugly as sin but bright as an angel'.[5] Toner has stated that early in his career Logue was self-conscious over his physical appearance to such an extent that he found it difficult to make friends and was reluctant to speak in public.[6]

Regardless of his own self-image, Logue had McGettigan's confidence. In 1866 he was encouraged to apply for a position teaching theology in the Irish College in Paris by the rector of the Dunboyne course, James O'Hanlan. He was appointed on McGettigan's recommendation and ordained on the way to Paris in a private ceremony by the Bishop of Pamiers, Guy Alouvry, on 22 December. The Rector of the Irish College, James Lynch, was impressed with McGettigan's recommendation. In October he thanked the bishop for his 'exceeding great kindness', in allowing Logue to come to Paris, 'and to give our national college the benefit of his excellent character, his extensive knowledge and distinguished talents'.[7] Toner believed that Logue might have become one of Ireland's foremost theologians had he not joined the hierarchy.[8] His rapid rise from seminarian to teacher suggests that Logue was certainly not lacking in talent or ability in the field of theology. Indeed, he won the Dunboyne course prize. He settled well into life in Paris, enjoying 'the esteem of students and superiors of the college'. He also frequented the state functions thrown by Napoleon III and rubbed shoulders with ennobled Irish exiles such as Count Nugent and Viscount O'Neill de Tyrone.[9] This comfortable obscurity was broken on 3 April 1870 when Logue published a treatise in *Le Monde* on the burning issue of Papal Infallibility.

Logue had been ordained at a time of great crisis for the Papacy and the European Church. Since the middle of the nineteenth century the shifting political landscape of Europe had diminished the temporal authority of the Pope. Papal lands in Italy were being swallowed up by nationalists in the *Risorgimento* and the Pope, Pius IX, was dependent on foreign troops to defend the remaining Vatican territory. In Catholic countries across Europe ecclesiastical appointments were handed out as court patronage, while the hierarchies in Protestant countries, including Ireland, were very much left to their own devices. Duffy has suggested that such was the lack of deference for the Papacy in Europe that most states 'wanted to reduce the Pope to a ceremonial figurehead'.[10]

In order to reiterate the centralised ecclesiastical authority of the Holy See, Pius convened the First Vatican Council in December 1869. The move to concentrate power, including authority over Church appointments to Rome, was a controversial one. Many hierarchies across Europe were reluctant to relinquish their independence and this was especially true of the French Church. As a response to the challenges facing the temporal authority of the Pope, it was proposed to recognise formally his status as the mouth of God on earth and declare him infallible.

The idea of Papal Infallibility divided the European Church and the debate was fought with great passion in the pages of the press and ecclesiastical journals.[11] Logue intervened in a dispute between Victor Cardinal Deschamps, Archbishop of Namur, and René Alexander Dupanloup, Bishop of Orléans, over whether Infallibility was opportune at this moment for the Church or even possible to define. Dupanloup, a renowned theologian, published an article in *Le Monde* in March 1870 in which he argued that the weight of Catholic theology precluded a definition of Infallibility. Moreover, he furnished a list of over fifty Catholic writers whom he said upheld this view. Logue's rebuttal took the form of a fourteen-page examination of Dupanloup's position. Rather than attack the bishop directly, he presented a meticulous critique of every theologian cited in the bishop's article, arguing that none of them precluded Infallibility. He concluded respectfully that Dupanloup had based his arguments on dubious and contradictory sources.[12]

Logue's article may have been submitted as part of some kind of collective declaration for Pius on the part of the Irish College. It was also entirely possible that he did not compile his treatise alone.[13] Nevertheless, it remained a clever and telling defence of the temporal and spiritual authority of the Pope and bore the signature of Michael Logue. This defence was symptomatic of his deep reverence and respect for the person and office of the supreme pontiff, a trait that would remain throughout his life.

On 18 July 1871 the Vatican Council voted to elevate the status of the Pope and declare him infallible in matters of faith and doctrine. Further proceedings, however, were interrupted by the outbreak of the Franco-Prussian War. In Protestant countries across Europe the doctrine of Papal Infallibility was denounced. In Prussia, for example, Bismarck launched his *Kulturkampf* against German Catholics. Bishops and priests were imprisoned and by 1876, more than a million Catholics had been barred by the Prussian Government from receiving the sacraments.[14] In Britain, William Gladstone denounced the moral and mental submission now demanded of Catholics by an infallible Pope. Moreover, he questioned the ability of Catholics to remain loyal to the state, given the deference now owed to Rome.[15] The Franco-Prussian War signalled the collapse of the temporal power of the Papacy. As French troops left to defend Paris, papal lands were swallowed up in Italian unification. The Pope became a virtual prisoner inside the tiny limits of the Vatican City.

Logue, who had left France along with the rest of the Irish College staff, returned to Paris at the end of the war where he remained for three apparently uneventful years. During his time spent in Ireland, however, Daniel McGettigan had been appointed primate and translated to the see of Armagh. His successor in Raphoe, James McDevitt, obtained a papal doctorate for Logue, presumably on account of his bold and erudite performance during the Infallibility debate.[16] In 1874 Logue applied for a vacant chair in theology in Maynooth. There were two other candidates for the position, Father John Mahoney of Cork, and Thomas Carr of Tuam. On a majority vote of the trustees, the post was offered to Carr.[17] Logue was prepared to return to Paris but McDevitt persuaded him to take up a pastoral position in the diocese of Raphoe and he was appointed as curate in the parish of Glenswilly near Letterkenny.[18] Although Toner was not explicit on the subject, it is reasonable to assume that Logue's superiors believed that such a move would benefit his ecclesiastical training. He appeared to settle well into parish life and in later years would recall his experiences in Glenswilly with fondness. In 1926 the parish priest there,

James Walker, told Toner that 'no priest could be more deservedly loved than Doctor Logue was when he was serving as curate in Glenswilly. He worked day and night for the spiritual and temporal welfare of the people.'[19] He remained in Donegal until 1876 when he applied for the vacant chair in Irish at Maynooth.

Logue was a proficient Irish speaker and he was appointed to the post. In addition he was also given the deanship of the seminary and the pressure of both posts weighed heavily on him. He resolved to return to Paris but was appointed to the chair of first-year theology on 27 June 1878. The following year, however, the see of Raphoe became vacant with the death of James McDevitt and McGettigan put Logue's name forward for the *terna*. Prior to the reform of canon law in the 1920s, bishops were appointed following an election conducted among the parish priests of the diocese. The result was ratified in Rome on receipt of confirmation of the result. Towards the end of a prelate's career it was customary to hold an election to nominate a successor, or coadjutor, to ensure a smooth transition from one administration to the next.

Before the election, however, the Logue family was caught up in the murder of the Earl of Leitrim, William Clements, who was bludgeoned and shot to death on 2 April 1878. The earl's driver and clerk, Charles Buchanan and William Makin, were also killed in the attack as they drove past Cratla Wood near Millford in Donegal.[20] Leitrim was a vociferous and litigious opponent of land reform with a propensity for evicting his tenants and the murders were blamed on agrarian extremists.[21] At the inquest, Logue's father (Michael Senior), who had been the driver of a second carriage in the earl's party, was praised for his actions in restraining the valet from intervening in the attack and thereby saving his life.[22] In the *Northern Whig*, Michael Senior was identified as the father of Professor Logue of Maynooth, but the controversy did not alter McGettigan's determination to have Logue stand in the *terna* for Raphoe. In truth, there was no real scandal as there had been no suggestion in the press that Logue's father was complicit in the attack. The primate's choice to succeed McDevitt had been made known before the *terna* in February 1879 and Logue won eighteen out of twenty of the votes of the priests in the diocese.[23]

He resigned his post in Maynooth and was consecrated Bishop of Raphoe on 20 July by McGettigan in the pro-cathedral in Letterkenny. The ceremony was attended by his colleagues and pupils from Maynooth and the Irish College in Paris. The *Freeman's Journal* described the consecration as the most 'impressing and interesting' of events. The presence of so many representatives of the hierarchy and the priesthood indicated 'the greatness of the event, the popularity of the new bishop and the depth of sincerity of Catholic feeling which prevails in the district'. In the opinion of the *Freeman*, Logue had 'distinguished himself as few contemporaries could have' and he was the natural successor to the late bishop who had been much admired.[24]

Logue inherited a diocese with a Catholic population of 110,000. In his diocesan report to Rome in 1881, he revealed some of his concerns over education, poverty and issues such as the abuse of alcohol and gambling.[25] Despite the positive experiences of his own childhood, Logue was surprisingly condemnatory of Catholic parents who sent their children to Protestant schools. He believed that attendance at such schools was inherently dangerous to the faith and morals of Catholic children because of the lack of structured and supervised teaching. For the parents, the penalty for sending their children there was severe. They were denied the sacraments 'in punishment for their carelessness about the faith and moral life of their offspring'. Logue was also of the opinion that the attitude of Protestant landlords had contributed to a chronic shortage of school places because they refused to sell land for the purpose of building Catholic schools.[26]

In many respects, Logue's ecclesiastical career had been guided by Daniel McGettigan. For a priest to advance because of the intervention of an influential patron was not unusual. William Walsh, for example, had enjoyed a close relationship with the Archbishop of Dublin, Edward McCabe, whom he eventually succeeded. In such a fashion, a senior prelate could ensure continuity and a safe pair of hands for his diocese or archdiocese after his death. The system, however, was not without its flaws. In 1880, for example, the archdiocese of Tuam descended into acrimony when Archbishop John McHale rejected a successor foisted upon him by a *terna*. The Bishop of Galway, John McEvilly, had been elected by the priests of the archdiocese but McHale refused to acknowledge the result, preferring to conduct all administrative business through his nephew.[27] In McGettigan, Logue had the example of a rather placid archbishop who was reluctant to enter into politics or controversy. Although the Primate of All Ireland in Armagh was nominally in charge, the hierarchy had been led from Dublin by Cardinal Paul Cullen and this trend continued when the cardinal was replaced by Edward McCabe as archbishop in 1879. In some ways a safe and obscure episcopacy suited Logue. He had shown little interest in politics during his priesthood and, if Toner was correct, retained a self-consciousness that precluded his taking the political centre stage. However few, if any, in the hierarchy could ignore or stand idle in the political and social upheaval heralded by events in 1879.

Notes

1 Toner Biography, Logue Papers, ADA, box 10, folder 2, ch. 2, p. 4.
2 *Ibid.*, p. 8.
3 McCaffery to Toner, 10 Dec. 1926, Logue Papers, ADA, box 4, folder 7, 'Letters'.
4 Logue to McGettigan, 26 Apr. 1865, McGettigan Papers, ADA, box 1.
5 Toner Biography, Logue Papers, ADA, box 10, folder 3, ch. 2, p. 5.
6 *Ibid.*
7 Lynch to McGettigan, 15 Oct. 1866, McGettigan Papers, ADA, box 1.
8 Toner Biography, Logue Papers, ADA, box 10, folder 3, ch. 2, p. 6.
9 Boyle to Toner, 4 Mar. 1926, Logue Papers, ADA, box 10, folder 3, 'Biography-letters'.
10 Duffy, *History of the Popes*, p. 95.
11 See Chadwick, *History of the Popes*, pp. 181–214.
12 Boyle to Toner, 4 Jul. 1926, Logue Papers, ADA, box 10, folder 1, 'Biography-letters'.
13 *Ibid.*
14 Duffy, *History of the Popes*, p. 234.
15 Gladstone, *Vatican Decrees*, p. 4.
16 Walsh, 'Cardinal Michael Logue', p. 117.
17 Toner Biography, Logue Papers, ADA, box 10, folder 3, ch. 3, p. 4.
18 *Ibid.*
19 Walker to Toner, undated 1926, Logue Papers, ADA, box 10, folder 3, 'Biography – letters'.
20 *Northern Whig*, 4 Apr. 1878.
21 *Ibid.*, 5 Apr. 1878.
22 *Ibid.*, 4 Apr. 1878.
23 Toner Biography, Logue Papers, ADA, box 10, folder 4, ch. 5, p. 12.
24 *Freeman's Journal*, 21 Jul. 1879.
25 Canning, *Bishops of Ireland*, p. 153.
26 *Ibid.*
27 See correspondence between McEvilly and McCabe, 1880, McCabe Papers, DDA, box 346/1.

2

Land and politics

The Land War

The upsurge in political violence after 1879 posed a series of complex problems for the Catholic Church in Ireland. The nature of violence, its scope and scale, and its origin all presented challenges which were in many ways new. The violent protest associated with the land question after 1879 heralded, or was symptomatic of, sweeping political change. Previously, it was quite often simply a matter of condemnation for the Church. Insurrection, such as the Fenian revolt, could be dismissed as the work of a small group of malcontents or of nefarious secret societies. The Land War, however, presented an altogether different challenge. Violence was protracted and supported by a large constituency that included members of the clergy. Political violence seldom provoked a unified response from the hierarchy. Some, finding themselves in agreement with the aims of the political movements that accompanied the agitation, sought accommodation. There were others, however, for whom the violence, or the potential for violence, negated any positive response to the political changes underway.

By his own admission Logue played only a minor role in the great events which constituted the Land War. Speaking in Armagh in 1891, he told the assembled clergy of the diocese that he had never been fond of thrusting himself forward and taking the lead in political movements. He preferred, he said, to do things quietly as there were abler hands at the helm and he was quite satisfied to assist them as far as he could.[1] When the Land League was founded in 1879, Logue was a newly consecrated bishop from a minor diocese. Although secretary to the bishops' Standing Committee, he was privy to, but still removed from, the makers and shapers of policy in the hierarchy. Nevertheless, his vote was recorded at the meetings and his name was included with the other bishops on the statements issued afterward. Publicly, Logue cultivated a studiously neutral attitude to the new political movement and the land agitation in general. It is difficult to find any statements made by him on the League or the legitimacy of the land campaign. There is evidence that he retained a great deal of sympathy with the plight of Irish tenants and even the objectives of the Land League. Privately, however, he was deeply worried by the tactics of the new movement and the involvement of the clergy in the campaign. He also bitterly resented the response of the British Government to what, at times, resembled a popular uprising.

The Land League had its origin in the disastrous economic decline in Irish agriculture after 1876. Between 1876 and 1879 the value of total Irish crop yields fell by almost £14 million. The economic downtown was worsened by a sustained period of exceptionally bad weather. In 1879, rain was recorded on two out of every three days. In the same year the potato yield was roughly a third of the normal average.[2] Despite the real and present threat of famine, the precarious existence of Irish smallholder tenants was exacerbated by the obligation to pay rent to their landlord. With barely enough to subsist on, paying rent and arrears proved difficult; and, by 1878, evictions on a large scale were underway in western counties.

Historians have differed as to the true nature of the land movement which sprung into existence in 1879. It has been argued that the Land League was merely the latest and most successful of the old associations and that its principal methods, the boycott and attacks on livestock and property, had been tried and tested in previous years.[3] Lee has described the Land League as Europe's first truly mass movement. For the first time in Irish history, he has argued, 'the masses came onto the political stage as leading figures rather than actors'.[4] Yet, it was not a movement dedicated to fundamental changes in the land system or Irish society as a whole in terms of proprietorship. Instead, it challenged the social and political power of the landlords by focusing on the ever-problematic relationship between landlord and tenant.[5] Thus, as it became formalised, the League's demands centred on grievances – fair rent, fixity of tenure and freedom of sale. Some of the factions, however, which gravitated towards the movement, such as the Fenians, ensured that the potential for violent confrontation would be an inherent part of its dynamic.

The bishops met to discuss the situation in October 1879. Out of the twenty-eight members of the hierarchy there were five active supporters of the League, five willing to give support privately, nine outright opponents and nine neutrals. Larkin has recorded Logue as one of the neutrals along with James Donnelly in Clogher, Francis Kelly in Derry and Nicholas Conaty in Kilmore. The majority of those who opposed the

League outright formed a bloc around the Archbishop of Dublin, Edward McCabe, along with the Archbishop of Tuam and his coadjutor, John McEvilly in Galway. The chief supporter of the League was the brash and outspoken Archbishop of Cashel, Thomas William Croke.[6]

As the bishops struggled with the social and political challenges of the new movement, Logue threw himself into economic relief efforts in Donegal. By the end of 1879 the number of farmers facing the real prospect of famine had risen drastically and the new bishop responded with compassion and zeal. Even before national efforts got underway in December, Logue had tapped into a general enthusiasm for relief, especially in America.[7] By January 1880 there were two central funds in Ireland for the relief of distress. The Dublin Mansion House Committee was modelled on the relief committees which had operated during the famine of the 1840s and was intended as a hub through which funds could be dispersed to committees across Ireland. The membership of the Dublin Committee included MPs, the Lord Mayor of Dublin, Edmund Dwyer Gray, and Protestant and Catholic senior clergy. A separate fund was established under the auspices of the wife of the Lord Lieutenant, the Duchess of Marlborough. Other funds included one operated by the *New York Herald* and another by the Irish community in Liverpool.

Logue presided over the first meeting of the Donegal Relief Committee on 4 January 1880. Other members of the committee included the Anglican Bishop of Derry and Raphoe, clergy from all denominations, doctors, Poor Law guardians and local merchants. The situation in Raphoe, although not the worst affected region, was sufficiently dire to demand Logue's constant attention. In the parish of St Johnstone alone, for example, the parish priest, Michael Martin, advised him that he had received applications for aid from some 1,400 people.[8] By July 1880 the Donegal Committee was helping some 60,000 local people with money, seed, food and clothing.[9]

The distribution of aid was not without controversy. Logue received complaints from many of his priests that Catholics were being discriminated against. Michael Martin told him that the local Protestant clergy were refusing to donate at all, denying that a crisis existed. They were taking their information, he said, from the larger farmers 'who say there is no distress . . . in order to get the labour of the poor starving man and his family for little or nothing'.[10] J. McKenna Edwards wrote from Belleek to inform Logue that no Catholic in the area had been assisted by the Duchess of Marlborough Relief Fund. Applicants, some 700 out of 1,000 in total, were turned away when found to be Catholic.[11]

In a letter to the *Derry Journal* in January 1880, Logue vented his frustration at the lack of Government intervention in the crisis. 'So powerless are individual efforts and private resources to cope with the evil', he wrote, 'that I fear the best disposed and most sanguine will abandon the task in despair, leaving our people, as our leaders seem disposed to leave them, to die by the road side'.[12] He was equally scathing about the attempt of the leadership of the Land League to politicise the relief effort. At the end of 1879 Charles Stewart Parnell and John Dillon embarked on a tour of America to garner support and funding. In an interview with the *New York Herald*, Parnell accused the Duchess of Marlborough Relief Fund of giving only enough money to tenants to pay their rents. He further alleged that only those tenants who held aloof from the League were assisted.[13] Doubts about the Mansion House Committee also surfaced with the result that, after a personal plea from Dwyer Gray, Logue published an angry letter in support of the fund. He branded the accusations from the League leadership as crimes against the famine-stricken people of Ireland. It was, he said, an even greater crime to shake the faith of the generous people of America in the various funds. 'Surely the authors of such charges', he went on, 'would be more cautious did they remember that in making them they snatched the scanty dole of charity from the mouths of weak women and helpless children'.[14]

Despite the controversy the League could not help being drawn into the relief effort. Indeed, the Donegal Committee benefited directly from League contributions. In January 1880, Patrick Egan, Treasurer of the Land League, sent Logue a cheque for fifty pounds. He apologised for the size of the amount but added 'with the aid of our generous countrymen in America our committee will soon be in a position to largely supplement the sum'.[15] The Mansion House Committee was wound up in October and in his final report, Logue revealed that the Donegal Committee had distributed over £34,000, not including clothing and seed.[16]

As the economic crisis deepened, the League stepped up its activities and the leadership embarked on a radical and aggressive strategy. The 'rent at the point of a bayonet' campaign was just short of an all-out rent strike. Tenants would withhold rents to the point where they faced forcible eviction.[17] In the face of what was tantamount to a general uprising, the Government responded with coercion. The Chief Secretary, W. E. Forster, told the cabinet in May 1880, 'by law, evictions must be carried out. We have no discretion as regards the humanity or moral justice of the eviction but we have simply to consider whether we allow the law to be defied or not.'[18] In August a Compensations Bill which would have provided some relief for evicted tenants was defeated in the House of Lords. The result was the trigger for an unparalleled upsurge in violence. Of the 2,585 violent crimes recorded in 1880, no fewer than 1,696 occurred after August. In response, the Government passed the Peace Preservation Act and suspended *habeas corpus*. It was believed that the sudden imprisonment of those instigating the violence would 'strike terror in a way that nothing else would'.[19]

The disturbances in Ireland and the growing clerical involvement in the land agitation drew the attention of the authorities in Rome. In the Irish situation, Pope Leo XIII saw an opportunity to foster links with London. The reign of his predecessor, Pius IX, had ended ignominiously with the loss of much of the papal lands in the *Risorgimento*. The temporal influence of the Holy See was at its lowest since the Reformation. Diplomatic links with Britain offered Leo the tantalising prospect of an alliance with a great power in his struggle with the Italian Government.[20]

Roman interference began in June 1880. The Prefect of Propaganda, under whose jurisdiction the Irish Church fell, wrote to the bishops condemning their apparent disunity and ecclesiastical disorder. Cardinal Giovanni Simeoni declared that 'dissensions have gone so far that the greater part of the people has separated itself from the clergy; preferring instead the counsels of protesting'. Such a grave evil was greatly to be feared, he went on, and boded ill for the future. The Cardinal Prefect demanded unity of action among the clergy in all matters. Any dissension should be referred to the Holy See for judgement and guidance.[21] The reason for the rebuke was helpfully explained to the Archbishop of Dublin by Tobias Kirby, Rector of the Irish College in Rome. 'The object of it', he told McCabe 'is that their Lordships should agree on a course of action and thus avoid even the semblance of dissension in their body before the public'.[22] But rather than encouraging unity, Simeoni's letter merely galvanised anti-League bishops into an offensive.

The following month McCabe issued a pastoral outlining his objections to the League. He expressed sympathy with the cause of Irish tenant farmers and conceded that aspects of the land laws in Ireland constituted 'oppression'. But before God's blessing could descend on any movement, he said, it would be necessary to make certain the work engaged in was good 'and the means employed for its accomplishment must be those which have the sanction of eternal justice'.[23] On 15 October, Tobias Kirby wrote from the Irish College to inform the Archbishop of Dublin that his pastoral letter would give pleasure to all the authorities in Rome.[24] McCabe's views, however, did not sit well with some of his colleagues.

Patrick Duggan, the Bishop of Clonfert, told the archbishop that the Land League was an expression of the popular will and was attempting to stop the violence in the countryside.[25]

The tempting promise of political support offered by the vocal British lobby in Rome encouraged the Pope to act again. In December 1880 Leo published a letter in the Italian press reminding the Irish clergy that the fundamental principle of the Catholic religion held that the end did not justify means which were anarchical and reproved by conscience.[26] Once more, McCabe issued a pastoral criticising the League and the land campaign. He upheld Leo's warning against Irish Catholics casting aside 'the obedience due to their lawful rulers' and against besmirching the good name of Ireland with illegal acts. Justice, he went on, might be violated and a cause, 'however right in itself, might be forced by the influence of passion into the flame of sedition'.[27]

The supporters of the League in the hierarchy, and indeed the League itself, remained undaunted by the Roman interference. Just before Leo's letter appeared in the press, the Archbishop of Cashel had written a strong letter arguing the League's case to Cardinal Simeoni. The cause was just, Croke argued, and the Irish people were strongly devoted to their religion and to the Holy See. Nine-tenths of the Irish people at home and abroad were in favour of the League, as were almost all of the junior clergy in Ireland.[28] The bishops' meeting in March 1881 proved a stormy affair. There was much bitterness over McCabe's unilateral pastoral and his crusade against the League.

However, there was a point around which every bishop could unite. They had been called together specifically to discuss word from Rome that the Holy See was contemplating the establishment of a papal nuncio in London. Such a move held the prospect of the Irish Church becoming subservient to a Roman representative based in Westminster. In Rome the Bishop of Ossory, Patrick Moran, had been received in audience by Monsignor Jacobini at the Secretariat of State where he was consulted about Irish reaction to the proposals. A horrified Moran immediately wrote to the primate, Daniel McGettigan, to warn the bishops of impending disaster. He argued that such a move would leave little room 'for that liberty of action in all disciplinary matters which has been the secret of the wonderful development of the Irish Church during the past fifty years'.[29]

Before the March meeting McCabe had sounded out each bishop on the proposals. With the possible exception of McGettigan, who was rather fatalistic about the scheme, the rest of the hierarchy viewed developments in Rome with alarm.[30] Logue advised McCabe that he would be unable to attend the meeting but would like his vote recorded in the negative. He argued that to subjugate the affairs of the Irish Church to a nuncio in London would be a disaster. Even the suspicion that the British Government could exert any influence over Church affairs in Ireland would create distrust and give the impression that appointments and utterances of the bishops were orchestrated by the Government and the Chief Secretary. 'I fear it would give a death blow', he argued, 'to the enthusiastic affection with which our people regard the Holy See'.[31] On 12 March he repeated his opposition to the proposals. He told McCabe he believed they would useful to England but ruinous for Ireland: 'It will be regarded by many as an attempt to coerce the clergy by means of the influence of Rome, just as the laity have been brought under a rule of terror by the suspension of the constitution.'[32]

This was a shrewd assessment. The British lobby in Rome was already interfering in the confirmation of ecclesiastical appointments. In the end, the line suggested by Logue was almost exactly that taken by McCabe in a letter to Simeoni sent on 15 March. A nuncio in London would weaken 'if not destroy the filial confidence which has hitherto bound our people to the Holy See'. McCabe also argued that 'it would fill this country with alarm and would create in the minds of the Irish race distrust for the decisions and appointments coming to them . . . from the Holy See'.[33] A relieved Moran wrote to McCabe on 21 March to tell him that, in the face of the unified opposition of the bishops, the scheme had withered.[34]

On the issues of the Land League and the land campaign, in public at least, Logue remained neutral. His reluctance to pronounce on the League stemmed, in part, from a lack of activity in his diocese. In January 1881, he told McCabe that agitation in Raphoe had 'not gone beyond speechmaking and the passing of resolutions'.[35] Privately, however, he remained suspicious of the methods of the League and was concerned with the involvement of the junior clergy. In October Logue questioned his priests on the motives and activities of the Children's Land League. Father James McFadden replied that in the Derrybeg area of Donegal its activities had not gone beyond attempting to instil in children a sense of Irish history through stories and songs. He did, however, promise to keep an eye on it.[36] Logue was even more concerned with priests entering into public controversy in connection with the League. In November 1881, Father John Collins wrote to him to deny that he had supported the 'No Rent' manifesto issued by the League leadership from prison. 'I do not admit', Collins said, 'that I have discredited my character either as a priest or as a man by writing and publishing letters from time to time'.[37] His reply suggests that Logue's initial letter was one of stinging rebuke.

The 'No Rent' manifesto provided the last gasp of the Land League's campaign. In March 1881, the Liberal Government produced a Land Bill and, despite voicing concerns about the provisions therein, the committee of bishops nominated to examine it pronounced favourably.[38] The prospect of a settlement, however, did not diminish the level of violence. Along with the Land reform the Government introduced more stringent coercion measures in the form of the Protection of Persons and Property Act. Among the provisions therein was the ability to transfer cases out of disturbed areas and the creation of special magistrates to try cases arising from League activities. This did not amount to martial law but, with the suspension of trial by jury, the country was not far from it. In fact, by the summer of 1881, troop levels in Ireland had risen from just over nineteen thousand to twenty-five thousand.[39] Forster warned the Cabinet: 'It is all we can do, by arrests and proclamations and constant employment of force to get on until the act be passed without the collapse of authority and general disorder'.[40]

Despite the fact that thousands of tenants took advantage of the provisions of the Land Act when it became law in the autumn of 1881, violent crime did not subside. The arrest of the League leadership and the proscription of the Land League created such a vacuum of authority in the country at large that the violence spiralled. Without the steadying influence of the League the first four months of 1882 witnessed some of the highest incidence of violence recorded in the conflict to date.[41] The Government treated with the leadership of the League who were released from prison in May, causing Forster to resign in protest. Before Parnell could reassert control of the countryside, Forster's replacement, Lord Frederick Cavendish, and his Under-Secretary, T. H. Burke, were murdered in Phoenix Park.

The killings marked a watershed in terms of the violence. Unified in revulsion at the deaths, dissensions were also bridged in the hierarchy by the elevation of McCabe to the cardinalate. Even relations with Rome were slowly healed. On 11 June 1882 the bishops issued a united pastoral which gave retrospective approval to the League. On religious and political grounds it was 'the indisputable right of Irishmen to live on and by their own fertile soil and to be free to employ the resources of their country for their own profit'. Legal means to redress the injustice of the land system was deemed a 'noble work of justice and charity'. In terms of the violence, the bishops concluded that 'in our belief, they [outrages] would never have occurred had not the people been driven to despair by evictions'.[42]

Although relations were slowly improving with Rome and the general level of violence was subsiding, the Holy See had a final warning on clerical involvement in political agitation. On 1 January 1883, Leo wrote to the Irish bishops to congratulate them for their success in quelling the disturbances in the country and guiding the will of the faithful. He warned, however, that there were still in Ireland 'hangers-on of bad company' engaged in acts of violence. The just cause of the country must be separated from the efforts, advice and works of iniquitous associations. On the issue of clerical involvement, Leo advised that the junior clergy should be restricted from attending political meetings. If any clergy were deemed necessary to be in attendance it should be only those 'in whose wisdom you especially place trust'.[43]

The Plan of Campaign

At first glance there seemed little to distinguish the Plan of Campaign from the land agitation that had gone before. There was a similar intent of withholding rents deemed unfair. Violence followed a familiar pattern of confrontation, coercion and eviction. The tools of the National League which had replaced the Land League, such as the boycott, were the same; and so were agrarian crimes such as arson, intimidation and even murder. There were, however, crucial differences. The Plan was, at its heart, a political one directed by the National League and supported by a concerted effort on the part of Nationalist MPs at Westminster. Since the end of the Land War, Parnell had transformed the League into an effective grassroots political machine. Its role was to maintain electoral support for the Irish Party and its demand for Home Rule. Despite the National League's involvement in violent confrontation, the control exerted by the party leadership was such that the level of violence seldom reached the heights experienced previously.

The response of the Church was also crucially different. In place of the divisions and dissent experienced in the earlier conflict, a broad consensus was forged among most, though not all, of the Irish bishops. The architect of this clerical-nationalist alliance was William Walsh who replaced McCabe as Archbishop of Dublin in 1885. Acting in concert with the Archbishop of Cashel, Thomas William Croke, it was Walsh who shaped the policy of the bishops in terms of the Plan. Building on the approval of the unity reached in 1882, Walsh constructed an alliance in which, in return for the support of the bishops on Home Rule, the League and the Irish Party would take up the struggle for a Catholic university, under the direction of the hierarchy.[44] Not quite the establishment of an Irish state, this alliance was nevertheless an almost unparalleled concentration of nationalist power in Ireland.

In the winter of 1885–6, economic disaster once again threatened in the west of Ireland with its attendant result of wholesale evictions. Drafted by William O'Brien and John Dillon, the Plan was published in the League newspaper, *United Ireland*, at the end of 1885. It was envisaged that tenants on each estate should combine and offer their landlord what they deemed a fair rent. If the landlord refused to come to terms, tenants would withhold the rents and submit them to a central fund to fight evictions. The League would step in if these funds proved insufficient. Once again, the point of ignition for potential violence would be the actual act of eviction which would be vigorously resisted. Farmers who took up the land of an evicted tenant would face the boycott. Events in Ireland would be supported by an aggressive campaign in the House of Commons. Despite initial doubts about the Plan and having had little involvement in its inception, Parnell agreed to continue the agitation at Westminster.[45]

As Walsh and Croke positioned the hierarchy behind the League, Logue maintained his neutral stance. It was one thing, however, to support those 'abler hands at the helm', but quite another to permit his own priests to take a leading role in local League activities. In contrast to the Land War, the League was now very active in Raphoe. In the course of 1885, Logue found himself in conflict with one of his priests, Father James McFadden, over his presidency of the National League branch in Gweedore. Even before the Plan commenced, Logue had found cause to censure McFadden over his activities in the parish.[46] He was undoubtedly a compassionate priest who could not stand idle when faced with the privations of his poorer parishioners. Unfortunately, he was prone to rash and intemperate outbursts and was, at times, consumed with a sense of his own martyrdom.

By the end of 1885, Logue had moved to rebuke his priest privately because of his League activities. In a letter in December McFadden profoundly regretted that the course he had taken in public life had prompted censure. 'I accept', he told Logue, 'your Lordship's remonstrance in all humility and obedience and I place myself unreservedly at your Lordship's disposal'. Prior to writing to McFadden, Logue had summoned him to answer for his actions. At the meeting, the priest had offered to 'break all further connection with the National League'. But McFadden's impression had been that Logue did not want him to act 'in such a way as to give grounds for suspicion that you had interfered, but to drop off gradually'.[47]

This was a remarkable and cunning manipulation. McFadden, it would appear, knew well his bishop's reluctance to court publicity. On 19 December, he wrote thanking Logue for his forbearance and for realising that it was better to have a restraining influence on the local League than to have no control at all. 'I have this very night', he said, 'taken the first steps towards reforming the constitution of the branch in the direction your Lordship likely intends'. This had included passing resolutions against the boycott.[48]

By January 1886, however, McFadden's obsequious obedience had been replaced by reproachful sullenness. He told Logue that it had become common knowledge that it was he who had ordered the local branch to pass resolutions against boycotting. McFadden told how the local landlords and their agents were rejoicing at the news of the decline of the League in Donegal. 'So much did they dread and respect its power', he said, 'that they freely gave expression that the collapse of power here must necessarily bring with it the fall of the League throughout Ireland'. He told Logue that he had made an earnest appeal that no resistance or show of opposition should be given henceforth to the enforcement of the law in any way. He concluded with the hope that Logue would be satisfied that he had made a great effort and would sympathise with him 'in the bitterness of the humiliation that my enemies guess at the cause'.[49] Logue's interference in the workings of the Plan in Raphoe proved merely a temporary setback for McFadden. In truth, he never really abandoned or limited his League activities and remained politically active until the end of the 1880s.

At the end of 1886, following the defeat of the Home Rule Bill, Gladstone's Liberal Government was replaced by a Unionist administration under Lord Salisbury. The change in leadership heralded a more robust approach to the Plan than had been undertaken by the Liberals. The Government embarked on a concerted campaign aimed at pacifying Ireland. This approach was soon visible in the simultaneous enactment of two bills in the autumn of 1887. Land reforms improved the criteria under which tenants could have their rents reassessed under the terms of the 1881 act while the Criminal Law Amendment Bill was designed to bolster the powers of the Irish judiciary by introducing sweeping powers of arrest.

The new Chief Secretary, Arthur Balfour, was determined that, along with getting a 'licking', Ireland should have some measure of relief.[50] He also moved to meet head-on the challenge of clerical participation in the Plan by stiffening the resolve of the judiciary when prosecuting priests. Salisbury went as far as sounding out British ambassadors across Europe as to the efficacy of compelling priests to break the seal of the confessional by testifying in court.[51] In Rome, the cause of the British Government was fought by John Ross, a Catholic convert and Irish Unionist who had close links with leading Catholics in England such as the Duke of Norfolk. Throughout the Plan, Ross kept Balfour well informed of events in the Vatican and lobbied strongly for a permanent representative there to be appointed by the Government.[52]

The hierarchy condemned the introduction of the Criminal Law Amendment Bill, declaring that Ireland was free from grave crime. 'In common with our lay fellow countrymen', they added, 'we view with deep indignation this new attempt to despoil our country of her constitutional rights and liberties and to place her at the mercy of unfriendly and irresponsible Government officials'.[53] The resolutions were not quite a declaration that the Government in Ireland was illegal. Nevertheless, the strident language used pointed to one that was, at the very least, oppressive and unjust.

Logue was absent from the meeting in April 1887. He had just been nominated for the position of coadjutor in Armagh and was busy with his transfer from Raphoe. He did, however, contact Walsh before the meeting to advise him that 'your Grace may take me as assenting to anything the committee [of bishops] may decide'.[54] Logue's apology did have a ring of truth. He translated to the see of Armagh without his successor having been named, a fact that would not be remedied until December.[55] To a certain extent, therefore, his responsibilities would have been divided between Armagh and Letterkenny. While Logue was not disinterested in the land issue his letter illustrates his faith in the Archbishop of Dublin. Despite his misgivings over the Plan and his absence from the meeting, his prior agreement showed at least a willingness to defer to the direction of Croke and Walsh.

The Archbishop of Cashel, however, was not enthusiastic at the prospect of Logue presiding at the bishops' meeting as Primate of All Ireland. As Primate *of Ireland*, second in ecclesiastical authority, the Archbishop of Dublin, first McCabe and then Walsh, had presided at meetings in the absence of the ailing Daniel McGettigan. Croke expressed surprise at the ease with which McGettigan had been granted a coadjutor. Remarking that the Archbishop of Armagh must have 'worked up the oracle' with the authorities in Rome, he testily concluded by telling Walsh 'we must have you a cardinal' before the meetings fell to Logue.[56] Croke's prickly response to Logue's advancement was not borne out of personal malice. It was more a case, perhaps, of resenting any possible interference with the alignment of the bishops which he and Walsh had worked so hard to create.

By the summer of 1887, however, the Pope had decided to intervene directly in Ireland. Leo remained susceptible to the promises of the English lobby and his view of Ireland was rather typical of his general attitude towards nationalism in Europe. In the case of Poland, for example, Leo chose to conciliate Tsar Alexander III rather than appear favourable to Polish claims for independence from Russia. His policy went as far as finding bishops for vacant sees who would not antagonise the Tsar.[57] Thus, he resolved to send a papal envoy to assess the Irish situation. Despatched under the direction of the Cardinal Secretary of State, Archbishop Ignatio Persico arrived in Ireland at the end of July. Persico's brief, on the surface at least, was straightforward. He was to study conditions in Ireland so that the Holy See would be able to adopt provisions to remove the causes of difficulty. Persico was encouraged to exhort the bishops to have confidence in the British Government and report wherever clergy transgressed the papal letters of 1881 and 1883.[58]

In the course of his mission, Persico criss-crossed the country interviewing prelates, landlords and politicians, and viewing conditions in Ireland first hand. In August 1887, he visited Armagh where he was feted by Logue and Daniel McGettigan. Persico's secretary, Enrico Gualdi, later told William Walsh that the envoy had made quite an impression on the two.[59] For his part, Persico despised the Archbishop of Dublin from first meeting. He was also suspicious of his own secretary whose relationship with Walsh and closeness to the Irish bishops he found deeply troubling.[60] By the end of 1887, the atmosphere surrounding the Persico's visit had turned increasingly bitter. On 22 December 1887 Persico complained to Walsh about an article in the *Pall Mall Gazette* which branded him 'a vile intriguer' and 'betrayer of the Irish cause'. Walsh illustrated amply how he felt by underscoring heavily both descriptions on Persico's letter.[61]

Persico's final report, submitted at the end of 1887, read as a damning indictment of the Irish Church and the Plan of Campaign. He noted the precarious existence of the Irish peasantry and praised their religious devotion and respect for the Holy See. On the relationship between the Church and the national movement, however, the report was scathing. Persico concluded that the Irish clergy deluded themselves that they dominated the movement while it was Parnell and his associates who really did so. Persico wrote of the Irish Party and the National League as if they were secret societies.[62] His account of the involvement of the Church in the Plan was perhaps even more damning. In their acquiescence in boycotting, they had become 'executors of biased and despotic decisions issued by tribunals . . . leading to the unjust punishment of those accused'. Some of the clergy carried their enthusiasm for the Plan and antipathy towards the landlords to the point of illegality.[63] Despite painting a picture of complete ecclesiastical disorder, Persico recommended that no declaration should be issued by Rome on the Plan or the conduct of the Irish Church. Despite everything, he still believed that the hierarchy were the key to a settlement.

Persico's visit and report had far reaching consequences for Logue. On 3 December 1887, he inherited the see of Armagh on McGettigan's death. Persico was impressed by Logue's moderate nationalism. He noted in his report that the new primate was not 'obsessed with the need to publish letters or comments on political questions'. He was scrupulously conscientious, favoured strong ecclesiastical discipline and was indifferent to public opinion.[64] Persico noted that Logue's succession would prove advantageous. With a new primate installed the power of presiding at bishops' meetings would fall to Logue, not Walsh.[65] By February 1888, however, Persico was voicing his impatience that the new primate had not moved to assert his control over the bishops. He was convinced that Logue had the strength and courage to counter the influence of the Archbishop of Dublin but was hesitating.[66]

While Logue knew nothing of Persico's opinions he was quite aware of the climate of criticism the Irish bishops faced at Rome. His new position also accompanied a remarkable change in his attitude to the Plan. The shift was not centred on the violence or the operation of the Plan but rather the actions of the police and the Irish administration. That the role of archbishop would entail a much greater public prominence was starkly brought home in January 1888. At McGettigan's month's mind mass in Armagh, James McFadden was arrested by police and brought to Armagh gaol. Logue was incensed. He told a gathering crowd that the timing of the arrest could not be regarded as anything other than an insult to the memory of the late primate. He accused the police of conduct calculated to exasperate the people and drive moderates to excess. More importantly, Logue made a point of entering the cell of the priest he had censured in 1886 and warmly shaking him by the hand.[67]

The new primate backed this very public expression of solidarity with McFadden by writing a letter to Tobias Kirby to express his fury at events in Armagh. He could be fairly confident that the Pope would hear of the incident. Kirby was a former classmate and friend of Leo XIII and the two men retained a cordial and close relationship. Logue repeated the accusations he made at the arrest of McFadden. He pointed out that the priest could have been arrested anywhere along the route from Letterkenny to Armagh and the actions of the police were not only disrespectful but deliberately provocative. He concluded by declaring 'and these are the men trying to secure the alliance of the Holy Father in crushing Irish Catholics!'[68]

By February, his anger had not diminished and he once again contacted Kirby to vent his frustration. His account of a rally to protest against the arrest of McFadden and another priest illustrated the extraordinary reversal of his policy of non-intervention. Logue told Kirby that he had contacted the Chief Secretary's office to broker an arrangement on the rally. He would guarantee the behaviour of the crowds if the police were kept quiet. The protest passed off peacefully and Logue relayed the often quoted anecdote that an army officer declared that the people were more afraid of the umbrellas of the priests than of the rifles of the army and police.[69] Logue's purpose in writing, however, was not just to demonstrate his own ecclesiastical control. He told Kirby that after the rally the police went around in the dead of night, pulling from their beds all those who had attended the protest. Logue was outraged at the bad faith shown by the police and the unspoken moral was that that the Government could not be trusted.

The problem for the bishops was that such accounts of the British Government's villainy were being ignored in Rome. In December 1887, Walsh had left for the Holy See to celebrate the Pope's jubilee, unaware that a campaign of vilification was already being waged against him. In February, Persico told Cardinal Rampolla to be careful when dealing with the Archbishop of Dublin. Walsh, he said, exercised too much influence over his episcopal colleagues, even to the point of intimidating and silencing them.[70] Walsh had intended a leisurely trip to Rome but his plans were changed drastically by a terse and unexpected summons from Leo.[71]

Despite the ominous signals emanating from the Vatican, Walsh remained upbeat. He told Croke that what amounted to a calling to account for the Church had gone very well. Walsh was confident that his testimony to the Pope had been such that the British lobby in Rome had been 'routed all along the line'.[72] On 12 February, accompanied by the Bishop of Cork, Thomas O'Callaghan, he outlined his idea of an acceptable settlement to Leo. Walsh explained that the roots of the unrest in Ireland were to be found in the injustices of the land system. He explained the boycott and the operation of the Plan and argued that stopping evictions immediately through the introduction of a bill would go a long way towards restoring order. All in all, the archbishop believed that his mission had gone well and achieved an understanding at Rome of the situation in Ireland.[73]

The decree

But Leo had already set in motion a process which would have devastating consequences for the Irish Church. In the time that Walsh was in Rome, the Pope had referred the Plan and boycotting for consideration by the Congregation of the Holy Office. Formerly the Inquisition, the Holy Office dealt with heresies, threats to the faith and matters of doctrine. In a verdict issued in April 1888, Cardinal Monaco, Prefect of the Holy Office, declared boycotting and the Plan of Campaign contrary to the faith and morals of Catholics. Roman authority had reversed completely the verdict of the Irish Church, given in 1886, that the Plan was moral.[74]

Walsh was dumbfounded by the decision. Not only had he no inkling that a pronouncement was imminent but the decision was published in the press before being communicated either to him or to the Irish Church. Clearly at loss, he wrote to Croke seeking advice on the next move. 'It is hard to say what is to be done', he said, 'the whole thing is deplorable. Ought anything to be done?'[75] For his part, Logue was rather sanguine about the decree. He had never been comfortable with the methods of the National League, despite deeply resenting the reaction of the Government. He told Croke on 30 April that the bishops had no choice but to publish the decree. The problem was how to do this without political mischief. He had no difficulty with the decree itself. He told the Archbishop of Cashel that it was a question of justice 'on which the Pope has every right to pronounce and to be heard'. However, danger lay in the reaction of the Irish Party incurring condemnation from the Holy See. 'Their mistake', Logue told Croke, 'is that they regard this as a question of politics which it is not'.[76] It was Logue's conviction that, in terms of Church-State relations, political actions were subject to the moral sanction of the Church. Religion and politics could not and should not be separated. He was also annoyed that his position as primate had been ignored. He complained to Croke that 'though there were two of our number in Rome, I have never received a line or a hint to indicate what was going on'.[77]

The attempts by the bishops to mitigate the immediate effects of the decree were undermined, almost from the outset, by the attitude of the Irish Party leadership. Following a meeting in Dublin on 17 May, a party committee dominated by more secular members such as John Redmond and William O'Brien condemned not only the decree but also the role of the Pope in Ireland.[78] The situation was worsened still by the development of a very public dispute between the Bishop of Limerick, Thomas Edward O'Dwyer, and the League leadership. On 25 May 1888 O'Dwyer published a letter to the Lord Mayor of Limerick ahead of a League meeting called to discuss the decree. He warned the nationalist leadership that the verdict of the Holy Office was binding in conscience. He also declared it a grievous sin to disobey it. The League responded by holding a public meeting in Limerick at which O'Brien accused O'Dwyer of disloyalty and cowardice. Whilst some in the hierarchy were appalled at such an attack on one of their colleagues, Croke was furious that O'Dwyer had spoken out at all. He told William Walsh that it had been agreed at the last meeting of the bishops that no individual statements were to be issued. The Bishop of Limerick, Croke reported furiously, had broken that agreement in the worst way – 'the little cur'.[79]

What should have happened, or what was expected in Rome, was that clerical involvement in the Plan would stop. It was not expected that the decree would be read in every church. There was, however, an expectation that the decree would be obeyed. The bishops met again on 30 May, declaring that the decree affected the realm of morals alone and the Pope had acted out of filial concern for the people of Ireland. The bishops warned the laity against intemperate and irreverent outbursts directed at the Holy See or the decree and reminded their flocks that the Roman pontiff had 'an inalienable and divine right to speak with authority on all questions appertaining to faith and morals'.[80] At the regular meeting of the hierarchy held in Maynooth on 27 and 28 June 1888, however, the bishops once again attacked the Government and the land system in Ireland.[81] There was no condemnation of the Plan and clerical participation in most areas remained undiminished.

It is not clear whether the decree had any direct effect on level of agitation which was already in decline before the Pope's intervention.[82] By the end of the year, there was disappointment in Government circles that the bishops in Ireland had not moved to condemn the Plan outright. In July, John Ross happily reported to Balfour from Rome that the decree would have to be obeyed. However patient Rome may have been, there was no intention of letting the Irish Church ignore it. Failure to comply on the part of the clergy would mean condemnation by the Holy See. Moreover, Cardinal Rampolla had told him that, if the Plan persisted, individual bishops would be called to account for events in their dioceses.[83] By March 1889, Ross's initial enthusiasm had turned to disillusionment. He complained to Balfour that the bishops could agree with the terms of the decree without actually enforcing it. The nationalists, he said, had 'debased the priests by converting them into their instrument'.[84]

The disapproval emanating from Rome made Logue nervous. If Persico had hoped Logue might wrest control of the bishops away from Walsh he was mistaken. Logue was content to follow the lead given by the archbishop and, as relations with Rome deteriorated, increasingly looked to Dublin for guidance. By November 1888, Rampolla was putting increasing pressure on the Irish bishops. Logue was particularly unnerved to receive an angry letter from the Cardinal Secretary in which 'he launches into denunciations of priests and laymen for their disrespectful, if not rebellious reception of the decree of the Holy Office'. He told Walsh that the letter had concluded with the reminder that the bishops were bound, at all hazards, to denounce and condemn the Plan and lay criticism of the Pope.[85]

In his reply, Logue defended the Church and the national movement, insisting that in the few areas where the Plan was in operation in the archdiocese, the priests were there to prevent trouble. Disturbances only existed on two estates and there the landlord had evicted Catholic tenants and replaced them with Protestants. He told Rampolla that much of the bitterness surrounding the decree had been exacerbated by the jeers and taunts of the Orange press.[86] In December 1888, Walsh informed Kirby that the decree had brought nothing but odium on the Holy See, despite the efforts of the bishops. The people now thought that the Pope was 'one of the strongest supporters of their oppressors' and he claimed that Ireland would experience the same kind of anticlerical nationalism seen in Italy during the pontificate of Pius IX unless something was done.[87]

In spite of Roman disapproval there was still an appetite for clerical involvement as the Plan ground on into 1889. Irish Catholics had been told that the Plan and boycotting were immoral but the Irish hierarchy had refused to condemn or separate itself from the national movement. In this equivocation the Plan was allowed to continue. By the end of the year, however, individual bishops had begun moves to rein in their more politically active priests. In Raphoe, the new bishop, Patrick O'Donnell, attempted to reason with James McFadden in an attempt to get him to moderate his League activities.[88] By October, however, his patience had snapped over the priest's continued indiscriminate involvement in the Plan and his numerous arrests. McFadden was forbidden to meddle in political or agrarian affairs under pain of suspension. He was not to speak publicly or publish anything on politics without the permission of his bishop for a period of five years.[89]

The final censure of McFadden was symptomatic of a wider disengagement by the hierarchy from the national movement. By 1890, the gulf between the bishops and the national movement had widened further. It was not just the continuing and vocal disapproval emanating from Rome. The British lobby at the Holy See was using the decree to interfere with episcopal appointments. John Ross explained to Balfour that the deportment, speeches and publications of prospective bishops would be examined for anything that contradicted the Papal edict. Such infractions could be passed on to the Prefect of Propaganda or Cardinal Secretary of State in the hope of overturning the result of the *terna*.[90]

Another factor in the rift was the periodic running battle between the Bishop of Limerick and the League leadership. Some bishops, such as the Bishop of Clonfert, Patrick Duggan, were irritated that O'Dwyer could not instruct on the decree without his usual 'flourish of trumpets'.[91] By 1890, however, the hierarchy had begun to close ranks around their colleague. In a letter to Walsh in July 1890 Logue called the dispute a crying scandal. On the one hand, he did not approve of O'Dwyer's public crusade which he believed had manufactured the controversy.[92] On the other, he deeply resented the attitude of the Irish Party leadership. They had compromised the bishops by not keeping quiet on the issue of the decree and the interference of Rome. Logue further fretted that O'Dwyer would be seen as the only bishop in Ireland willing publicly to defend the Pope and the Holy See. He complained to Walsh that the bishops had remained silent when many things were said and done that were anything but becoming in Catholics, to guard against the appearance of dissension. 'Now these gentlemen', he told Walsh, 'parade our silence as an approbation of every word they have ever said and every step they have ever taken'.[93] In August, Logue's fears were confirmed in a letter from Tobias Kirby from which he learned that Leo wished to thank O'Dwyer personally for his defence of the Holy See.[94]

There was a growing awareness among the bishops that the hierarchy had become very much the junior partners in the clerical-nationalist alliance.[95] Clerical support for the Plan and the League had brought the Irish Church little except disapproval from Rome. The alliance with the Irish Party had delivered little on the issue of Catholic education or even Home Rule. In October the bishops met to consider the worsening situation and issued a strident affirmation of the authority of the Holy See. They emphatically reminded their flocks that 'on all questions appertaining to morals, the Sovereign Pontiff, the Vicar of Christ on earth has an inalienable right and divine right to speak with authority'. The decision of the Holy Office on boycotting and the Plan was upheld in that they were both deemed morally unlawful.[96] To repair the rift with Rome, the bishops resolved to send a delegation, headed by Logue. By the end of 1890, however, matters were changed utterly by the O'Shea divorce. As the national movement split, the issues surrounding Parnell's leadership provided a catalyst for rapprochement between Rome and the Irish Church.

The accidental cardinal

The decision to appoint Logue as cardinal was greatly influenced by his conduct during the Land War. Persico had been impressed with Logue's moderate nationalism and his reluctance to court political controversy. He was not, however, disinterested or politically indifferent. Logue pursued his own agenda. He remained strongly averse to political violence and to priests becoming entangled in political agitation. In public, he closely supported the line determined by Croke and Walsh. The Plan of Campaign had the support of the bishops and his objections to it were not so pronounced as to persuade him to crusade against it in the way that O'Dwyer did. Neither was his sense of nationalism advanced enough to allow him to fully endorse the Plan like Walsh or Croke. However, Logue's elevation was also influenced by strong lobbying against the Archbishop of Dublin.

Along with his favourable impressions of Logue, Persico presented a stream of negatives regarding Walsh to the authorities in Rome. In 1888, for example, he described Walsh as being more politically compromised than any other bishop in Ireland.[97] Other voices in Rome joined the campaign. In February 1890 John Ross told Balfour that Cardinal Rampolla agreed with him that Walsh and Croke were 'both incorrigible' and had spoken quite openly about them as 'the two pillars of much of the evil that prevails in Ireland'.[98] Having been of little interest to the British lobby at Rome, by the 1890s Logue had suddenly become the centre of attention. As relations between the Holy See and the Irish Church thawed, it became common knowledge that Leo wished to seal the rapprochement by awarding a red hat.

The Archbishop of Dublin, however, did have supporters in the Church, who lobbied strongly on his behalf. The Bishop of Elphin, Laurence Gillooly, was particularly forthright in his praise of Walsh and his criticism of Logue. In September 1890 he wrote to Cardinal Simeoni at Propaganda to inform him of Logue's indecision in calling episcopal meetings. 'The primate is slow and indecisive', he said: 'he is not conscious of the importance of events or only partially understands them'.[99] This was as untrue as it was unfair, but Gillooly wanted Propaganda to reserve the authority of convening meetings to the see of Dublin.

At the same time, the Duke of Norfolk warned Rampolla that the elevation of Walsh would be a sign of encouragement 'to those who are striving to confound the cause of religion with disorder and misrule'.[100] Logue, he went on, had 'no doubt spoken in terms to be regretted but I think everyone admits that he is a bishop rather than a politician'.[101] Logue's moderation and general reticence were contrasted sharply with Walsh's appetite for political entanglements involving not just himself but the whole of the episcopate in Ireland. The primate was very much portrayed as a safe pair of hands. Norfolk's views might have been unfair to Walsh, but his estimation of Logue was true to a large extent. As we shall see, however, it was not the case that Logue lacked a political vision. It was rather that he had a bishop's view of politics.

But to assign responsibility for Logue's appointment solely to the opinions of others would be to do him a disservice. Following the bishops' October statement in 1890, he was in the happy position of being able to present Leo with a personal testimony of the realignment towards Rome of the Irish Church. Logue explained directly to both Leo and Cardinal Simeoni the difficulties faced by the Irish Church during the Plan and with the publication of the decree. O'Donnell, who accompanied him, told Walsh their audience with Leo had left nothing to be desired. 'His Grace, the primate', he said, 'explained the present situation most satisfactorily'. Logue had done 'great justice' to the cause of the Irish Church.[102] It is doubtful that the Pope would have appointed Logue as cardinal if he had found anything objectionable in him. Admittedly, the disqualification of both Croke and Walsh on political grounds and concerns about the age of John McEvilly in Tuam were critical factors in Logue's elevation. But he also had much to commend him to the position, other than simply the negative comparisons made with the other archbishops.

Whatever the reasons behind his appointment, the decision came as a complete shock to the Irish Church. Patrick Glynn, an Augustinian attached to St Patrick's Church in Rome, told Walsh that amazement was a poor word to describe feelings there. Rumours had been circulating the Vatican since November 1892 that a red hat was on its way to Ireland after an eight-year gap. Glynn had received assurances from Cardinal Vannutelli, Prefect of Ceremonies, that Dublin would receive the honour. Glynn told Walsh that he could hardly credit the news. Cardinal Vannutelli said that the sorrow he felt at the appointment was felt by nine out of ten cardinals in Rome.[103] Croke, who professed to being unsurprised, having had prior knowledge, was less than charitable about Rome's decision. 'So be it', he told Walsh, 'provided it is to be an adjunct of the primacy and not an exceptional favour to an individual'.[104] He later told Tobias Kirby that the announcement had taken everyone by surprise. It was generally expected that the distinction would go to Dublin. 'But Rome seems to glory in surprises and perhaps I had better say no more on the subject.'[105]

Perhaps the most considered and prophetic response to the news came from the Bishop of Raphoe. Writing to console Walsh in January 1893, Patrick O'Donnell said that with some reason he would be considered to have suffered at the hands of the enemies of Ireland's cause. 'Thus, though your influence for good under one aspect would go up through being clothed in scarlet', O'Donnell went on, 'the influence Lord Salisbury dreads and misrepresents so assiduously will rise very considerably by you being left as you are'.[106] To his great credit, Walsh was quick to congratulate Logue on the 'signal honour' conferred on him by the Holy See. He also added that he hoped this would be the means 'of strengthening your Grace's hand in the management of your unruly team'.[107]

Logue was under no illusions as to the nature of his appointment. 'Of course', he told Walsh, 'I know the choice was not determined by any personal consideration; for if it were, there could be very little found in me to deserve it'. The news had left him miserable and out of sorts and all he wanted was a quiet Christmas. He recognised that his red hat was due to the circumstances of his being in Armagh. 'I did not leave Raphoe willingly', he confessed, 'and I never regret having done so more than now'.[108] It is, perhaps, an irony of history that one who did not seek high station, was convinced of his unworthiness for the role and lacked the confidence and the inclination to undertake public responsibility, should become the spiritual leader of Catholic Ireland.

Notes

1　*Freeman's Journal*, 12 Jan. 1891.
2　Cullen, *Economic History*, p. 149.
3　Townshend, *Political Violence*, p. 115.
4　Lee, *Modernisation*, p. 73.
5　Vaughan, *Landlords and Tenants*, pp. 9–11.
6　Larkin, *Modern Irish State*, p. 24.
7　Toner Biography, Logue Papers, ADA, box 10, folder 4, ch. 5, p. 12.
8　Martin to Logue, 25 Feb. 1880, Logue Papers, RDA, no. 107 (1880).
9　*Dublin Mansion House Relief Committee Proceedings*, p. 325.

10 Martin to Logue, 25 Feb. 1880, Logue Papers, RDA, no. 107 (1880).

11 Edwards to Logue, 14 Mar. 1880, Logue Papers, RDA, no. 140 (1880).

12 *Derry Journal*, 2 Jan. 1880.

13 *Freeman's Journal*, 14 Jan. 1880.

14 *Ibid.*, 4 Feb. 1880.

15 Egan to Logue, 20 Jan. 1880, Logue Papers, RDA, no. 14 (1880).

16 *Dublin Mansion House Relief Committee Proceedings*, p. 327.

17 Bew, *Land and the National Question*, p. 116.

18 Forster to the Cabinet, 10 May 1880, TNA, CAB 37/2 (23).

19 Townshend, *Political Violence*, pp. 128–32. For statistics, see p. 183.

20 Macaulay, *Holy See*, p. 94.

21 Simeoni to McGettigan, 1 June 1880, McGettigan Papers, ADA, box 1, 'Holy See' (Translation).

22 Kirby to McCabe, 16 June 1880, McCabe Papers, DDA, box 331, folder 346/1.

23 *Freeman's Journal*, 11 Oct. 1880.

24 Kirby to McCabe, 15 Oct. 1880, McCabe Papers, DDA, box 331, folder 346/1.

25 Duggan to McCabe, 27 Oct. 1880, McCabe Papers, DDA, box 331, folder 346/1.

26 Larkin, *Modern Irish State*, p. 67–8.

27 *Freeman's Journal*, 10 Jan. 1880.

28 Larkin, *Modern Irish State*, pp. 68–70.

29 Moran to McGettigan, 5 Mar. 1881, McGettigan Papers, ADA, box 5, 'Seminaries'.

30 McGettigan to McCabe, 6 Mar. 1881, McCabe Papers, DDA, box 332, folder 346/1.

31 Logue to McCabe, 9 Mar. 1881, McCabe Papers, DDA, box 332, folder 346/1.

32 Logue to McCabe, 12 Mar. 1881, McCabe Papers, DDA, box 332, folder 346/1.

33 Larkin, *Modern Irish State*, p. 84.

34 Moran to McCabe, 21 Mar. 1881, McCabe Papers, DDA, box 332, folder 346/1.

35 Logue to McCabe, 9 Jan. 1881, McCabe Papers, DDA, box 332, folder 346/1.

36 McFadden to Logue, 13 Oct. 1881, Logue Papers, RDA, no. 17 (1881).

37 Collins to Logue, 1 Nov. 1881, Logue Papers, RDA, no. 27 (1881).

38 *ICD*, 1882, p. 242.

39 Townshend, *Political Violence*, p. 141.

40 Forster's Memorandum to the Cabinet, 30 June 1880, TNA, CAB 37/5 (45).

41 Townshend, *Political Violence*, p. 177.

42 Larkin, *Modern Irish State*, pp. 172–3.

43 Leo XIII to McGettigan, 1 Jan. 1883, McGettigan Papers, ADA, box 1, 'Holy See'(Translation).

44 See Larkin, *Modern Irish State*, chs 8 – 10.

45 Larkin, *Plan of Campaign*, p. 16.

46 Gallagher to Logue, 11 Feb. 1885, Logue Papers, RDA, no. 3 (1885).

47 McFadden to Logue, 17 Dec. 1885, Logue Papers, RDA, no. 16 (1885).

48 McFadden to Logue, 19 Dec. 1885, Logue Papers, RDA, no. 17 (1885).
49 McFadden to Logue, 4 Jan. 1886, Logue Papers, RDA, no. 1 (1886).
50 Curtis, *Coercion and Conciliation*, p. 178.
51 Salisbury's circular, 12 Apr. 1887, TNA, CAB 37/20 (30).
52 Ross to Balfour, 10 Mar. 1887, Balfour Papers, BL, MS 49821, fols 1–6.
53 Resolutions, 21 Apr. 1887, Walsh Papers, DDA, box 359, folder 402/6, 403/1–3.
54 Logue to Walsh, 12 Apr. 1887, Walsh Papers, DDA, box 359, folder 402/6, 403/1–3.
55 Maguire to Walsh, 21 Dec. 1887, Walsh Papers, DDA, box 359, folders 402/6, 403/1–3.
56 Croke to Walsh, 21 Jan. 1887, Walsh Papers, DDA, box 359, folders 402/6, 403/1–3.
57 Chadwick, *History of the Popes*, p. 432.
58 Macaulay, *Holy See*, p. 90.
59 Gualdi to Walsh, 3 Aug. 1887, Walsh Papers, DDA, box 359, folders 402/6, 403/1–3.
60 O'Callaghan, 'Persico Papers', *Collectanea Hibernica*, xxxiv/xxxv, p. 274.
61 Persico to Walsh, 22 Dec. 1887, Walsh Papers, DDA, box 359, folders 402/6, 403/1–3.
62 Macaulay, *Holy See*, pp. 118–20.
63 *Ibid.*
64 *Ibid.*, p. 127.
65 O'Callaghan, 'Persico Papers', *Collectanea Hibernica*, xxxvi/xxxvii, p. 294.
66 *Ibid.*, nos. 34/35, 1992–93, p. 185.
67 *Freeman's Journal*, 21 Jan. 1888.
68 Logue to Kirby, 20 Jan. 1888, Kirby Papers, AICR, no. 31 (1888).
69 Logue to Kirby, 15 Feb 1888, Kirby Papers, AICR, no. 74 (1888).
70 O'Callaghan, 'Persico Papers', *Collectanea Hibernica*, xxxiv/xxxv, p. 185.
71 Morrissey, *William Walsh*, p. 98.
72 Walsh to Croke, 23 Jan. 1888, Croke Papers, NLI, P0612.
73 Walsh to Croke, 12 Feb. 1888, Croke Papers, NLI, P0612.
74 Larkin, *Plan of Campaign*, p. 202.
75 Walsh to Croke, 29 Apr. 1888, Croke Papers, NLI, P0612.
76 Logue to Croke, 30 Apr. 1888, Croke Papers, NLI, P0612.
77 *Ibid.*
78 Larkin, *Plan of Campaign*, p. 224.
79 Croke to Walsh, 14 June 1888, Walsh Papers, DDA, box 360, folder 406/4–6.
80 Walsh to Logue, 26 May 1888, in Walsh, *William Walsh*, pp. 352–4.
81 *IER*, 3rd ser., ix (July 1888), p. 672.
82 Townshend, *Political Violence*, p. 195.
83 Ross to Balfour, 1 July 1888, Balfour Papers, BL, MS 49821, fols 51–2v.
84 Ross to Balfour, 19 Mar. 1889, Balfour Papers, BL, MS 49821, fols 23–6.
85 Logue to Walsh, 14 Nov. 1888, Walsh Papers, DDA, box 360, folder 403/4–6.

86 Macaulay, *Holy See*, p. 235.
87 Walsh to Kirby, 14 and 28 Dec. 1888, Kirby Papers, AICR, nos. 434 and 454 (1888).
88 O'Donnell to McFadden, 15 Mar. 1889, Kirby Papers, AICR, no. 47 (1889).
89 O'Donnell to McFadden, undated, O'Donnell Papers, RDA, no. 67 (1889).
90 Ross to Balfour, 26 Sept. 1889, Balfour Papers, BL, MS 49821, fols 28–31.
91 Duggan to Walsh, 21 June 1889, Walsh Papers, DDA, box 361, folder 404/1–3.
92 Logue to Walsh, 17 July 1890, Walsh Papers, DDA box 362, folders 404/4–6, 405/1–2.
93 Logue to Walsh, 31 July 1890, Walsh Papers, DDA box 362, folders 404/4–6, 405/1–2.
94 Logue to Walsh. 16 Aug. 1890, Walsh Papers, DDA box 362, folders 404/4–6, 405/1–2.
95 Larkin, *Fall of Parnell*, p. 158.
96 *IER*, 3rd ser., xi (Nov. 1890), p. 1048.
97 O'Callaghan, 'Persico Papers', *Collectanea Hibernica*, xxxviii, p. 171.
98 Ross to Balfour, 6 Feb. 1890, Balfour Papers, BL, MS 49821, fols 43–4v.
99 Larkin, *Fall of Parnell*, p. 193.
100 Macaulay, *Holy See*, p. 344.
101 *Ibid.*, p. 354.
102 O'Donnell to Walsh, 6 Dec. 1890, Walsh Papers, DDA box 362, folders 404/4–6, 405/1–2.
103 Glynn to Walsh, 19 Dec. 1892, Walsh Papers, DDA, box 401 Aug-Dec.
104 Croke to Walsh, 19 Dec. 1892, Walsh Papers, DDA, box 401 Aug-Dec.
105 Croke to Kirby, 28 Dec. 1892, Kirby Papers, AICR, no. 618 (1892).
106 Macaulay, *Holy See*, p. 357.
107 Walsh to Logue, 18 Dec. 1892, Logue Papers, ADA, box 3, 'Dublin archdiocese'.
108 Logue to Walsh, 19 Dec. 1892, Walsh Papers, DDA, Aug-Dec, box 401.

3

The university campaign

The question

The issue of university education in Ireland was a constant source of grievance for the bishops. The university system in Ireland was 'at the centre of a network of proselytism and indifferentism which the hierarchy had come to regard as the characteristic of the Protestant constitution in Ireland'.[1] The Roman Catholic Church demanded the same rights and recognition which the state extended to Protestants in terms of state-funded, denominational university education. The demand for national justice, however, masked other concerns and preoccupations. The challenges to traditional faith thrown up by the intellectual revolution and the advent of Darwinism made a truly Catholic university not only desirable, but essential.

It was not that the universities of Ireland were closed to Catholics, but that those universities remained theologically unacceptable to the bishops. Trinity College in Dublin with its Anglican seminary and Protestant ethos was deemed a danger to faith and morals. Likewise, the Queen's Colleges in Belfast, Cork and Dublin were also condemned because of a lack of ecclesiastical control over teaching and a ban on religious education. The bishops demanded that Irish Catholics refuse to send their children to either institution. With its generous funding and modern facilities Trinity College was often the object of covetous glances as well as condemnations from the sees of Armagh and Dublin. Despite the bishops' nationalist rhetoric, however, Trinity was not exclusively funded by the Government or from the spoils wrested from Catholics during the Penal days. The lion's share of monies came from the revenue from estates and college fees.[2]

Having condemned the Queen's Colleges and Trinity the bishops set out to establish a university of their own. In 1854 the Catholic university was established in Dublin under John Henry Newman. The university provided teaching in the arts and languages as well as science and medicine. The intention was to give Ireland a 'Catholic Oxford' but the new institution rapidly began to deteriorate. Funding and students dwindled and Newman clashed frequently with Cardinal Cullen over the direction of the university.[3] It also suffered from the fact that it could not confer recognised qualifications in any subject except medicine. Thus the Medical School, based in Cecilia Street in Dublin, for a long time remained the university's only unqualified success. In 1883 the university was reconstituted as University College, Dublin, under the direction of the Jesuits. Under an outstanding Rector in William Delaney, the college underwent something of a renaissance so that by the 1890s attendances had risen sharply.

The University Question at times proved as divisive for the bishops as the issue of political violence. In 1879 Benjamin Disraeli's Conservative Government moved to reform the university education system in Ireland. The Universities Act set up a central examining body, the Royal University of Ireland. As well as awarding degrees to students at the three Queen's Colleges, the Royal University could also confer degrees on any affiliated college. Residency was not required for matriculation except in the medical faculty. Direct funding of the Queen's Colleges continued but there was also indirect funding for Catholic colleges in the form of scholarships, fellowships and prizes. Although falling well short of the central demand for a state-funded university of their own, the Royal University was accepted as an interim measure that would bring some educational relief to the Catholics of Ireland.

That acceptance, however, was obtained by the narrowest of margins. Logue recalled that at the meeting convened to discuss the scheme, the bishops assembled had more or less decided to reject Disraeli's proposals. In a letter to Walsh in 1889, he recounted that the meeting had already voted to denounce the scheme but the following day Edward McCabe, the Archbishop of Dublin, reversed the decision and a statement was issued grudgingly accepting the Royal University. Logue was permanently suspicious of the institution. 'My view', he told Walsh, 'is that the bishops, as a body, should publicly sever all connection with it'.[4] It must be said, however, that all the public utterances and condemnations did not prevent Catholics from attending the Queen's Colleges or even Trinity.

Having replaced Cardinal McCabe in 1885, William Walsh rapidly became the foremost ideologue and spokesman for the Irish Church on the university issue. A former student at the Catholic University and President of Maynooth, he wrote prolifically on the subject and displayed a tenacity which often bordered on obsession. Walsh's position as the spiritual head of the most populous area in Ireland, his proximity to Dublin Castle and his prowess as an incisive and persistent pamphleteer made him almost uniquely suited to lead the university campaign. His proximity also to Trinity College meant that that institution was seldom far from his thoughts. Nevertheless, even he remained circumspect when dealing with the issue of the Queen's Colleges.

Despite couching their campaign in the rhetoric of the national question, the bishops remained preoccupied with securing control over the teaching, staffing and ethos in present and future universities in Ireland. Non-denominational education was as unworkable as it was undesirable. Speaking in 1889, Walsh said it was a 'fixed principle' that religiously mixed institutions were inherently dangerous to the faith and morals of Catholic students.[5] Logue was even more scathing. In 1898 he declared that an 'unsectarian' university was impossible. The Queen's Colleges, he said, were merely traps, baited with the odd Catholic professor to ensnare the few Catholic 'stray rats'. Europe, with its penchant for mixed education, was now being consumed by self-inflicted wounds. The continent was now afflicted by 'communism, socialism and anarchism in the masses and peculation and corruption in the classes!'[6]

This was an agenda which the Church was often at pains to conceal, especially in the midst of the scientific revolution. It would be disastrous for the campaign if the bishops fulfilled the worst predictions of their critics who accused them of medievalism and merely seeking state funding for Catholicism in Ireland. In truth, Church policy demanded that local hierarchies retained powers to dismiss and to appoint only in faculties of theology. However, anyone deemed to pose a threat to the faith and morals of students should be deprived of their appointment. Likewise, an institution could find itself condemned as a danger to the faith if the teaching of science there was adjudged contrary to the precepts of the Catholic Church.[7] There is little doubt that the Irish bishops sought at least some control over teaching at universities. But there was a difference between what was, in effect, the weight of Roman expectation regarding the form of a university for Catholics in Ireland and what the Irish bishops would accept. Logue, however, remained uncompromising in his approach, as might be expected from one who had to justify any settlement to the Holy See. But the same could not be said of some of his colleagues. Indeed, it was a major concern for him that the hierarchy would go too far in compromising ecclesiastical control in return for a university they could claim as being 'Catholic'.

He was content, however, to leave the direction of the campaign to William Walsh. Under Cardinal McCabe, the statements issued by the bishops on education were often critical and condemnatory but lacked direction. Walsh's impact as Archbishop of Dublin was immediate. In forging the clerical-nationalist alliance he succeeded in convincing the national movement to undertake political agitation on the university issue. In return the Irish Party received the support and moral sanction of the bishops for the Plan of Campaign and for the goal of Home Rule.[8] Barely a year after his consecration, Walsh was engaged in negotiations with Dublin Castle on the university issue. The talks with the Chief Secretary, Sir Michael Hicks-Beach, and his successor, Arthur Balfour, collapsed. The archbishop was convinced that the British had only dangled the university carrot in the hope of securing ecclesiastical support against the Plan of Campaign.[9]

Despite the failure of the negotiations, the process had confirmed Walsh as the central figure in the bishops' campaign. What also emerged from the discussions was a clearly defined strategy for the future conduct of the campaign. Two statements issued by the Standing Committee on 21 March and 25 June 1889 declared that the bishops would abstain from formulating any scheme for the settlement of the University Question, thereby passing the onus onto the Government. The bishops also announced that their demands and wishes would be best served by 'the establishment, in an exclusively Catholic, or in a common university, of one or more colleges conducted on purely Catholic principles'. On the question of safeguards for faith and morals, the Standing Committee would accept a university on the Senate of which there existed 'an adequate number of representatives enjoying the confidence of the Catholic body'.[10]

Not all of the bishops were content to follow Walsh's lead but, crucially, he had Logue's support. The campaign against Parnell had forced Logue to abandon his reluctance to enter the spotlight and his consecration as cardinal pushed him further to the fore in the university campaign. Despite his confession to Walsh that he was unprepared to assume his assigned role, Logue's pastorals and speeches reflected a growing confidence in his position in the 1890s. There was a new belligerence among the bishops on the university question. Reflecting the redress of land grievances and the general climate of unrest which had persisted following Parnell's demise, the Standing Committee asserted that 'we are made to feel bitterly the uselessness of constitutional agitation on our part. Violence and excess obtain ready hearing and lead to redress of grievances; but the constitutionally expressed desires of the Irish people . . . count for very little'.[11]

Logue's performance at an Armagh rally on the university issue in 1898 revealed his eloquence and his ability to play to the gallery. Again, the familiar themes were rehashed but Logue added a new grievance. He returned to an idea first expressed in 1896 that the taxes of Irish Catholics were being used to fund not only the 'Godless' Queen's Colleges but Trinity as well. He argued that those 'who pay the piper had the right of calling the tune' and Catholic money was being diverted by English bigots into the exclusive education of the Ascendancy. Logue incorporated in his speech all the elements designed to appeal to the nationalist sentiments of his audience. The Penal days, he declared, were alive and well in Ireland in matters of education and Irish Catholics were as much victims of bigotry now as they were then. He concluded with a rousing rallying cry for Catholics to 'persevere in their agitation till prejudice shall have yielded to reason, till the light of public opinion shall have flooded the dark places of bigotry and till victory shall have crowned their efforts!'[12] The aplomb of Logue's performances, however, belied his uncertainty when confronted with an actual proposal for a Catholic university. It was one thing to rouse an audience on the University Question but quite another when, in 1898, he was presented with a possible solution.

The demise of St Patrick's University

The impetus for this solution came from Arthur Balfour, now First Lord of the Treasury and Leader of the Commons in Lord Salisbury's Unionist Government. Balfour may have seemed a surprising champion of the cause of university education for Irish Catholics. By the 1890s, the Plan of Campaign was dead and the Irish Party was hopelessly divided, as were the Liberals. It was not quite the case, however, that the university issue had outlived its usefulness as a political bargaining chip. Balfour was one of the chief architects of the policy of constructive unionism which aimed at 'killing Home Rule with kindness'. It was the intention to address Irish grievances through root and branch reforms which, it was hoped, would diminish nationalist agitation on the issue of the Union.[13] The removal of Church grievances on education might have garnered valuable support from the episcopate but Balfour was also generally committed to educational reform. He was a keen amateur scientist and philosopher with a passion for study and enough of an educationalist to seek reform for its own sake.[14]

Balfour declared that it was not his aim to conciliate the views of the Catholic hierarchy, but to afford to Irish Catholics some measure of the educational privileges enjoyed in the rest of the United Kingdom.[15] In 1887, during the talks with Walsh, he had gone as far as proposing the creation of a Catholic college within the Queen's Colleges. The scheme collapsed, however, amid opposition from members of the Cabinet and Conservative backbenchers.[16] Balfour's enthusiasm for reform, however, remained undiminished. In a speech in London on 22 January 1897, he declared that unless an acceptable system of university education could be contrived in Ireland, it would be vain to hope that higher education would be practically brought within reach of that community.[17]

The positive signals coming from Westminster were reciprocated in an episcopal statement issued in June 1897. The Standing Committee gave its clearest indication as to the extent to which the bishops were willing to compromise on the issue of ecclesiastical control. Any new university would provide secular teaching only, but priests should not be barred from holding office or attending to attain degrees after ordination. The new institution should have a faculty of theology but the bishops accepted that the chair might not be not endowed from public money. They were prepared to agree that any monies voted by Parliament should be 'applied exclusively to secular knowledge'. They also remained flexible on the issue of staffing and the university would be open to students of all faiths.[18]

An opportunity for Balfour to begin negotiations with the episcopate arose during committee wrangling on a London Universities Bill which was passing through the Commons. Opposition from Irish MPs was delaying the passing of what seemed a fairly innocuous piece of legislation. Richard Haldane, Liberal MP for Haddingtonshire and the sponsor of the bill, enquired the reason for Irish obstruction. He was told by Tim Healy, MP for North Louth, that the Irish Party had no objection to the scheme in itself. However, the price of Irish support and assistance on the bill would be a commitment to tackle university education in Ireland. Haldane was a close friend of Balfour but could not undertake such a move without consulting the Government first. Balfour, however, was 'not only sympathetic but anxious' that Haldane should try his hand. He was also content to have him act as intermediary and emissary of the Government. Moreover, the initiative also had the support of the Chancellor, Sir Michael Hicks-Beach, who promised to back any proposals with fifty thousand pounds from Irish Church surplus monies.[19]

Logue was not enthusiastic at the prospect of fresh proposals coming from Westminster. Neither was he enamoured at the new spirit of compromise abroad amongst the bishops. Despite his support for Walsh, and the fact that his name appeared on the statement as chair, the 1897 declarations proved something of a watershed and the source of much anxiety. In January 1898, the Bishop of Limerick, Edward O'Dwyer, called on him to suggest that he seize the initiative and open a dialogue with the Government. Logue was appalled at the idea and wrote to Walsh confessing that he 'could not think of taking any steps in so grave a matter without consulting your Grace and knowing your views'. O'Dwyer had also asked him to convene a meeting of the Standing Committee to issue details of compromises on the appointment of professors but Logue declined. He told Walsh that the bishops were just as likely to get what they wanted by sticking to their guns. 'In fact', he went on, 'it appears to me we have already reached the boundary line which divides from the Queen's College system and if we go further, I do not see what there is to fight for'. The kind of university that Logue hoped for was one which would be able 'to take its place beside Trinity, not a mere collection of miserable provincial colleges'.[20]

Logue remained uncertain of his own role in the unfolding developments and suspicious of Balfour. In August 1898 he wrote to Walsh to tell him he had been informed by Sir John Ross, Balfour's former Roman agent, that the Government had no intention of introducing a bill in that parliamentary session. He was also unsettled by the attitude of some of the bishops, especially the Bishop of Limerick. 'I have always feared individual action on the university question', he told Walsh, 'especially as I saw a disposition to waive the principles we have been so long contending for and to take *any* measure provided it gave the *name* of a university for Catholics'.[21] Whether Logue's fear concerned his own actions or the actions of other individuals breaking ranks was not made clear.

Regardless of Logue's concerns, events were unfolding rapidly. Armed with the support of Balfour, the promise of money from the Treasury and a draft set of proposals, Haldane set out for Dublin in October. He was well aware of a need to be circumspect. He told Balfour on 20 September that 'the ground is thoroughly rotten and requires careful walking'.[22] In his autobiography, he gives an extraordinary account of his travels which, at the time, must have seemed surreal. His first meeting was with the Archbishop of Dublin, who expressed his support for the draft proposals. Following the meeting, Haldane immediately set off to present the draft to Logue in Armagh. Walsh had advised travelling under cover of darkness as the Archbishop was sure Haldane 'was being watched closely'. As per instruction, he left his luggage at Armagh station and proceeded, in darkness and on foot, to *Ara Coeli*. Walsh had admonished Haldane to ask only women for directions as men might recognise him. On reaching the cardinal's residence he was met at the door by Logue who was dressed in full canonical scarlet. Haldane had been warned by Walsh to expect a frosty reception but this was certainly not the case. Logue informed him that he was a friend of the proposals and, when told that the Archbishop of Dublin supported the scheme, replied, 'then I approve it also'. Logue proceeded to offer a very surprised Haldane such 'little hospitality' as the rules of the Church would allow. 'He opened the door', Haldane recalled, 'and there was a table with two chairs, and on the table was an enormous dish of oysters flanked by a bottle of champagne'.[23]

Haldane reported to Balfour that, despite some initial doubts among the bishops, there was a positive response overall to his mission. He had learned from a 'private source' that a majority within the episcopate were favourable to the draft proposals but others required more information. These had 'probably placed themselves under the leadership of the primate, Cardinal Logue'. Walsh had told Haldane that the Holy See would probably accept a university that was 'permeated by Catholic influence' rather than one which was under the authority of the Irish bishops. He was adamant, however, that the hierarchy should have a say in the composition of the governing body and retain powers of dismissal over staff. Having been warned prior to his meeting with Logue of his hostility to the university proposals, Haldane was surprised to find him so positive. Logue told him that ratifying the proposals would be a mere formality, requiring only the calling of a general meeting of the episcopate. If the scheme could be successfully brought forward in England, he said, 'matters would be made easy so far as the Catholic Church was concerned'.[24] Balfour was encouraged by the positive reception Haldane had received. 'I earnestly hope', he told him, 'that all the labours you have undergone will bear fruit'.[25]

Despite Haldane's attempts at secrecy, word had leaked and details of the scheme appeared in the press. The thawing of relations between the Government and the Irish bishops was greeted with growing resentment by both Liberal and Conservative MPs.[26] Moreover, by the end of the year Balfour was facing growing sectarianism and rebellion from his party's grass roots. At a conference of the National Union of Conservative and Constitutional Associations held in Bristol in December 1898 a motion was approved which asserted that the introduction of a bill to establish a Catholic university in Ireland would be disastrous for both the Government and the party and would alienate Ulster Unionist support.[27]

By January 1899 the situation had become such that Balfour was forced to meet his critics head on. When the Manchester Conservative Union passed a motion condemning the 'endowment of Romanism' in the form of a Catholic university he chose the occasion to deal publicly with the sectarianism spreading in the party.

On 23 January 1899 he published an open letter which contained a strong rebuttal and rebuke not just for the Manchester Union but for Conservative associations throughout Britain. 'I think I am not mistaken', he said, 'in supposing that it is the religious aspect of the university question which disquiets my friends in East Manchester and elsewhere'. Balfour identified the objections to any scheme as arising from fears that a Catholic university 'would augment the power of the Irish priesthood and depress the cause of Protestantism'. He argued that this could not be further from the truth. What he proposed was 'not a scheme for making Roman Catholics but only a proposal for educating them'. Balfour asserted that, far from diminishing Protestantism, such a university would serve Protestant interests as 'the evils of priestly influence' would be negated by a 'broadening of knowledge and a more thorough culture'.[28]

Almost at the same time that Balfour published his letter, Haldane forwarded a more detailed set of proposals to Logue. Recalling their meeting the previous October, he felt sure that what was in the draft scheme came close to what they had discussed. As stated in the press, what was proposed was the establishment of two new universities. The Queen's University would be based in Belfast and was primarily intended as an institution which would appeal to Presbyterians and other Protestant denominations. St Patrick's University, to be established in Dublin, was intended for Catholics. Each Senate would be appointed by the Government and both bodies would have sole responsibility for the appointment of staff. Powers of dismissal would reside with the Senate with a right of appeal to a board of visitors appointed by the Crown. Three-fifths of the Senate would always consist of persons 'not ministers of religion'.

The endowment of both institutions was fixed at twenty-five thousand pounds per annum. No part of the proposed endowment would be applied for construction, maintenance or improvement of any place of religious worship. There would be no funding for chairs in either philosophy or modern history. Haldane informed Logue that Balfour would introduce a bill if he received a favourable response from the bishops. He was not asking for a public statement from the cardinal. Indeed, Haldane was most anxious that Logue's part in the negotiations be kept private. He told Logue that he believed Balfour would, 'without quoting or making any reference to you, be prepared to make a grave step for a statesman by making the definite step of inducing his party to accept the scheme'.[29]

Logue did not reply immediately and his silence worried Haldane. At the end of 1898 it had been decided that the St Patrick's scheme would be presented by Haldane to Parliament in the form of a private member's bill. Balfour had promised him the support of the Government and had even helped draft the bill.[30] Walsh had told Haldane that, despite the silence of the bishops and his own inability to approve the scheme, he believed a deal could still be done. He was anxious to increase the size of the endowment. 'The Catholics of Ireland', he said, 'would regard it only as an insult to be put off with an endowment on a low scale whilst Trinity College was on a far higher level in that respect'. The archbishop informed Haldane that Logue was now quite hostile to the scheme as it stood. He added wryly, 'the effect of your visit must have been quite evanescent'.[31] Haldane was disappointed in the attitude of the Archbishop of Dublin, believing he was 'only trying for more money'. He told Balfour that, if this was the case, the scheme was dead as no more money could be found. The continuing silence from Armagh was cause for grave concern.[32] On 25 January 1899, however, Logue sent a telegram confirming he had received the proposed bill and asking permission to show it to the bishops' Standing Committee. Haldane was relieved. 'I think well of Logue's telegram', he told Balfour; 'he is the straightest of them'.[33]

Despite what he told Haldane in October and despite assenting to the proposals because they had received a nod from Walsh, Logue was uneasy about what was on offer. He confessed to Walsh on 3 January that he had 'a nervous fear of whittling down our demands to what is scarcely within the bounds of orthodoxy'.[34] He repeated his belief that the Government would just as soon grant a liberal measure as easily as a 'niggardly one' and it was dangerous to soften their position any further. He told Walsh on 16 January, 'it is hard to see where the proposed universities would differ in their constitutions from the Queen's Colleges'. Logue was outraged at the financial arrangements of the scheme. But it was the issues of ecclesiastical control of teaching and the reaction of Rome which caused him most concern. He told Walsh, 'I don't see what security we have for the character of the teaching. There is no test so that a professor may be an infidel as far as the proposed bill is concerned.' He also doubted that St Patrick's would escape papal censure. 'I believe', he told Walsh, 'that if the policy of the Holy See were the same as at the time the Queen's Colleges were established, the whole scheme would likely be condemned'.[35]

Logue's concerns were shared by the Standing Committee. At a meeting convened to discuss the proposed bill on 23 February 1899, the bishops drafted a set of amendments designed to make the scheme more palatable. The senate should exclusively comprise Catholics and have bishops represented adequately at all times. The monies for St Patrick's should be equal in every way to the funding received by Trinity. The Chancellor should always be a Catholic and at least two of the visiting body should be Irish bishops. No head of faculty or department should be excluded from that appointment on the grounds of being a priest. The Committee also utterly rejected the exclusion of philosophy and modern history from the curriculum. Finally, the bishops demanded that 'means should be provided by the university statutes for removing from office teachers or professors who propound doctrines in opposition to the faith and morals of Catholics'.[36] The objections of the bishops had been summed up in a letter to Haldane from Walsh prior to the meeting. 'Trinity has its Protestant complexion practically secured', he said, 'whilst there is no effective code [or] responding provision on our side'.[37]

It is extremely doubtful whether Balfour would have countenanced *any* of the proposed changes demanded by the bishops. Likewise, it was to be expected, perhaps, that the bishops could not have been enamoured of a scheme designed to undermine 'the evils of priestly influence'. Logue was well aware of the impact that these amendments would have on the attitude of the Government and also how they would play in English public opinion. Rather than publish, he decreed that the resolutions should remain confidential. On 1 March he wrote to Walsh informing him that rumours had reached *Ara Coeli* that the Government would not now press ahead with any university scheme for Ireland. Rather than give Balfour an excuse to paint the bishops as unreasonable, Logue wanted to hold back on any statement. If they published anything, it should contain no mention of draft proposals or acknowledgement that the bishops had received a scheme from London. Such a statement should merely welcome the spirit in which matters were proceeding and state that the bishops could not make a pronouncement on proposals they had not seen.[38]

The difficulty for Balfour, which Logue shrewdly recognised, was that his initiative was not Government policy at all. St Patrick's was the product of a personal collaboration with a member of the Opposition and despite support from key Government figures, such as Hicks-Beach, he had yet to sway the Unionist parliamentary party. Any prospect of this receded rapidly in the early months of 1899. The St Patrick's proposals suffered from the fact that they were presented amid a bitter and vitriolic debate between High and Low Church within Anglicanism. The controversy centred on the retention of Roman ritual and traditions such as the Benediction and Church societies such as sodalities and confraternities. Unfortunately for Balfour, the volume of criticism from within his own party was significantly increased as the vitriol from the Anglican debate spilled over. As early as September 1898, he had expressed anxiety over the effect of the controversy on the St Patrick's proposals. 'All this ritualistic row', he told Haldane, 'has come at a most unfortunate moment'.[39] On 13 February 1899 Logue told Walsh that he had received a letter from Haldane intimating that Balfour's resolve was wavering. Haldane had also alleged that ministers were receiving threatening letters from their constituents on the religious issue.[40]

In the face of opposition from his own party and daunted by the sectarian vitriol in the press, Balfour quietly withdrew his support for the scheme. Logue was absolutely furious. In an angry letter to Haldane on 6 March 1899, he declared, 'seeing the spirit of bigotry which has lately developed . . . it is useless to seek the redress of a Catholic grievance from the English Parliament'. There was only one hope left, he went on, 'that is to cease agitating for particular remedies and to go in with all the energy the country can command for Home Rule'.[41] Logue waited until June to comment publicly on the collapse of the scheme. At a prize-giving ceremony in Maynooth he launched a scathing attack on the Government. He told his audience that a university was denied them simply because they were Catholics. 'Still, it would seem', he went on, 'that the cries of bigotry have once more been allowed to stifle the voice of justice and that the Unionist Party is prevented by the bigotry of a number of its members from remedying the long-standing grievance of the Catholics of Ireland'.[42]

Having tarred the Unionist Government with the sectarian brush, Logue turned his attention to the Irish Party. The performance of Irish MPs on the university question remained a source of disappointment for him. While previous statements had urged the party to unite behind the bishops and the university campaign, Logue's pronouncement was of a different hue altogether. He called on Irish Catholics to 'exclude from any representative position in their gift, any man who will not put this question of educational equality for the Catholics at the forefront of his political programme and labour honestly to secure it'.[43] In a letter to the Archbishop of Dublin, Logue derided the efforts of the Irish Party. He told Walsh that 'the country would just as well be unrepresented as being in the hands of the present squabblers!'[44]

Victory and consolidation

Logue's statement drew a line under the Balfour initiative and the university question receded for the next two years. From 1901, however, a series of Royal Commissions sparked the issue into life once again. The impetus for the first of these came from the Bishop of Limerick, Thomas O'Dwyer. Separating himself from the bishops' policy of 'wait and see', he forged an alliance with John Healy, Bishop of Clonfert and coadjutor in Tuam, and the Rector of University College, William Delaney.[45] The move was a radical departure from the course set by Walsh. Logue was appalled that the university issue would be discussed in such a public and unpredictable forum as a Royal Commission.[46] Moreover, the fact that O'Dwyer and his allies had drafted a university scheme in defiance of the agreed policy of the hierarchy caused a bitter rift between the sees of Dublin and Limerick.[47]

The Royal Commission under Lord Chief Justice John Robertson sat from September 1901 until June 1902 and heard from a hundred and forty witnesses. Its report was not unanimous and found favour with none of the factions among the bishops. The final report included a recommendation that the Royal University be reconstituted as a teaching university made up of the three Queen's Colleges. A university college should be established in Dublin for Catholics, which would effectively mean an endowment for a Catholic university.[48] The schemed proved unacceptable to all sides. A series of subsequent talks between the Chief Secretary, George Wyndham, William Walsh and John Healy, failed to make headway. A further Royal Commission also added little to the university debate. Logue despaired of the whole process and fretted about the direction of the campaign. In a letter to Walsh on 11 November 1906 he confessed: 'I have long seen that things are drifting and drifting rapidly. I believe that drift began when the bishops [watered down] their requirements for a Catholic college or university to the point that such an institution would be barely distinguishable from the Queen's Colleges.' He also voiced concern over the disunity among the prelates and the fact that this had 'got abroad'. He told Walsh, 'if we do not speak with one voice it is all up for us'.[49]

The Liberal landslide in 1906, however, brought with it fresh prospects and a change in personnel. The final settlement of the University Question owed much to the personality and persistence of the Chief Secretary, Augustine Birrell. Appointed in January 1907, Birrell brought a fresh perspective to Ireland and a flair for educational reform. The reasons for the ultimate success of the Birrell plan lay in his willingness to work with Walsh from the outset and his ability to persuade the archbishop that there could simply be no settlement that involved Trinity. He was also able to capitalise on a political atmosphere lacking the kind of sectarianism that had so undermined Balfour's initiative. As he told Walsh in December 1907, 'unhappily no one in England *really* cares a straw about the University Question in Ireland'. Unhappily, perhaps, for Birrell's attempt to raise support from Liberal MPs; but also fortunately in that the Chief Secretary could afford to ignore a certain 'fanatical crowd who, terrified of the neo-Catholicism of the Church of England, see Popery writ large over the whole subject'.[50]

Logue played very little part in the negotiations, preferring to trust to the judgement of the Archbishop of Dublin. Having received an outline of the proposals in November 1907, Logue gave a cautious response. He told Walsh that 'a perfectly satisfactory arrangement for Catholics' could be found along the lines contemplated by Birrell, but warned that substantial reform of the Queen's Colleges would be required to make them acceptable. He was, however, obviously weary of schemes and proposals and he continued to be extremely wary of compromise. 'It seems to have been the policy of the Chief Secretaries of both parties to get the bishops to make concessions and then throw them over', he told Walsh. 'We have gone to the very edge of what principle will admit; and we are now like men wedged between two immovable walls.' He would rather, he said, have things left the way they were rather than have things so constituted that they would be left with nothing but 'seminaries of indifference'.[51]

The Chief Secretary forwarded a draft copy of his plan to Logue in December to be sure he was 'on the right lines'. The attraction of the plan was that it offered a completely new university system for Ireland. The Queen's College in Belfast would be reconstituted as a university in its own right. The Royal University would be abolished and in its place a 'National University' would be established with a new Catholic University in Dublin and constituent colleges in Cork and Galway. There would be no religious tests but no funding for religious education of any kind. However, there was no ban on clerics becoming teachers or holding positions in the Senate, which would be nominated by the Crown.[52]

Logue still had some concerns. In January 1908 he wrote to Walsh expressing his fear that the Senate would be dominated by people from Trinity or the Queen's Colleges.[53] For his part, Walsh was busy attempting to bully Birrell into releasing more funding for the proposals.[54] By the end of January 1908, the bishops had met to discuss the proposals and, as there were no resolutions drafted, Walsh reported the disposition of the Standing Committee to Birrell himself. The bishops were generally satisfied with the provisions of the proposals. However, concern was expressed over the position of Maynooth and the lack of provision for its affiliation with the new university. Aside from that, Walsh reported that there was the 'greatest possible readiness to consider the matter in all its various aspects'.[55]

In April 1908, Logue was sufficiently confident in both the bill and Walsh's abilities to leave Ireland to attend centennial celebrations in the archdiocese of New York. The engagement was a long standing appointment which he had accepted in the previous year, but before leaving he informed Walsh that he had forwarded a copy of the bill to Cardinal Gotti, Prefect of Propaganda.[56] In his absence, the bishops met to consider the bill again in May. Concern still remained over the position of Maynooth and the composition of the Senate and Walsh wrote to Birrell to warn him of a mood of dissatisfaction. He told the Chief Secretary that 'seeing as the Holy See condemned the system of the Queen's Colleges it is pretty obvious that if things are in any way worse in this respect in the new college the outlook will be a gloomy one!'[57] Birrell moved quickly to address these concerns and, following some trouble in the committee stage, the bill was passed virtually unopposed.[58]

On Logue's return to Ireland in June, the Standing Committee issued a statement in support of the university bill. Their acceptance was explained not so much with bad grace as with a desire to declare, in no uncertain terms, the extent to which they had compromised. The new university, they pointed out, was not framed in accordance with the 'religious sentiments and convictions of this Catholic nation'. However the bishops did 'freely recognise the limitations which existing parliamentary conditions impose upon the government and desire to solve this question as easily as possible'.[59] The bill did encounter some opposition towards the end. In July, the Presbyterian General Assembly voiced concerns over the introduction of denominational education into Ireland. Logue complained bitterly to Walsh that 'the impudence of these people in dictating what will suit the majority of the Irish people is intolerable!' He told the archbishop to make sure that Birrell was aware that 'any concession to such bigotry would get a hostile reception from Catholics'.[60] Despite these last-minute hitches, the bill passed into law as a triumph of compromise and practicality. On 1 August 1908 the bishops' university campaign finally came to an end.

Logue was very relieved when Walsh secured the position of Chancellor of the National University. In December 1908 he wrote to convey his hearty congratulations at what he described as a 'fit crowning of many long years of hard work'. Having Walsh at the helm, he was sure, would give Catholics a security of faith and morals which they would not have had otherwise.[61] Despite this, Logue's support for the National University was grudging at best. The proscription against religious teaching and the inexplicable denial of chairs in modern history and philosophy, both of which were available at Queen's in Belfast, dampened his enthusiasm considerably. Speaking at the Marist College in Dundalk in June 1909 he told his audience that the university, like all concessions they received from their friends in England, 'bore the brand of slavery impressed upon it'.[62] In his view the institution was far, far short of what Catholics in Ireland would wish for themselves. Nevertheless, he did encourage Catholic youth to avail themselves of the university, safe in the knowledge that with Walsh as chancellor, the danger to faith and morals would be diminished.

The National University enabled the Church to tighten its ban on Catholics attending Trinity, now that students had a viable and safe alternative. Birrell's settlement had effectively introduced educational partition, a situation in which Trinity found itself increasingly isolated. It was not enough, however, that the new university would have the name 'Catholic' and the support of the bishops. The National University was guided by some brilliant individuals who recognised that if it was to succeed, it must provide the very best in higher education. As Bertram Windle, President of the National University at Cork, told Walsh in 1910, any mistakes which were made in the beginning would increase the pull of Belfast and Trinity.[63]

In some respects, Logue hindered the settlement of the University Question. His lack of confidence on assuming the primacy at the end of the 1880s caused him to dither over the calling of episcopal meetings. Walsh, who dominated the bishops on the education question in the same way as he had led on the Plan of Campaign, was exasperated by the indecision in Armagh. In March 1889, during the Plan of Campaign, as Balfour was formulating a draft scheme, Logue forgot to summon a meeting. Walsh told the Bishop of Elphin, Laurence Gillooly, 'I see quite plainly that as long as the initiative is left to him, nothing will be done, and we shall simply be effaced'.[64] However, as cardinal after 1893, Logue was a powerful voice against compromise with the British Government. His preoccupation with ecclesiastical control was one of the main reasons for the collapse of the St Patrick's scheme in 1898, though deflecting possible criticism of the bishops on to the Government was a deft touch.

However, Logue's determination to have a university acceptable to Rome ultimately ensured the success of the campaign. There would have been little point in accepting a university which was deemed 'Catholic' only to then have it condemned by the Holy See. Logue trusted Walsh to deliver an institution that would not only meet the requirements of Rome but also be of sufficient prestige to redress Catholic grievances on the status of Trinity College. This cooperation eased whatever early tension existed in the relationship between the two men, though the partnership between Armagh and Dublin sometimes dismayed others within the episcopate. Walsh undoubtedly remained the intellectual mainspring of the university campaign but Logue played his part. He was a forceful and eloquent speaker on the issue who successfully painted the demand for a university in terms of the national question and religious intolerance towards Catholics. His preoccupation with ecclesiastical control was a reflection not only of his orthodoxy but also of the need felt by within the Church to protect the faithful from the intellectual revolution currently underway in Europe.

Notes

1 Norman, *Catholic Church*, p. 33.
2 McDowell, *Trinity College*, p. 510, also Luce, *Trinity College*, chs 10 and 11.
3 Morrissey, *William Walsh*, p. 6.
4 Logue to Walsh, 5 Feb. 1889, Walsh Papers, DDA, box 361, folder 404/5.
5 Walsh, *University Question*, pp. 154–60.
6 *Drogheda Argus*, 19 Feb. 1898.
7 See Daniel Coghlan, 'The Church and Human Liberty' and 'The Church in Countries of Mixed Religion', *IER*, 4th sec. xix and xx (Jan. and Oct. 1906).
8 *ICD*, 1886, p. 439.
9 Walsh to Kirby, 19 Dec. 1886 and 30 May 1887, Kirby Papers, AICR, nos. 538 and 284 (1886 and 1887).
10 William Walsh, *University Question*, pp. 400–1.
11 *Ibid.*, p. 423.
12 *Drogheda Argus*, 19 Feb. 1898.
13 Gailey, *Death of Kindness*, p. 26.
14 Correspondence between Balfour and R. B. Haldane, Haldane Papers, NLS, MS 5904.
15 Walsh, *University Question*, p. 202.
16 Larkin, *Fall of Parnell*, pp. 108–14.
17 Walsh, *University Question*, p. xviii.
18 *ICD*, 1898, p. 377.
19 Haldane, *Autobiography*, pp. 128–9.

20 Logue to Walsh, 30 Jan. 1898, Walsh Papers, DDA, box 370, folder 357/6.

21 Logue to Walsh, 9 Aug. 1898, Walsh Papers, DDA, box 370, folder 357/6.

22 Haldane to Balfour, 20 Sept. 1898, Balfour Papers, BL, MS 49724, fols 10–11*v*.

23 Haldane, *Autobiography*, pp. 130–2.

24 Haldane to Sandars (Balfour's private secretary), 20 Oct. 1898, Balfour Papers, BL, MS 49724, fols 14–15.

25 Balfour to Haldane, 24 Oct. 1898, Haldane Papers, NLS, MS 5904.

26 *The Times*, 4 Mar. 1898.

27 *Ibid.*, 8 Dec. 1898.

28 *University Education in Ireland*, Logue Papers, ADA, box 8, folder 5, 'Universities'.

29 Haldane to Logue, 21 Jan. 1899, Logue Papers, ADA, box 8, folder 5, 'Universities'.

30 Haldane to Balfour, 3 Jan. 1899, Haldane Papers, NLS, MS 5904, fol. 179.

31 Walsh to Haldane, 19 Jan. 1899, Balfour Papers, BL, MS 49724, fols 47–8*v*.

32 Haldane to Balfour, 23 Jan. 1899, Balfour Papers, BL, MS 49724, fols 51–2*v*.

33 Haldane to Balfour, 25 Jan. 1899, Balfour Papers, BL, MS 49724, fol. 54*r–v*.

34 Logue to Walsh, 3 Jan. 1899, Walsh Papers, DDA, box 371, folder 364/3.

35 Logue to Walsh, 16 Jan. 1899, Walsh Papers, DDA, box 371, folder 364/3.

36 Resolutions, 23 Feb. 1899, Logue Papers, ADA, box 8, folder 5, 'Universities'.

37 Walsh to Haldane, 5 Feb. 1899, Haldane Papers, NLS, MS 5904, folder 187.

38 Logue to Walsh, 1 Mar. 1899, Walsh Papers, DDA, box 371, folder 394/3.

39 Balfour to Haldane, 24 Sept. 1898, Balfour Papers, BL, MS 49724, fols 12–13*v*.

40 Logue to Walsh, 13 Feb. 1899, Walsh Papers, DDA, box 371, folder 364/3.

41 Logue to Haldane, 6 Mar. 1899, Balfour Papers, BL, MS 49724, fols 64–7.

42 *Freeman's Journal*, 21 June 1899.

43 *Ibid.*

44 Logue to Walsh, 1 Mar. 1899, Walsh Papers, DDA, box 371, folder 363/3.

45 Morrissey, *William Walsh*, p. 83.

46 Logue to Walsh, 25 July 1901, Walsh Papers, DDA, box 384, folder 358/2.

47 Walsh to Logue, 17 Dec. 1901, Logue Papers, ADA, box 3, 'Dublin Archdiocese'.

48 *Royal Commission on University Education (Ireland)*, 1902, Cd 900, p. 131.

49 Logue to Walsh, 11 Nov. 1906, Walsh Papers, DDA, box 378, folder 374/4.

50 Birrell to Walsh, 13 Dec. 1907, Walsh Papers, DDA, box 1, folder 14, 'Birrell's University Scheme'.

51 Logue to Walsh, 19 Nov. 1907, Walsh Papers, box 379, folder 381/2.

52 Birrell to Logue, 31 Dec. 1907, Logue Papers, ADA, box 8, folder 5, 'Universities'.

53 Logue to Walsh, 3 Jan. 1908, Walsh Papers, DDA, box 380, folder 375/1.

54 Walsh to Birrell, 6 Jan. 1908, Walsh Papers, DDA, box 380, folder 375/1.

55 Walsh to Birrell, 23 Jan 1908, Walsh Papers, DDA, box 1, folder 14, 'Birrell's University Scheme'.

56 Logue to Walsh, 16 Apr. 1908, Walsh Papers, DDA, box 380, folder 375/1.

57 Walsh to Birrell, 8 May 1908, Walsh Papers, DDA, box 1, folder 14, 'Birrell's University Scheme'.
58 Walsh to Birrell, 28 May 1908, Walsh Papers, DDA, box 1, folder 14, 'Birrell's University Scheme'.
59 *ICD*, 1909, p. 514.
60 Logue to Walsh, 17 July 1908, Walsh Papers, DDA, box 380, folder 375/1.
61 Logue Papers, 18 Dec. 1908, Walsh Papers, DDA, box 380, folder 375/1.
62 *ICD*, 1910, p. 478.
63 Windle to Walsh, 21 Jan. 1910, Walsh Papers, DDA, box 1, folder 4, 'National University'.
64 Larkin, *Fall of Parnell*, p. 107.

4

Evolution and docility of mind

The new science

The nineteenth century was theologically fraught not just for Catholicism but for Christianity in general. As the Church struggled to face the challenges thrown up by modern science, Logue maintained a simple faith. Along with a commitment to the idea of clerical control over education, he retained an orthodox view of the role of the clergy in Ireland. The bishops stood as guardians over the faith and morals of their flocks and it was the duty of the priesthood to hand down the faith and traditions of the Church as interpreted by Rome. For Logue, true piety among Catholics could only be maintained through what Leo XIII described as 'docility of mind'.[1] This necessary acquiescence on the part of the faithful in matters of doctrine and belief, however, became increasingly difficult to maintain in the latter half of the nineteenth century.

For Christianity, and Catholicism in particular, evolution theory as outlined by Charles Darwin in *Origin of Species* and later *Descent of Man*, appeared to present considerable challenges. In suggesting a natural explanation for the creation and development of life in the form of the idea of natural selection, Darwin not only contradicted the biblical account of creation but offered a universe which could run quite well without the Christian God at all. Evolution was creation and development devoid of conscious purpose.[2] Historically, the Catholic Church has not often been associated with scientific endeavour and engagement with modern thought. In Ireland and across the Catholic world, however, a passionate debate on science developed among the clergy. Certain priests embraced the discoveries of modern science and actively sought to reconcile their faith with evolution theory to defend the Church from accusations of medievalism. Others, alarmed at the pace of theological change, offered passionate resistance, believing modern scientific theory was nothing more than dangerous heresy.

Ireland lagged behind in terms of the debate on science in the wider Catholic world. In the years following the publication of *Origin of Species* in 1859 and even *Descent of Man* in 1871 there was a remarkable reluctance among the clergy of Ireland to discuss science in the journals of the day. Even in Ireland's national seminary at Maynooth, there was little discussion of scientific ideas or modern thought. Father Walter McDonald, Professor of Theology and Prefect of the Dunboyne Course at Maynooth from 1881–1920 was amazed at this lack of debate during his tuition there in the 1870s. At a time when the ideas of Darwin, T. H. Huxley and Herbert Spencer were setting the intellectual world alight, he wrote, 'our strong child-like faith kept us safe in the Middle-ages which was well for those of us that could stay there but full of danger for any that could not'.[3]

This lack of scientific discussion is not easily explained. Compared with England, conditions in Ireland were not conducive to a wide ranging debate. By the 1860s half of the British population lived in cities, there was an affluent middle class and a printed media with large circulations fed a general hunger for scientific debate.[4] In contrast, less than a quarter of Irish people in 1881 lived in towns with a population of over two thousand and the majority of Catholics remained tied to the land.[5] The Catholic middle class in Ireland was much smaller than its counterpart in England. Yet, as Jones has shown, Catholic Ireland did have an intelligentsia and there was a strong demand for higher education and an interest in science among the Catholic middle class.[6] Ireland also had an established scientific culture. There was a vibrant network of scientific and natural history field clubs that enabled engagement between amateur and professional scientists. Trinity College in Dublin became a hotbed of evolutionary debate.[7] But the clubs were dominated by Protestants and Protestant clergy, and the ethos of Trinity, despite Catholic attendance there, remained overwhelmingly Protestant.

Perhaps one event more than any other set the parameters for the relationship between the Catholic clergy and science in Ireland. In 1874, John Tyndall, an Irishman and president of the Royal Institute, addressed a meeting in Belfast of the British Association for the Advancement of Science (BAAS). Tyndall presented a militantly materialistic interpretation of Darwin's theory of evolution by natural selection. He told his audience that 'we shall wrest from theology the entire domain of cosmological theory'.[8] He also dared trespass upon the question of Catholic education in Ireland, declaring the hope that Irish youth would be emancipated by science; that they would imbibe and be leavened by it.[9]

It was too much for Paul Cullen, Cardinal Archbishop of Dublin. In an angry pastoral to the Irish people Cullen condemned Tyndall and his address. He also took the opportunity to pronounce on the nature of true science. Proper science, he claimed, 'is the observation of facts as they *are* in the material world, not *how* things came to be'. It is perhaps unsurprising that the man who drafted the final wording of the declaration of Papal Infallibility in 1870 should issue such a vehement and vitriolic attack.[10] What Catholics heard in chapels across Ireland was a strident reiteration of the intellectual authority of the Catholic Church. Tyndall, he said, had 'obtruded blasphemy against this Catholic nation'. The address to the BAAS was dismissed as 'the pride of intellect that exalteth itself against the knowledge of God' and evolution was merely a rehash of the old pagan naturalism rejected by the ancient Church and 'reprobated by the Holy Spirit as unpardonable sin'.

Evolution, then, had been portrayed to ordinary Catholics as pagan and sinful and anathema to Catholicism. Moreover, Tyndall's views on education were seized upon as vindication of the bishops' condemnation of the universities of Ireland and the episcopal ban on Catholics attending Trinity or the Queen's Colleges. In these institutions, Cullen declared, 'the chairs of science . . . are ever converted to pulpits whence infidelity and irreligion are disseminated'. Far from being the enemy of science, the Church was a promoter of all knowledge which, if rightly handled, would lead back to God from whence it came.[11]

Given the vehemence of Cullen's attack it is not surprising that the clergy of Maynooth should remain reluctant to discuss science. Although the most public condemnation of Darwin in Ireland, Cullen's pastoral was not the first. In May 1873 an article was published in the *Irish Ecclesiastical Record* under the pseudonym J. G. C. which set out to ridicule Darwin and his theories. Evolution was dismissed as fantasy containing less truth than the legend of Prometheus. J. G. C. scoffed at the notion of the mutability of species and derided natural selection as Moloch, 'only appeased by the ruthless extermination of the unsuccessful competitors'.[12] Similar themes were repeated in a pamphlet by J. K. C. published in 1875, this time in mocking verse:

> Our Darwin, I own, is too bold for a flunky,
> Since he holds that all mankind have come from a monkey.
> Will he tell us how long till his monkeys shall speak
> And become great proficients in Latin and Greek?[13]

Bad verse aside, although the overall tone of both articles remains scornful they represent at least some engagement with and consideration of science among the Irish clergy.

The response in England and elsewhere was different. In 1869 St George Jackson Mivart published a series of articles in response to *Origin of Species* in the *Quarterly Review*. Mivart was a convert to Catholicism and had been a lecturer in St Mary's Hospital Medical School in London since 1862. He was initially encouraged by Darwin himself to publish and the articles formed the basis for *On the Genesis of Species* published in book form in 1871. Fiercely protective of Catholic tradition and critical of natural selection, he nevertheless conceded the plausibility of evolution. Moreover, Mivart argued that evolution may have been the means by which God shaped the cosmos. This 'theistic evolution' sought to take the materialistic sting out of Darwin's theory and make it more palatable to Catholic orthodoxy.

This willingness in England to engage with evolution and modern science head-on was repeated elsewhere. In France, for example, the clergy and Catholic intellectuals had long been accustomed to publishing on science. In 1869, Gillaume-René Meignan, Bishop of Chalons-sur-Marne and later Cardinal Archbishop of Tours, presented an interpretation of the historical character of the biblical account of creation which did not clash with scientific ideas on geology in *Le Monde primitif selon le Bible*.[14] In the United States, the Catholic clergy engaged in scientific discussion with the blessing of members of the hierarchy such as James Gibbons, Cardinal Archbishop of Baltimore.[15]

In Ireland, however, by 1880, articles on modern science remained purely condemnatory. In June, another vitriolic attack on Darwinism appeared in the *Record*. 'Revelation, geology and the antiquity of man' was published by a priest under the pseudonym H. E. D. The essential argument presented was that the Bible contained the one true account of creation: 'we prove the truth of our assertions by the authority of the oldest book in the world, the veracity and authenticity of which are demonstrated by inherent and outward evidence'. H. E. D. denied the idea that humanity was older than events portrayed in the Bible and dismissed Darwin's 'animated leaves and intellectual shellfish and talking baboons'. Evolution remained a theory of 'coincidences and verisimilitudes, tracing fancied resemblances and incipiencies and hiding its improbability under supposed ages of interminable length'.[16]

The first signs of a coherent debate on Darwin in Ireland emerged in 1884. James McCaffery, Professor of Ecclesiastical History at Maynooth, identified the two sides in the ensuing controversy as Traditionalist and Concessionist. Traditionalists looked to the biblical account of creation as the only orthodox view. They sought to defend traditional doctrine and belief from the challenges of modern science. Concessionists were those clergy for whom the discoveries of modern science had forced a reinterpretation of traditional doctrine and theology. As Brundell has argued, rather than perceive science as a threat, they felt an 'imperative to try and resolve the tensions between religion and science and preserve a coherent Christian world view'.[17] Labels such as Traditionalists or conservatives and Concessionists or progressives, however, are misleading. They suggest that 'progressives' were not conservative on matters of faith and were therefore insufficiently orthodox. Likewise Traditionalists or conservatives were not all unthinking obstructionists.[18]

The position of the Pope played a crucial role for both sides. Leo XIII was a pontiff for whom the social questions of the day were paramount. No pronouncement on evolution or science was forthcoming from Rome, leaving Traditionalists with little framework on which to mount a defence of their position. Concessionists revelled in the doctrinal vacuum and used the general spirit of scholarship fostered by Leo to push the boundaries of orthodoxy. The only encyclical Leo offered for guiding Catholics engaging in science was a re-emphasis of scholastic philosophy and the teaching of St Thomas Aquinas in *Aeterni Patris* issued in 1878.

Thomism was intended to provide Catholics with a medium through which to approach science and engage the secular world.[19] It was the epitome of the observation of facts that *are* in the material world and its intricacies defy more than the briefest of descriptions here. Essentially, the philosophy held that there could be no conflict between the natural and supernatural world since both had the same author in God. The material world existed in two states – Potentiality and Act. Act means perfection and Potentiality imperfection. Only something existing in a state of Act could move another in a state of Potentiality towards a state of Act. Since God is the source of all perfection, Thomism, in part, represented the observation of God's interaction with all things in the state of Potentiality.[20] Both sides in the debate used Thomism in their central arguments. Traditionalists used it as an alternative to the rationality of modern science. Progressive theologians, like Mivart, would interpret the process between Potentiality and Act as a proto-evolutionary theory which could provide the basis for an accommodation with science.

In an article entitled 'Darwinism', published in the *Record* in September 1884, Jeremiah Murphy, secretary to the Bishop of Cloyne, argued that the Bible was valid proof of the immutability of species. Evolution simply did not exist since complex and primitive organisms could be readily observed interacting in the modern world. He angrily denounced Darwin for elevating the beasts of the field to the same level as human beings with immortal souls. Murphy pointed to evolution as the new enemy of the Church, as 'Protestantism, with its cognate broods of heresy, is beneath contempt as an adversary now'.[21] The overall tone of the article was one of sneering dismissal but it also revealed something of the inherent insecurity in the Traditionalist position. There was, perhaps, something fearful in Murphy's allegation that the evolutionists 'would take from us the God whom our fathers adored, the religion that is our sole consolation here and our passport to happiness hereafter and as a substitute they would give us nothing – absolutely nothing'.[22] In December, Murphy published a further article condemning as contrary to Catholic doctrine the application of evolution theory or natural selection to humankind.[23]

In July 1885, John S. Vaughan of St Bede's in Manchester published 'Evolution and faith' in reply to Murphy. There was nothing particularly unusual in an English priest publishing in an Irish ecclesiastical journal. The *Record* had a wide audience, as did that other clerical mainstay, the *Irish Catholic Directory*. In the same way, Irish priests contributed regularly to *The Tablet* in England. Vaughan, who would become Bishop of Salford in 1908, criticised Murphy's rejection of evolution out of hand. He upheld the right of Catholics to accept evolution as a 'plausible hypothesis' in the absence of any firm definition. Vaughan argued that the Church needed to debate the issue freely. There was no dispute that God created human beings and gave them souls. However, the manner in which that creation took place was very much up for interpretation as scripture remained unclear and there was no theological consensus in the Church. Vaughan argued that the way in which the first human body was formed possessed a strong interest for many. 'But to suppose that it has any deep rooted connection with our religious interests', he went on, 'or that it can affect in any appreciable way our attitudes towards God or towards each other is surely a profound mistake'.[24]

A flurry of articles then followed between Murphy and Vaughan, each growing ever more strident in defence of their respective positions. In 'Faith and evolution', published in the *Record* in August 1885, Murphy returned to materialism in evolution theory. 'Surely no system of exegesis could be more suicidal for Catholics to adopt', he argued, 'than one which, while it fails to satisfy their own principles, gives to the enemies of Revelation a handle for the total rejection of the whole of sacred scripture as a collection of meaningless jargon'.[25] Vaughan replied that Catholics could freely hold with evolutionary theory and the mediate creation of Adam's body without being condemned as heretics and hell-bound.[26] He accused Murphy of being misleading in his logic, 'while rhetorical flourishes and fervid apostrophes are too often called upon to do duty for the more prosaic, but less easy process of reasoning'.[27] The controversy was ended abruptly in November 1885 when the *Record's* editor, Robert Browne, called a halt. Further articles had been received from Vaughan but Browne had had enough of two priests bickering in public and the matter was deemed 'fully discussed'.[28]

Two priests squabbling over science hardly constituted an open clerical debate, but gradually more priests began publishing on Darwin and other scientific subjects. The continued absence of a definitive doctrine on the question of evolution was a telling factor in the development of the general debate in the Irish Church and in the wider Catholic world. The lack of dogma forced clerics to look inward to existing theology to help justify or condemn in their respective positions. In the 1890s, for example, a spirited argument developed around the writings of St Augustine and his interpretation of Genesis. Philip Burton, a Vincentian or Missionary Father from Cork, asserted that St Augustine's work precluded a consideration of the mediate creation of Adam's body or any other aspect of creation.[29]

The article was prompted by the publication in the United States of *Evolution and Dogma* by John Augustine Zahm. Zahm was a priest of the Holy Cross and Professor of Physics at Notre Dame. Like Mivart, he was fascinated by science and modern thought and regarded neither as a threat to traditional Christianity. He claimed it was perfectly acceptable for Catholics to believe that Adam had developed from some kind of anthropomorphic ape. Moreover, in *Catholic Science and Catholic Scientists*, Zahm passionately pleaded for reconciliation between science and Catholicism. It was his 'sole ardent desire' to show that there was nothing in true science or in evolution, when properly understood, that was contrary to scripture or Catholic teaching.[30]

The idea that St Augustine could provide some arguments to bridge the gap between Catholicism and modern science was supported by Patrick Coakley, an Augustinian from Donegal. In reply to Burton's article, Coakley argued that the theory of evolution was not synonymous with atheism. Evolution had suffered from the militant anticlericalism of some of its most vociferous advocates. Coakley drew attention to Huxley's assertion in *Darwinia* that the theory of evolution, 'in addition to its truth, has the great merit of being in a position of irreconcilable antagonism to that vigorous enemy of the highest life of mankind – the Catholic Church'.[31] He asserted that evolution was not antagonistic to Catholicism. It was the uses to which the theory had been put that caused misgivings in the Church. At the very least, the lesson given by Augustine was that Genesis was not a literal account of creation and was open to interpretation.[32]

By the end of the 1890s, however, Roman authority had begun to stir. The vacuum in doctrine, so necessary for the debate on Darwin, was slowly and quietly being filled, not by papal decree, but by the Sacred Congregations. Leo remained aloof from the debate but both Propaganda and the Index moved to enforce an orthodoxy based on tradition rather than definition. No public statement was issued. Rather, the Congregations pursued a policy of silent censure and condemnation. In 1894, M. D. Leroy's *Evolution des espèces* was condemned by the Index at the instigation of the Jesuit newspaper *La Civilta Cattolica*. The paper had been founded in the 1850s by Pius IX and, since the publication of *Origin of Species*, had fought a running battle with evolutionists in Europe and America. Leroy's work was found to be in error but the Index resisted issuing a public definition of orthodoxy on the science question, despite the exhortations emanating from *La Civilta Cattolica*. The Index settled for a public recantation from Leroy and the withdrawal of his book from public sale. Zahm's *Evolution and Dogma* was placed on the Codex in 1897 but again, the Index preferred to censure the author privately through the head of his order rather than go public.[33]

For *La Civilta Cattolica* and for the Index, Catholic flirtation with a theory that treated humankind as merely another species to be catalogued and studied was a step too far. At the same time, Leo's pontificate, based as it was on the semblance of liberalism and engagement with the modern world, could ill-afford the ignominy of creating another Galileo in the person of Darwin.[34] Nevertheless, in 1899 the Sacred Congregation of the Index had increased powers bestowed by the Holy See. The faithful were forbidden to read, publish or even possess forbidden books under pain of excommunication. Powers of censure were no longer confined to the Congregation or the Pope but were extended to local primates and bishops. Moreover, the breadth of censure was expanded to include 'persons who deny the spirituality of the soul, as materialists do, or persons who deny the existence of God as atheists do'.[35]

Logue's elevation to the cardinalate in 1893 made it impossible for him to remain aloof from the controversy over science. In him, the Irish Church 'recognised the authority of the ancient See of Rome', as the clergy of

Dungannon put it in 1896.[36] Logue was orthodox in his views and his vision of the role of the clergy meant that he could only be alarmed at the debate on science. In his address to a public meeting on university education in Armagh in February 1898, he argued that any future university for Catholics in Ireland should have its own department of natural science under episcopal control. In secular education, he argued, natural science and mental philosophy were 'availed of not only to discredit Catholic teaching but even to assail the fundamental truths of Christianity'. Logue continued the notion first expressed by Cullen there were two kinds of modern science. He told the gathering that 'Catholic teaching has nothing to fear from true science. It is only the perversion of science which leads even to an apparent opposition with it.' He concluded that science 'may be perverted and young men who hang upon the words of a professor without sufficient knowledge to put his opinions to the test may be perverted also'.[37]

The difficulty for the Church was in distinguishing between the two kinds of science. It was not simply a question of identifying true science as that which held no opposition to traditional beliefs. The debate on science itself had already witnessed the pushing of boundaries far beyond traditional orthodoxy by respected and renowned Catholic theologians. Far from considering science as a threat, many in the Church were, by the 1890s, incorporating modern science in their interpretations of traditional and established doctrine.

'A nest of heresy'

Logue's first confrontation with potential heresy occurred in 1898 with the publication of *Motion: Its Origin and Conservation* by Walter McDonald. At first glance, McDonald would seem an unlikely rebel. He was educated in St Kieran's College in Kilkenny before attending the seminary at Maynooth. Following his ordination in 1876 he returned to St Kieran's but left to take up a position as Professor of Theology in Maynooth in 1881. In 1888 he was offered and accepted the position as Prefect of the Dunboyne courses, a post wherein he found 'no emoluments – only trouble'.[38] McDonald, by his own admission, was an indifferent scholar until he was presented with a collection of the works of St George Jackson Mivart in 1884 by William Walsh, then President of Maynooth. Mivart's treatises stimulated McDonald in a way he had 'never felt before. It was the beginning of a new life.'[39]

With the zeal of a convert he began a new approach to his theology, one which set out to treat the subject in the same manner as natural science, with constant enquiry and experimentation leading to discovery. McDonald was set firmly within the Concessionist camp. He was convinced that traditional arguments could and should be modified so that 'they received new strength from the now so much clearer teaching of natural science'.[40] Besides, as he declared in the preface to *Motion*, it was 'a mistaken view of the duty of the theologian . . . to propound in the face of modern physical science, whatever he may find to have been received commonly two or three hundred years ago'.[41] It was not biology or evolution which fascinated McDonald but physics, specifically theories surrounding the nature of matter and energy.

It is difficult to encapsulate briefly the complex theories contained in *Motion*. McDonald's book is a fusion of Thomistic theology and theories of kinetic energy borrowed from modern physics. The main contention of the book is that all motion or energy has been present in various forms since the creation of the universe. Since God created the universe He remained the source of all motion. Tying in the Thomistic theories concerning Potentiality and Act, McDonald concluded that all motion, even that which prompted the actions of human beings, came from God. Such a teleological approach to the cosmos might have been palatable to traditional doctrine but McDonald went further. He argued that God was the source for *all* acts in nature and in humankind and sought proof for his theories in contemporary works on the physical cosmos from controversial authors such a Herbert Spencer. His arguments left little room for the central Christian doctrine of free will and, despite its main concern with physics, *Motion* also contained the contention that science and not religion could tell us the true origin of the cosmos. 'The anterior history of the earth and of the heavenly bodies', McDonald argued, 'has to be learned from physical science and theologians and metaphysicians should be prepared to accept the conclusions of the scientists on this matter'.[42]

There is every indication that, despite its content and time of publication, *Motion* would have gone unnoticed by Logue and the Irish hierarchy. Although the book received Walsh's *imprimatur*, he later confessed that he had not read it and the ecclesiastical censor, Father John Hickey, saw nothing but mild controversy in the book.[43] The first alarming notes were sounded when *Motion* was denounced in an article sent to the *Record* by another theology professor at Maynooth, Daniel Coghlan. He had first objected to McDonald's ideas in 1894, reporting the thesis '*De Modo Agenda Gratia in Natura*' to the Council of Studies at Maynooth for containing heterodoxy. 'The teaching you enunciate', Coghlan had told McDonald, 'seems to me clearly opposed to faith'.[44]

The editor of the *Record*, J. F. Hogan, pulled the article before publication and sent it to Walsh who then passed it along to Logue in a letter on 14 February 1898. Coghlan alleged that *Motion* presented ideas which were contrary to Catholic doctrine. More incendiary was the accusation that McDonald was teaching his unorthodox ideas to the students at Maynooth.[45] Walsh confessed that he was under the misapprehension that the book was a treatise on physics and recommended to Logue that if the allegations proved to be true, the book should be submitted to Rome for examination with a view to having it quietly withdrawn.[46]

Logue voiced his concerns in an immediate reply to Walsh on 15 February. He agreed that Coghlan's article should be withdrawn and the allegations therein investigated thoroughly. Secrecy was vital as the bishops had nominated McDonald as Prefect of Studies at Maynooth in October 1897 and had communicated this to Rome. It would be a considerable embarrassment if their nominee were publicly censured by the Holy See. Moreover, Logue was supremely conscious of the fact that this was a controversy over a 'scientific subject' and the Irish Church could ill-afford accusations that it was engaged in a witch hunt. Arthur Balfour had begun to address the Irish University Question and Logue was anxious not to disrupt the positive signals which had been emanating from London. In addition, the Holy See was considering a request from the Irish bishops that Maynooth should be granted the facilities to confer degrees under Papal charter. Logue believed that the matter should be approached with delicacy and if the book contained error 'the author should be charitably induced to withdraw it from circulation'.[47]

On 21 February Logue again wrote to Walsh expressing fears over the content of *Motion*. The bishops, he said, were the guardians of the faith in Ireland and 'I think they would fail in their duty did they permit a book written by one of their professors to circulate among the people while it contained unusual doctrine'.[48] He was also concerned by the allegation that McDonald was teaching dubious doctrine at Maynooth. 'It would be a nice thing', he wrote to Walsh, 'if our national college became a nest of heresy!'[49] By March, Logue had actually read the book and passed copies along to other members of the hierarchy. He was not impressed by McDonald's 'unconscious materialism' and complained that such controversy among Irish theologians was a waste of time and talent.[50]

Despite his misgivings, Logue was reluctant to condemn the book himself but voiced concerns over McDonald's motives. 'He has started on a voyage of discovery in doctrine', he told Walsh, 'a very dangerous thing to say the least of it'.[51] Rather than judge the matter for himself he resolved that they should proceed with their first idea and have McDonald submit *Motion* for consideration and pronouncement by Propaganda. This was communicated to McDonald through a letter drafted at a meeting of the Visitors at Maynooth in April 1898. Patrick O'Donnell, Bishop of Raphoe and a former classmate of McDonald, was given the task of explaining the bishops' decision and delivering the letter.

McDonald was impressed by the conciliatory tone of the bishop's communication. He was, however, less certain about the admonishment that, 'in giving full effect to their lordships' directions, there does not appear to be any reason for the college body to be told what is being done'.[52] He also expressed his deep and sincere regret that he should have been the occasion of bringing about this controversy. However, he told O'Donnell that he could not 'withdraw from it without disparagement to a doctrine which I regard as of the very first importance in the controversy between the Catholic and materialist philosophy'.[53] Despite the obvious sincerity of his motives, McDonald's *Motion* was condemned as unsound and placed on the Codex of Forbidden Books. The condemnation issued from Cardinal Ledochowski at Propaganda in December 1898 was never made public. In July 1899 a further rescript was sent by the Cardinal Prefect ordering the complete withdrawal of all copies of the book from sale. He also demanded that McDonald refrain from teaching any of the theories mentioned in *Motion*.[54]

McDonald dutifully wrote to Browne & Nolan, *Motion*'s publishers, and had the book withdrawn but he refused to capitulate on his teaching without protest. He wrote to Logue on 29 July 1899 to inform the cardinal that he was challenging the decision of Propaganda regarding his teaching of the theories on kinetic energy. Not only was he unhappy that Rome was structuring his lessons but he questioned the very nature of the decision itself. McDonald had sent over twenty theses to Propaganda in support of *Motion* and Ledochowski replied with six pages detailing the errors adjudged to be therein. The problem for McDonald was in the fact that the opinions given in these *animadversiones* were rendered only by two theologians appointed by the Congregation, as was customary. He complained to Logue that it was difficult to determine whether the documents 'contained the authoritative teaching of the Holy See' which would bind him in obedience or, rather, the private opinions of two theologians who did not understand his ideas.[55]

McDonald was given leave to challenge the ruling of Propaganda in what was, in the current climate of condemnation, an extraordinary act of forbearance by Logue and the Visitors at Maynooth. But for McDonald, the matter had gone beyond questions of orthodoxy. He was passionately committed to his theories and the issue now was his freedom and right to teach all aspects of theology as a college professor. His appeal, predictably perhaps, was rejected. Not only was the charge of dubious orthodoxy upheld but, in a further rescript from Propaganda, McDonald was forbidden from teaching his theories in Maynooth. Logue was empowered to oversee his lessons and to issue punishment to the extent of removing him from his position.[56] Later in the year, McDonald was brought before the Visitors and admonished by Logue that he should confine himself to traditional teachings on the relationship between God and living things.[57]

For McDonald, the ending of the *Motion* controversy in such a fashion was a setback but not a fatal one. He certainly found it increasingly difficult to have his theological works published in the *Record* for which he blamed Logue and Walsh rather than the editor, J. F. Hogan.[58] Despite the close watch kept on his more scientific or theological work, McDonald continued to irritate the hierarchy and Logue in particular. He published essays in various journals, away from the eyes of the ecclesiastical censor, on socialism, nationalism and the education question. An exasperated Logue wrote to Walsh in 1908 to complain that McDonald had 'been running wild for some time now' and his criticism of the hierarchy on various questions had gotten out of hand. The question was what should be done with him. 'I fear he can never be kept quiet and his example, considering the position he holds, is ruinous', Logue told Walsh. He concluded, 'I am told some of the young priests have picked up and are propagating his ideas. It is a terrible thing if our own ecclesiastical college is to be turned into nest of liberalism and anti-clericalism!'[59]

The controversy over *Motion* illustrated that Ireland was not exempt from the growing backlash against the intellectual movement in the Church. However, Logue's deft handling of *Motion*, and McDonald, avoided embarrassment or accusations of medievalism. Despite the censure of prominent intellectuals such as Zahm there remained an appetite for scientific discussion among the Irish clergy. The excommunication of Mivart in 1900 for heterodoxy did little to dampen this enthusiasm, even at Maynooth.[60] In 1903, Peter Coffey, professor of logic and metaphysics at the seminary, published 'the hexahemeron and science'. The article was a very measured consideration of the relationship between the Church and science. He concluded that fault existed on both sides. Scientists were dazzled by their discoveries and had attacked the Church. Its defenders denied authenticated facts in their zeal and forgot that 'scientific certainty is better than doubtful exegesis'.[61] In the same year, Edward Selley, a Dublin Augustinian, published 'The nebular theory and divine revelation'. This article fully embraced developmental ideas on the formation of planets. He asserted that the Bible was there to teach people about God, not geology or astronomy, and he praised the idea of God as the great 'Evolver of the universe'.[62] The conditions for discussing science, however, were about to change sharply.

Modernism

The problem for those engaged in progressive theology and discussing science was that, by 1900, science and evolution had moved on from debating the origins of life. Evolution theory had outgrown its biological cradle was now a facet of almost every branch of speculative study. Scientists may have differed on the finer points of the theory but there was a general acceptance, even among Catholic scientists, that evolution had played some part in the origin of life on earth and in the origins of humankind. The challenge for the Church now came from those who had adapted evolutionary theory to the study of the social sciences, history and anthropology. It was one thing to try and incorporate evolution into existing dogma but quite another to accommodate theories which identified religion itself as merely another evolutionary construct. As theologians grappled with the new ideas of science the boundaries of dogma were pushed ever further. In addition, some Catholic scholars were increasingly adopting principles and methods borrowed from secular history-writing and science when treating theological subjects.[63]

Perhaps the best example of the latter was contained in the works of the French ecclesiastical historian Alfred Loisy. In the 1890s Loisy had published a paper on what was known as the Johannine Codicil, an ancient text concerning the divine nature of the Trinity. He argued that, in purely historical terms, the Codicil was part of a later tradition and, therefore, could not have been written by John the Evangelist. The paper caused uproar and was immediately condemned by the Index. Pope Leo XIII, partly in response to it, issued *Providentissimus Deus* which emphasised the need to 'defend biblical truth from rationalists and the children of the Reformation, and rejected the theory that the truth of the Bible was guaranteed only in the realm of faith and morals, saying that in authentic scripture there were no errors'.[64] Loisy, however, received nothing more than a reprimand. In 1903 he published *L'Évangile et L'Église* in which he argued that there was no historical proof for the divinity of Jesus Christ. Loisy stated that Christ and his followers, believing that the end of the world was imminent, did not found a Church nor was an account of the Resurrection contained in the original Gospel texts. As historical events, a historian could not recognise in them anything in the way of objective truth or reality.[65] Other theologians stepped outside the boundaries of traditional doctrine altogether in an attempt to incorporate science into the Catholic faith. In 1906, Father George Tyrell attempted to explain the development of Catholicism, and religion in general, in wholly evolutionary terms. In *Apologetics of Immanence* Tyrell explained revelation not as a direct gift from God, but as an evolutionary product of the individual's moral sense.[66]

Leo XIII died in 1903 and his successor, Giuseppe Melchiore Sarto of Venice, who assumed the title Pius X, reacted in a very different way to the advanced theology abroad in the Church. As Chadwick has pointed out, Pius was a simple pastor who did not understand what was happening and saw only that it was his duty to maintain the apostolic truths.[67] The first action in his campaign to do so was contained in an address given at St Peter's in December 1904. He told the assemblage that 'Catholic writers must, in all that touches the action of the Church in society, subject themselves entirely in intellect and in will, like the rest of the faithful, to their bishops and to the Roman Pontiff.'[68]

In July 1905, Pius issued the encyclical *De Christiana Doctrina Tradenda* which reaffirmed the Church's role as supreme teacher and guardian of truth. The language used left no doubt that the new Pontiff regarded this a time of peril for the faithful. He warned that they were under attack by an enemy of subtle cunning. These intellectuals, he said, were the ravening wolves that St Paul had warned of, entering the flock and sparing none.[69] In contrast to the emphasis placed on the social question by his predecessor, Pius elevated those who taught the faith above those who alleviated the suffering of the poor. Welfare of the soul came before welfare of the body. The encyclical placed heavy emphasis on catechetical instruction, in a way ordinary people would understand, as the antidote to the evils of intellect devoid of the knowledge of God.

In Ireland, the shift in Roman attitude galvanised Traditionalists, who immediately went on the offensive. There was a sharp increase in articles attacking science and Catholic apologists for science in the *Record* after 1905. Regular Traditionalist contributors such as Daniel Coghlan, who had written condemnatory articles on both Tyrell and Loisy, were joined by new voices such as that of the Reverend R. Fullerton of St Malachy's College in Belfast, who attacked the 'new' sciences of ethnology and anthropology. In 'The evolution of culture' Fullerton argued that both sought to make a human being 'nothing better than his dog or his horse' and ignored the essential truth of the Bible.[70]

Both *Tradenda* and the statement on the obligations of Catholic writers led to a tightening of ecclesiastical censorship. *Imprimatur* became much more than the rubber stamp of episcopal approval it had been in the past. Such was the level of scrutiny of the *Record* in March 1905 that the theology professors at Maynooth met to discuss the creation of a new journal dedicated exclusively to the higher branches of theology. The idea, unsurprisingly, came from Walter McDonald, but his proposal had the support of the majority of the faculty. Of those present at the meeting all bar one voted to begin work on the journal. The assembled professors were Patrick McKenna, Joseph MacRory, James McCaffery, Walter McDonald, John Harty, Patrick Toner and Daniel Coghlan. McKenna voted for the proposal but excused himself from active participation because of poor health while Coghlan voted against and left the meeting after the vote.[71]

It was the general idea that the journal should remain outside the control of the bishops and be published in a spirit of 'filial confidence' without ecclesiastical censorship. McDonald wrote to Walsh about this possibility and was encouraged by the positive reply he received. The Archbishop of Dublin even went as far as discussing ways in which the censor could be avoided. However, Walsh wrote again in February to inform McDonald that he had changed his mind. Since their last correspondence, a disagreement had arisen among the bishops on the new publication. 'This being so', Walsh went on, 'you will kindly see that my name does not appear on any list of subscribers'. He told McDonald that he did not want to appear to be taking sides against any of the bishops who opposed it.[72]

In fact, Logue had written to Walsh on 24 October expressing his misgivings about the proposed publication. Considering the nature of McDonald's articles in the past, Logue certainly did not wish to subscribe to a publication of which he was a 'leading director'. He told Walsh that 'unless the periodical be kept under strict censorship, its publication will be a dangerous experiment'.[73] The first issue of the new *Irish Theological Quarterly* was thus published in January 1906 under Walsh's *imprimatur* and the censorship of Canon Jacob Dunne of Holy Cross College, which was close to the Archbishop's palace in Dublin. There was really nothing the bishops could do to stop the publication without creating a massive scandal. Logue, however, had ensured that it was kept under tight scrutiny. Despite the pressure from the cardinal and the Board of Trustees of Maynooth, the professors went ahead with the journal although 'with an uncomfortable feeling that we were all under suspicion and disliked'.[74]

That is not to say that the *Irish Theological Quarterly* became a forum for unfettered experimental theology. Following the edict on Catholic writers and the publication of *Tradenda*, the climate was not one conducive to debate of any kind. In his review of the state of the Church in 1906, James McCaffery described how the European Church was gripped by condemnations by the Index, papal interference in the running of seminaries and the forced resignation of college professors.[75] Indeed, even in Maynooth, McDonald recalled a change in atmosphere to one in which critics were continually 'on the pounce' for heresy and disrespect for authority.[76] McCaffery pointed out in his article that 'the leaders of the new intellectual movement are, in general, as loyal sons of the Church as those who light-heartedly undertake to stone them'.[77] But this sentiment was not shared by the Irish hierarchy, particularly Logue, who did not trust the editors of the *Irish Theological Quarterly* sufficiently to allow its publication without censorship. Ultimately, this ensured it was never the journal envisaged by McDonald. Disillusioned, he resigned as editor after only two years.

The condemnation of Modernism in 1907 effectively not only ended the open and passionate debate on science within the Church, but smothered the intellectual movement. In the first of two encyclicals, *Lamentabili Sane*, published in July, Pius X condemned over fifty authors, Tyrell and Loisy among them, for works contrary to doctrine and the faith. This was followed by *Pascendi Dominici Gregis* which was published in September. *Pascendi* clearly identified the enemies of the Church as coming from within and who were dedicated to the ruin of religion. 'In the very veins and vitals of the Church', Pius wrote, 'is the living peril menacing certain harm because they know her inmost secrets'.[78]

Pascendi was a meticulous condemnation of every facet of progressive theology and the attempt to conciliate dogma with science. Tyrell's theory of immanence was denounced along with Loisy's interpretation of scripture.[79] It is worth noting, however, that amid all the indictments, evolution was only condemned if applied to sacred scripture or the Church. Special condemnation was reserved for those who attempted to reinterpret scripture for science's sake. Thus, the Concessionist desire to reconcile religion and science was branded as treachery, and those engaged in it were denounced under the blanket term of Modernism. Pius believed Modernists could only reconcile religion with science by subjugating the former to the latter. Philosophy and science could never prescribe what was to be believed. Their duty was not to investigate the mysteries of God, but to regard them with humble and pious reverence.[80] Modernists had succeeded in gathering to them all the heresies that had ever been, the result of curiosity unrestrained. Perhaps more than anything else, *Pascendi* was a declaration that the interpretation of belief, faith and Catholicism itself was the sole preserve of Roman authority.

Pascendi was not only a condemnation of Modernism or Concessionism, although that in itself may have been enough to end the debate on science. Pius included a series of definitive measures designed to combat the spread of the evils of Modernism throughout the whole Church. Those suspected of unorthodoxy were to be rooted out of positions of authority in colleges and seminaries. Pius ordered that the study of natural science in seminaries and Catholic colleges should be strictly regulated. Professors, too, would come under scrutiny before appointment. *Pascendi* demanded: 'rejecting all other considerations let those who have in any way been imbued with Modernism be excluded from offices of either ruling or teaching'. If professors already in post were found to be 'imbued with Modernism', they should be summarily dismissed.[81]

For the Irish hierarchy, the timing of *Pascendi* could not have been worse. Logue and the bishops, after all, had given their assent to a new university in which they could not have the kind of control over teaching and staffing envisaged by Pius. There were certain safeguards in the National University. Many of the teaching staff had simply decamped to the new institution from University College. The potentially sensitive subjects of botany and zoology, for example, remained in the safe hands of George Sigerson.[82] The problem for the bishops was how to maintain a Catholic ethos at the new university when the teaching of religion and philosophy was prohibited under its charter. As the hierarchy grappled with this difficulty, others pushed hard for an aggressively Catholic agenda. The President of Cork College, Bertram Windle, a noted Catholic scientist, accused the bishops' Standing Committee of timidity. He voiced his concerns in a letter to Walsh in 1910 declaring that enough was not being done. He wanted his Catholic students to be able to go out and meet the challenges of modern thought 'built up by their faith and be apostles of the same all over the world'.[83]

Following protracted consultation and a period of fundraising, the bishops created a theology faculty adjoined to the National University in Dublin. Its purpose was the same as a statutory faculty, offering courses in theology and postgraduate studies. However, details of the syllabus, examinations and degrees would not appear on the university programme.[84] Nor would the new faculty use the resources or buildings of the university. With the establishment of the faculty, the bishops hoped to, in Logue's words, baptise the 'pagan bantling' that was the National University.[85] By encouraging priests to commit to the courses in the new faculty, the bishops hoped that the Irish priesthood could be 'worthily represented in the scientific defence of religion'.[86]

In addition to the new strictures and responsibilities placed on the clergy, Pius demanded that the laity also play a part. Catholic booksellers were ordered to remove and refuse to stock objectionable literature. Councils of Vigilance were to be set up in every diocese to 'watch for the encroachment of error and Modernism'.[87] To show that the Church was a true friend of science, Pius announced the creation of a special institute in Rome. He envisaged a place that would 'gather together the most illustrious representatives of science amongst Catholics and which will have for its object, with Catholic truth for a guide and direction, the progress of all kinds of science and learning'.[88]

Towards the end of 1908, Pius augmented the restrictions contained in *Pascendi* by reserving the right to interpret scripture solely to the Papal Biblical Commission under pain of excommunication.[89] The final counterstroke against the intellectual movement in the Church came in 1910 with the Oath against Modernism. It was to be sworn by all clergy, pastors, confessors and professors of philosophy and theology. The oath bound the taker to adhere to and accept any definition of the Church, particularly those issued to correct the errors of modern times. Clauses reaffirmed that the Church was instituted by Jesus himself. It rejected the use of rationalist principles in the study of the scriptures and any modern aberration from traditional doctrine. The oath basically bound the taker to acceptance of every stricture laid down in *Lamentabili Sane* and *Pascendi*.[90]

Although the encyclicals did not represent an infallible declaration, there was scant difference, in Catholic perception, between that and the declarations of an infallible pontiff. It was not just the threat of excommunication or dismissal which prompted clergy to retreat from science. James McCaffery was correct in his estimation that Concessionists were loyal sons of the Church. The Pope had spoken and the vast majority of clergy fell in behind him. Chadwick, for example, puts the number of priests who refused to take the oath worldwide at fifty.[91] McCaffery, writing in December 1907, pointed out that certain theologians had gone too far and embarked on a course 'which had for its object the overthrowal of received interpretation of the Christian faith'.[92]

For his part, McDonald complained bitterly that the action of a few theologians within the Church had destroyed any chance of reconciling science and religion. He resented that fact that Loisy had remained in the Church after the 1890s (he was eventually excommunicated in 1908) and that theorists like Tyrell had pushed too far. Moreover, he blamed the identification of Concessionism with Modernism for the odium and heavy censorship which accompanied the launch of the *Irish Theological Quarterly*. 'We were unfortunate at the time at which our project was commenced', he wrote, 'as the Modernists not only lamed but killed us. They aimed at progress, so did we; therefore we were Modernists.'[93] The vacuum in doctrine that fostered the debate on science no longer existed. However, it was filled not by definition on evolution or science but by the wielding of papal authority. Pius had told Catholics what not to believe and how not to approach science without defining in any way an official doctrine on evolution or any other scientific question. Also, in reserving for the Holy See all biblical interpretation, past, present and future, Catholic theologians were denied room to manoeuvre on questions of creation, the development of life or the origin of humankind.

This lack of direction prompted one baffled academic, Professor D. T. Barry, Professor of Physiology at Queen's College in Cork, to seek clarification in the pages of the *Record*. In January 1920, Barry published 'Descent and selection: a query' in the hope of gaining some guidance on how he should approach the question of evolution while teaching students. The problem was that 'a Catholic student frequently announces his inability to discriminate in scientific writings what might be acceptable as orthodox and what should be rejected as heterodox'.[94] Barry pointed out that Darwin's theory of natural selection had a fascination for many students but there was a general belief that it was condemned by the Church as 'godless and untenable'.[95] It was his own belief that evolution, as a theory, lacked absolute confirmation but was the best one that accounted for the facts. Darwinism had been sullied and misappropriated by the 'causo-mechanical pilferers' like Spencer and Huxley.[96] The clarification sought was not forthcoming, certainly not in later editions of the *Record*.

In the post-*Pascendi* era, however, science posed the same difficulty for Traditionalism as it had for Concessionism. It mattered not that all theology, or the theology that was published, was now 'Traditional' in nature. Science was ever-changing and Catholic theologians had more to grapple with than theories concerning the development of life on earth. In 1917, for example, the first detailed consideration of the moral impact of abortion appeared in the *Irish Theological Quarterly*. In 'The sacredness of fetal life' John Harty, Professor of Dogmatic and Moral Theology at Maynooth, explored the theological implications of the termination of pregnancy and the rights of the unborn child over that of the mother. The article was basically an examination of the ways in which modern science and medical ethics concurred with theology on the subject of abortion. All agreed, for instance, that termination to protect the good name or social standing of the mother was unacceptable. More interesting perhaps was the use of language and terminology borrowed from eugenics. Harty did not just consider the moral choice between the life of mother and child. The national value to society of each life was weighed; the potential benefits of a fertile mother against the potential genius and eventual fertility of a child. Indeed, the whole article was set within the context of eugenic fears and concepts.[97]

He was not the first to display sympathy with eugenics. In 1911, Thomas Slater, a professor from St Beuno's Jesuit College in Wales and an inveterate opponent of Concessionism and scientific engagement, published 'Eugenics and moral theology'. Slater explained eugenics as the science of good breeding, the attempt to apply the laws of heredity to improve the human race. He pointed out the contention of eugenicists that the modern trend was for weaklings in body and mind to survive in greater numbers owing to conditions in society. He also vented their fears that the growing numbers of 'the insane, the neurotic, the feeble-minded, sickly, unhealthy, degenerates and undesirables' were threatening to poison the life of the nation.[98]

For someone who had attacked Concessionists for warping dogma to suit the times and warned of the dangers in the positivism of modern science, this was an extraordinary article.[99] Slater argued that much in the theories advanced by Francis Galton, the founder of the eugenics movement, fitted with Christian morality. 'The object of eugenics', he wrote, 'the physical and mental good of the race of mankind, is part of the object of charity, the chief and the noblest of Christian virtues'.[100] He differed, however, on the methods which should be employed to improve the race. He disapproved of compulsory sterilisation and abortion, noting wryly that the calendar of Christian saints would be much shorter if all the degenerates had been removed. Slater concluded that eugenics posed no problems for the moral theologian who would also deplore 'race suicide'. He approved of eugenic measures to improve the race, including granting diplomas to those couples found to be eugenically sound and rewards for the production of healthy stock. The Church, he argued, would not approve of forced segregation of the unfit but he believed that if this were shown to be in the common interest, she might change her discipline on the matter.[101]

Slater's sympathies were not shared by the Irish hierarchy. In 1919 Logue commissioned a report into proposals for the introduction of a Medical Treatment of Children Bill for Ireland. The inquiry was made in order that the bishops would be 'able to form a reliable estimate of the dangers which may arise' from such a bill becoming law. The report was compiled by Robert Browne, Bishop of Cloyne, and Dennis Kelly, Bishop of Ross, and presented to Logue at a meeting of the hierarchy in October 1919. The proposals, which the bishops had obtained, envisaged the setting up of a post of a Schools Medical Officer under whom a scheme would be established requiring the compulsory examination of school-children by doctors and dentists. The prospect of children being examined individually caused the greatest concern. It was pointed out to the bishops that it was in this private examination, especially for girls, that any grave danger to faith and morals might occur. These dangers seemed all the greater 'when it is remembered that it is the Eugenics Society of England that is at the back of the movement which has led to recent legislation for the schools of this country'.

The bishops pointed to the recent statement made by Sir George Newman of the Eugenics Society in which he argued that it would be highly desirable for girls of thirteen to be given lessons in mothercraft and sexual hygiene. This showed clearly the aims of those who had been at work for some years 'to improve the breed of human beings on lines that are purely materialistic'. The bishops resolved that school managers should be encouraged to insist that parents give written permission for any exami-nation. Moreover, no individual examinations would go ahead without the presence of a parent, and girls would only be examined by a 'lady doctor'.[102]

The effect on the Irish hierarchy of the condemnation of Modernism was cathartic. Freed from the shackles of indecision arising from the gap in doctrine, the bishops enthusiastically set out to implement the guide-lines and strictures laid down by Pius. The establishment of the National University meant that the bishops no longer needed to be circumspect when dealing with science or scientific subjects and could condemn or condone as they pleased without fearing the consequences. In June 1907, the hierarchy published the decrees from a general synod held two years previously. Among them was the introduction of oral and written tests on doctrine for priests for up to five years after ordination. The synod also recommended the reading of wholesome literature for all Catholics and called for the establishment of parish libraries to further this aim.[103]

Indeed, the campaign against dangerous literature was the most public manifestation of the bishop's commitment to honour the papal edicts.

Despite the initial enthusiasm of the hierarchy, the campaign did not take off until 1911 when it benefited from the upsurge in Catholic Nationalist fervour over Home Rule. The issue of contentious or immoral literature was one in which Logue had long been interested and he remained one of the campaign's most constant and influential supporters. In his Lenten pastoral of 1902, for example, he had complained that 'the benches of our public book marts still groan under the weight of tons of washy, sensationalist, materialistic and often sensual trash which are weekly and daily imported'.[104]

The campaign against objectionable literature was conducted by various Vigilance Councils or Committees but these remained most active in urban areas. Their level of success and indeed their intended targets remained unclear. There was, for example, no Codex of Forbidden Books for Ireland. Logue was most enthusiastic for the project. In a Lenten pastoral published on 1 March 1912 he urged that the movement be extended to every part of the country. The evil of pernicious literature could only be met by 'sleepless vigilance and active, earnest, persevering work'. He urged the faithful to boycott newsagents who refused to remove objectionable literature. 'No ostracism', he said, 'could be more legitimate or more lawful'.[105] Under Logue's patronage, the Vigilance Committees established to watch for heresy and Modernism would become the moral censors of Irish culture. The campaign, and Logue's commitment to it, had surprising longevity, lasting until well after the First World War. In 1915 Logue wrote a congratulatory letter to the secretary of the Dublin Vigilance Committee, Lawrence O'Dea, expressing his satisfaction at the work. He spoke of the need to expand the movement into the countryside and approved of the efforts of the Dublin branch to 'purify the theatres, music halls and picture houses'.[106]

One of the main results of the Vigilance campaign was the establishment of the *Catholic Bulletin* in 1911. Just as the *Record* had been established to convey doctrine to the clergy, the *Catholic Bulletin* was intended to give a popular interpretation of theology which would be accessible to ordinary Catholics. It was also intended to provide a list of approved reading and to pioneer a library of Catholic literature, sanctioned and 'approved to the last page' by Catholic ecclesiastics.[107] It was perhaps no surprise that Daniel Coghlan should contribute the first of the new journal's articles. Indeed, Coghlan remained a steady contributor, even after his elevation to be Bishop of Cork in 1912. On taking office, he changed his name to Cohalan, causing a degree of ecclesiastical and historical confusion. The tone of the article illustrated the populism intended for the *Catholic Bulletin*. In 'Modernism and the old faith', Coghlan painted Modernism, science and evolution as being somehow reserved for Protestants.[108]

The reaction of both Protestant and Catholic clerics to John Tyndall's claim in 1874 to 'wrest from theology the entire domain of cosmological theory' was remarkably similar. In his presidential address to the Belfast Naturalists Field Club given on 18 November 1874, the Reverend William McIlwaine, a Church of Ireland minister, branded Tyndall's speech as reckless and needless. 'Might not anyone possessed of half the intelligence of the speaker', he asked, 'have foreseen the inevitable consequences of the basis of the religious faith professed by this auditory being assaulted as he assaulted it'?[109] While he could not, as a Protestant, associate himself with much of Cullen's condemnation, McIlwaine deemed its objections 'valid and weighty'.[110] By the twentieth century, however, evolutionary science appeared much less problematic for sections of Protestantism than for Catholicism. Perhaps the early debates on Darwin in the environment of higher education enabled Anglicanism to reach an accommodation with modern thought. Trinity College produced a generation for whom evolution was an integral part of modern scientific thought and, therefore, was not seen as a threat. Catholicism, in contrast, remained hamstrung by its reliance on Roman authority for doctrine and dogma. The debate on Darwin among the clergy came late and was eventually crushed under the weight of Roman orthodoxy. A position on Darwin was never defined.

Throughout the controversy over science, Logue worked hard to maintain ecclesiastical discipline and safeguard the Irish Church from embarrassing accusations over its attitude to science. He remained deeply respectful of the person and office of the Pope and had no difficulty enacting the strictures of *Pascendi*. The ideas on pernicious and dangerous literature fitted perfectly with some of his own convictions. Despite his exasperation with Walter McDonald, however, Logue was reluctant to take the kind of severe action demanded under *Pascendi*. Even armed with a Propaganda rescript in 1908 from Cardinal Gotti, Ledochowski's successor, reminding McDonald that his theories constituted novel doctrines as condemned in *Pascendi*, Logue took no action other than to give McDonald a stern talking to.[111] This was despite an angry letter to Walsh in which he vented his fury at the professor for continuing to include his condemned theories in class. 'I think he should be called before [the Visitors]', he told the archbishop, 'and plainly told that if he does not cease to promulgate his singular and mischievous opinions within his class or the press, the bishops would dispense with his services'.[112]

Logue's tactics during the *Motion* controversy and his approach to the problem displayed a deftness of touch when it came to ecclesiastical politics. In referring the matter to Rome, he was able at once to disassociate himself from any decision made by Propaganda and to increase the likelihood of that decision being obeyed, as carrying the weight of Roman authority. *Motion* also illustrated his penchant for delegating some of the more unpleasant tasks. Following his angry letter to Walsh and McDonald's ticking off by the Visitors, Logue fretted about a forthcoming meeting of the Maynooth Union. 'I take it there will be none of the bishops present', he told Walsh, 'and no one knows what imprudent course some of the junior clergy, infected, as I am told, as some of them are, with Doctor McDonald's views may take it into their heads to pursue'.[113] Logue nominated Walsh to preside, saying he had a prior engagement opening a church in Kilkenny. The archbishop duly attended and the meeting passed off without incident.

Despite his distaste for personal controversy, Logue remained most comfortable when dealing with religion and faith. Chadwick's description of Pius X as a simple, conservative pastor could equally have been applied to him. Unlike Cullen, he responded to challenges to the faith not with confrontation but with a quiet determination. His enforcement of orthodoxy and ecclesiastical discipline was carried with little fanfare, but his championing of the Vigilance Committees, and other propaganda organisations such as the Catholic Truth Society, had, as we shall see, far-reaching consequences.

Notes

1 *In Amplissimo*, Letter of Leo XIII to the Archbishops and Bishops of the United States of America, 15 Apr. 1902, *IER*, 4th ser., xii (Sept 1902), pp. 272–4.
2 Paul, 'Religion and Darwinism', p. 419.
3 Gwynn, ed., *McDonald*, p. 17.
4 Hodge, 'England', pp. 7–8.
5 Vaughan, ed., *Irish Historical Statistics*, p. 27.
6 Jones, 'Catholicism, Nationalism and Science', p. 47.
7 Jones, 'Darwinism in Ireland', pp. 2–6.
8 Brooke, 'Darwin and Victorian Christianity', p. 203.
9 *IER*, 2nd ser., x (Nov. 1874), p. 54.
10 Norman, *Catholic Church*, p. 412.
11 *IER*, 2nd ser., x (Nov. 1874), pp. 49–61.
12 J. G. C., 'Darwinism', *IER*, 2nd ser., ix (May 1873), p. 344.
13 J. K. C., *Tyndall and Materialism*, p. 11.

14 Paul, *Edge of Contingency*, p. 24.

15 Appleby, 'Exposing Darwin's "hidden agenda" ', p. 174.

16 H. E. D., 'Geology, Revelation and the Antiquity of Man', *IER*, 3rd ser., i (May 1880), pp. 262–72.

17 Brundell, 'Catholic Church Politics and Evolution Theory', p. 83.

18 Appleby, 'Exposing Darwin's "hidden agenda" ', p. 174.

19 Brundell, 'Catholic Church Politics and Evolution Theory,' p. 83.

20 Hastings, *The Encyclopaedia of Religion and Ethics*, xii, p. 323.

21 Murphy, 'Darwinism', *IER*, (Sept. 1884), p. 586.

22 *Ibid.*, p. 594.

23 Murphy, 'Faith and Evolution', *IER*, 3rd ser., v (Dec. 1884), pp. 756–67.

24 Vaughan, 'Evolution and Faith', *IER*, 3rd ser., vi (July 1885), pp. 413–14.

25 Murphy, 'Faith and evolution', *IER*, 3rd ser., vi (Aug. 1885), p. 491.

26 Vaughan, 'Faith and evolution', *IER*, 3rd ser., vi (Oct. 1885), p. 652.

27 *Ibid.*, p. 651.

28 Editor's note, *IER*, 3rd ser., vi (Nov. 1885), p. 820.

29 Burton, 'Was St Augustine an Evolutionist?', *IER*, 4th ser., v (Feb. 1899), p. 345.

30 Brundell, 'Catholic Church Politics and Evolution Theory', p. 83.

31 Coakley, 'Was St. Augustine an Evolutionist?', *IER*, 4th ser., v (Apr. 1899), p. 346.

32 *Ibid.*, pp. 358–9. The work referred to was St. Augustine's *De Genesi ad Litteram*.

33 Brundell, 'Catholic Church Politics and Evolution Theory', pp. 87–8. See also Appleby, 'Exposing Darwin's "hidden agenda" ', pp. 185–94.

34 Paul, 'Religion and Darwinism', p. 416.

35 Hurley, 'New Legislation on the Index', *IER*, 4th ser., vi (Nov. 1899), pp. 73–4.

36 *Irish News*, 4 Mar. 1896.

37 *Drogheda Argus*, 19 Feb. 1898.

38 Gwynn, ed., *McDonald*, p. 132.

39 *Ibid.*, p. 23.

40 *Ibid.*, p. 29.

41 McDonald, *Motion*, p. ix.

42 *Ibid.*, p. 447.

43 Walsh to Logue, 14 Feb. 1898, Logue Papers, ADA, box 12, folder 9, 'Publications'.

44 Gwynn, ed., *McDonald*, p. 30.

45 Coghlan, 'On motion', Logue Papers, ADA, box 12, folder 9, 'Publications'.

46 Walsh to Logue, 14 Feb. 1898, Logue Papers, ADA, box 12, folder 9, 'Publications'.

47 Logue to Walsh, 15 Feb. 1898, Walsh Papers, DDA, box 370, folder 357/1.

48 Logue to Walsh, 21 Feb. 1898, Walsh Papers, DDA, box 370, folder 357/1.

49 Logue to Walsh, 28 Feb. 1898, Walsh Papers, DDA, box 370, folder 357/1.

50 Logue to Walsh, 5 Mar. 1898, Walsh Papers, DDA, box 370, folder 357/1.

51 Logue to Walsh, 20 and 21 Mar. 1898, Walsh Papers, DDA, box 370, folder 357/1.

52 Gwynn, ed., *McDonald*, p. 33.

53 McDonald to O'Donnell, 1 May 1898, Logue Papers, ADA, box 12, folder 9, 'Publications'.

54 Ledochowski to Logue, 25 July 1899, Logue Papers, ADA, box 12, folder 9, 'Publications' (Translation).

55 McDonald to Logue, 29 July 1899, Logue Papers, ADA, box 12, folder 9, 'Publications'.

56 Ledochowski to Logue, 17 Apr. 1900 (no. 38025), Logue Papers, ADA, box 12, folder 9, 'Publications' (Translation).

57 Gwynn, ed., *McDonald*, p. 38.

58 *Ibid.*, p. 195.

59 Logue to Walsh, 3 Mar. 1908, Walsh Papers, DDA, box 380, folder 375/1.

60 *ICD*, 1902, p. 431.

61 Coffey, 'The Hexahemeron and Science', *IER*, 4th ser., xi (Aug. 1903), pp. 144–53.

62 Selley, 'The Nebular Theory and Divine Revelation', *IER*, 4th ser., xi (Dec. 1903), p. 422.

63 Brundell, 'Catholic Church Politics and Evolution Theory', p. 87.

64 Chadwick, *History of the Popes*, p. 351.

65 Coghlan, 'Evolution, Darwin and the Abbé Loisy', *IER*, 4th ser., xix (June 1906), pp. 488–93.

66 Ranchetti, *Catholic Modernists*, pp. 43–6.

67 Chadwick, *History of the Popes*, p. 354.

68 *IER*, 4th ser., xvii (Jan. 1905), p. 177.

69 *De Christiana Doctrina Tradenda*, p. 3.

70 Fullerton, 'The Evolution of Culture', *IER*, 4th ser., xxi (Feb. 1907), p. 121.

71 Gwynn, ed., *McDonald*, p. 195.

72 *Ibid.*, p. 201.

73 Logue to Walsh, 24 Oct. 1905, Walsh Papers, DDA, box 377, folder 372/5.

74 Gwynn, ed., *McDonald*, p. 204.

75 McCaffery, 'The Church in 1906', *IER*, 4th ser., xxi (Jan. 1907), p. 2.

76 Gwynn, ed., *McDonald*, p. 205.

77 McCaffery, 'The Church in 1906', *IER*, 4th ser., xxi (Jan. 1907), p. 2.

78 *Pascendi Dominici Gregis*, p. 5.

79 *Ibid.*, p. 7.

80 *Ibid.*, p. 18.

81 *Ibid.*, p. 54.

82 Delaney to Logue, 2 Oct. 1909, Logue Papers, ADA, box 8, folder 5, 'Universities'.

83 Windle to Walsh, 11 June 1910, Walsh Papers, DDA, box 1, folder 4, 'National University'.

84 Standing Committee Report, 23 Sept. 1911, Logue Papers, ADA, box 1, folder 1, 'Meetings of the Hierarchy'.

85 *ICD*, 1913, p. 525.

86 Standing Committee Report, 23 Sept. 1911, Logue Papers, ADA, box 1, folder 1, 'Meetings of the Hierarchy'.

87 *Pascendi Dominici Gregis*, p. 61.

88 *Ibid.*, p. 63.

89 *ICD*, 1908, p. 406.

90 Oath against Modernism, 1910, Logue Papers, ADA, box 1, 'Hierarchy'.

91 Chadwick, *History of the Popes*, p. 355.

92 McCaffery, 'The Papal Encyclical on Modernism', *IER*, 4th ser., xxi (Dec. 1907), p. 563.

93 Gwynn, ed., *McDonald*, p. 208.

94 Barry, 'Descent and Selection: A Query', *IER*, 5th ser., xvi (Jan. 1920), p. 44.

95 *Ibid.*, p. 46.

96 *Ibid.*, p. 52.

97 Harty, 'The Sacredness of Fetal Life', *Irish Theological Quarterly*, xii (1917), p. 36.

98 Slater, 'Eugenics and Moral Theology', *Irish Theological Quarterly*, vi (1911), pp. 402–3.

99 See Slater's articles in the *IER*, 'Evolution in Doctrine and its Progress in Theology', 4s, xiv (June 1903), and 'The Roots of Liberal Theology', 4th ser., xxi (Jan. 1907).

100 Slater, 'Eugenics and Moral Theology', *Irish Theological Quarterly*, vi (1911), p. 408.

101 *Ibid.*, pp. 411–12.

102 Report to the Standing Committee, 21 Oct. 1919, Logue Papers, ADA, box 1, folder 1, 'Meetings of the Hierarchy'.

103 Luzio, 'The Maynooth Synod Decrees', *IER*, 4th ser., xxi (June 1907).

104 *Freeman's Journal*, 10 Feb. 1902.

105 *Catholic Bulletin*, ii (1912), p. 102.

106 Logue to O'Dea, 1 Nov. 1915, Logue Papers, ADA, box 12, folder 9, 'Publications'.

107 *Catholic Bulletin*, i (1911), p. 1.

108 Coghlan, 'Modernism and the Old Faith', *Catholic Bulletin*, i (1911), p. 27.

109 *Belfast Naturalists Field Club Reports*, 2nd ser., i (1874), p. 84. See n. 8 above.

110 *Ibid.*, p. 85.

111 Gotti to Logue, 25 Feb. 1908, Logue Papers, ADA, no. 79979, box 12, folder 9, 'Publications' (Translation).

112 Logue to Walsh, 28 Mar. 1908, Walsh Papers, DDA, box 380, folder 375/1.

113 *Ibid.*

5

Home Rule politics

Regicide

Logue was a nationalist. He retained a fundamental conviction that the Irish had the right to govern themselves and only self-government could effectively redress Catholic grievances. He supported and participated in the clerical-nationalist alliance forged by William Walsh in the 1880s. Although deeply concerned over the methodology of the National League, he offered nothing but support to the campaign in public. His disapproval of clerical participation in the Plan did not prevent his show of solidarity with Father James McFadden or his defence of the national movement to the Pope. His doubts over land agitation were balanced by outrage at the actions of the British Government. However, there has been a tendency among historians to question Logue's nationalist credentials and dismiss his contribution to the politics of the period. Miller, for example, has described him as having only 'sufficient acumen to realise that the Home Rule cause should not be opposed'.[1]

Logue was much enamoured with the clerical-nationalist alliance. He supported fully the bargain of mutual support struck in 1884 between the national movement and sections of the hierarchy. For him, a close relationship between politics and religion was not only desirable but essential. The example of the *Risorgimento* had shown that nationalism without clerical direction could be as dangerous to the interests of religion as socialism or science. Although he remained committed to the idea of self-government, Logue was far from being the 'quintessential nationalist' of the Home Rule era.[2] His difficulty was that, by the 1890s, he was increasingly unable to trust the leadership of the Irish Party. The political elite of the national movement would become the ruling elite in a Home Rule government and it was Logue's growing conviction that neither could be entrusted with Catholic interests.

Even before the O'Shea divorce case which heralded the split in the Irish Party, Logue was alarmed at the growing fissures developing in the clerical-nationalist alliance. It was not just the verbal attacks on Thomas O'Dwyer, the Bishop of Limerick. Logue could see a growing secularism among the Irish Party leadership. By July 1890, his resentment had boiled over. In a letter of bitter complaint to the Archbishop of Dublin, he declared that the Irish Party had 'climbed into their present influential position on the shoulders of the Irish priests and the Irish bishops'. It was the clergy who worked the electoral registers and contributed the 'sinews of war' in the form of funds. 'They now think', he told Walsh, 'they are secure enough to kick away the ladder by which they mounted'. Logue fretted that 'these gentlemen' had now got the people in their hands and might soon be able to attack the priests, bishops and even the Pope with impunity.[3] He worried that the growing rift between politicians and bishops was not only a bad business for the country but would put back the cause of Home Rule.[4] His doubts about Parnell's leadership and concern over the Irish Party's willingness to uphold Catholic interests had surfaced earlier. The occasion was a bill before Parliament which would allow a man to marry his dead wife's sister. Logue was disappointed that Parnell, someone he had 'greatly admired', would vote for such a proposal. 'Let not the vital questions of morality', he warned him, 'be mumbled by the smug Protestantism of English Liberals; but bid your followers to arise and maintain the discipline of the Catholic Church'.[5]

When Parnell was named in the O'Shea divorce case, however, there was a marked reluctance on the part of the bishops to side against him. Although the divorce case began at the end of 1889, Parnell was not named until 1890. Tim Healy, MP for North Louth, recalled in his memoirs his wonder at the spirit of incredulity maintained by the bishops about something that was almost common knowledge.[6] Indeed, L. P. Curtis has suggested that not only had Parnell's affair with Catherine O'Shea existed since 1882, but he was also the father of her three children.[7]

Logue displayed none of the reticence of some of his colleagues. While acknowledging the depth of the 'sin' and scandal involved in Parnell's adultery, he was also concerned about the political implications for the Irish Party and the prospects for Home Rule. Gladstone had moved to distance himself from Parnell and the whiff of scandal. Adultery played just as badly among English nonconformists as it did among Irish Catholics. Logue was convinced that if Parnell clung on to the leadership Home Rule would be a thing of the distant future. In a letter to Walsh from Rome he also vented his utter disgust at Parnell's actions and hoped for the sake of all he would retire quietly. 'A man having the destinies of a people in his hands', he said, 'and bartering it away for the company of an old woman, is certainly not a person to beget confidence'.[8]

There is no doubt that, as the Irish Party fragmented, Logue viewed the developing crisis as an opportunity for change within the national movement. He told Walsh of an audience with Cardinal Simeoni in which the Cardinal Secretary of Sate had voiced concerns over finding a replacement for Parnell. Logue told him not to worry, that they had 'plenty clever men in Ireland' and that 'Providence would provide a leader'.[9] He was convinced that the Church should take the field boldly and dismissed any prospect of peace with Parnell. 'Better fight him now', he told Walsh, 'for fight him we must in the long run'.[10]

As the crisis deepened, Logue went on the offensive. In a speech in Armagh in 1891 he condemned Parnell. Politics, he said, could never be exempt from the law of God and it would be disastrous for the whole country to keep a discredited idol in his place.[11] He returned to the same theme in his Lenten pastoral. Should the Irish people, he asked, sacrifice Ireland's glorious principles 'to minister to personal ambition; to submit the necks of a people struggling for freedom to the heel of a dictator?' They could never follow, he declared, 'a banner which we are ashamed to unfurl'.[12] In the midst of Logue's moral outrage, however, the pastoral also contained something of a political declaration. There could be no separation between Church and politics. Irish Home Rule under Parnell would be an abomination. It was Parnell's refusal to go quietly and preserve the national movement rather than the 'sin' of divorce that caused much of Logue's anger.

The bishops mounted a successful campaign against Parnell and his faction of the Irish Party. As well as a concerted effort to keep the junior clergy in check, they set about establishing the apparatus for a new national movement. A new grass-roots organisation, the National Federation, was created to counter Parnellite influences in the National League. In March 1891 a new newspaper, the *National Press*, was published in response to the Parnellite propaganda of the *Freeman's Journal*.[13] The personal feuding within the Irish Party was bitter, as was the rift between the Parnellites and the bishops. Parnell's death on 6 October 1891 did not resolve the leadership question or the party in-fighting. It did, however, mark the withdrawal of the hierarchy from the field. Aside from opposing Parnellite candidates, the bishops played little further part in the conflict.

Logue had been at the forefront of the campaign but had given little thought to what would happen should Parnell finally be ousted. His conviction that Providence would provide a leader was rather typical of a 'wait and see' attitude prevalent among the bishops. In Cashel, Thomas Croke was dismayed by the bickering in the national movement. He told Walsh in December 1891 that he was 'done with Irish politics'. He noted there were now three vying political factions in Ireland and concluded sadly that 'it must be survival of the fittest'.[14] Whether trusting in divine intervention or to political natural selection, the bishops made little effort to encourage unity among nationalists. Having conspired to commit regicide, they now rather abandoned the Irish Party to its own devices. Croke made a last ditch effort to enlist Logue's help in 1892 in getting an agreement between the warring parties. He told the primate that no one in the Irish Party would object to his arbitration. He himself had had enough. 'My heart has gone into my body', he told Logue, 'and I can see nothing before me but . . . chaos'.[15] However, this was a role for which Logue, by inclination and political acumen, was ill-suited.

Logue's prompt and resolute opposition to Parnell played well in Rome. His condemnation of Parnell in Armagh in January 1891 drew high praise from Tobias Kirby. On 15 January the Rector told him that he had adopted the language that a bishop should use at a critical juncture in the political life of the country. Catholic Ireland, he said, could never permit a convicted adulterer to be the leader of her representatives in her just political struggle.[16] Such praise could only bolster Logue's growing political confidence. Moreover, his unflinching performance in the leadership crisis undoubtedly strengthened his appeal as a possible candidate for the cardinalate.

Party politics

Parnell's death intensified rather than soothed the bitter divisions within the national movement. The Irish Party split into three factions whose differences remained slight on the surface but were for the time being insurmountable. All three factions had elements with which Logue and several of his colleagues might have found common cause. He was never enamoured of the Irish Party's reliance on English Radicals but the very sobriquet 'Parnellite' rendered John Redmond's faction unpalatable. John Dillon and William O'Brien had fought the good fight against Parnell but Logue trusted neither of them. The memory of O'Dwyer's ordeal in Limerick at their hands was, perhaps, still fresh. It was Tim Healy, however, who was to provide Logue with the kind of parliamentary representation he sought and who would be his closest and perhaps only real political ally.

The election of 1892 put the Liberals into government with a small majority which left Gladstone heavily dependent on the Irish Party. Despite the Liberal Party's tenuous grip on power and its slender lead indicating that it had no mandate in England, Gladstone pressed ahead with a second Home Rule Bill.[17] A modest measure, the bill could be more easily defined by the authority it withheld from the prospective Irish parliament than what it proposed to bestow. Westminster would retain control over customs and exercise, foreign relations and trade. Moreover, the Irish legislature was specifically prohibited from endowing theological professorships from public money or 'imposing any disability or conferring any privilege on account of religious beliefs'.[18] For Logue, the bill was less than useless. It simply did not provide the means or the opportunity for the redress of Catholic grievances or provide sufficient authority to enact real reform.

He told Walsh on 8 May 1893 that the bill would mean nothing but mischief for Catholic interests. He was convinced that if it passed, it would leave Irish Catholics languishing in their current state of inequality. The lack of authority which would be vested in an Irish parliament meant the whole thing was rather worthless. 'Justice could be fought out of the Imperial parliament by the influence of the Irish vote', he told Walsh, 'that vote would count for very little if the bill was passed'. Logue believed that a protest against the restrictive clauses of the bill should be passed directly to Gladstone as the Irish Party, in its current state, was next to useless. Gladstone should be told, he went on, 'that we look for no advantage but insist on equality as a right; that we are prepared to concede to Protestants where they have not already, anything we claim for ourselves'.[19]

The bishops' objections on the bill, specifically the clauses leaving a Home Rule parliament hamstrung on the education question, were passed to Gladstone. In June, Logue confessed that he was relieved but was furious that English Catholics had come out strongly against Home Rule.[20] Despite its flaws, he wished the bill well but was fatalistic as to its chances of success. He was also conscious of the opprobrium which would be heaped upon the bishops if they aired their objections in public. He told Kirby on 23 June 1893 that the bill would not pass but 'it would not be wise for the bishops to take upon themselves the odium of defeating it'. His view was that the bill would be rejected in its current form and redrafted. Happily, Gladstone would have the bishops' objections before him when redrafting it. Perhaps then Catholic interests would be provided for as they ought to be.[21] At the end of September, Logue reported to Kirby that the Home Rule Bill had been shelved but it was sure to come up again, 'and I trust in a form more acceptable to Catholics than the last bill was'. He was more upset that English Catholics had openly opposed the bill. 'Catholics in the Empire should combine for the good of the Church', he said, but 'such union was impossible given the contempt for Ireland shown by English Catholics'.[22]

With the Home Rule Bill gone, the bishops were left dependent on the Irish members to 'fight justice' out of the Imperial Parliament. It was a measure of Logue's political pragmatism that the demise of the bill did not occasion despair. The fact that he did not approve of the terms offered also helped. The defeat of Home Rule in 1893 began a period during which the Irish Party proved a source of constant disappointment to him. He simply had no confidence in the wisdom and prudence of Dillon, O'Brien and Redmond.[23] Such was Logue's concern at what he perceived as secularism within the Irish Party and growing separation between the Church and politics that in November 1894 he published a letter to the national movement in the press. He accused elements within the Irish Party of sacrificing Catholic interests 'for an alliance with English Radicals and Free Thinkers'. He declared that there was an attempt being made by some politicians 'to bring the political interests and aspirations of our people into conflict with their religious interests and Catholic feeling'. He believed that if such a course was pursued it would do more to 'discourage patriotism, paralyse national action, destroy cordial union and even break up the national movement' than all the divisions of the past.[24]

Logue's disaffection with the party leadership pushed him in the direction of Tim Healy. Healy was more willing to champion Catholic causes openly and he remained hostile to the Irish Party's alliance with the Liberals. His acerbic wit and 'artful sectarianism' appealed to Logue's sensibilities as did his cynicism regarding parliamentary politics.[25] His editorship of the *National Press* and bitter opposition to Parnell also enhanced his *bona fides* with the clergy. Healy's willingness to have his party, the short-lived People's Rights Association, used as an adjunct of the Church, or Church interests, garnered much support in clerical circles. Maume has observed that Healy and his supporters were perfectly willing to operate in much the same fashion as the German Catholic Centre Party. Such a policy may have appealed to Logue greatly but, given his innate aversion to political entanglements, to describe him as a 'Healyite' is perhaps an overstatement.[26] In return for giving Catholic interests a voice in the House of Commons, Healy received the consistent and powerful support of not only the cardinal primate but many others within the hierarchy. Even Walsh, who had described him in 1893 as representing 'a thoroughly dishonourable, dishonest and dangerous element in our public affairs in Ireland', became a convert to Healy's cause.[27]

Miller has argued that his relationship with Healy marked Logue's attempt to make his influence felt through the sponsorship of a sycophant but this is a rather harsh judgement.[28] Doubtless, Logue derived a certain pleasure in tweaking the political noses of Dillon and O'Brien but the same charge of pandering to sycophancy has not been levelled at Walsh who also came strongly to favour Healy in North Louth. In backing Healy, there was no sense that Logue was attempting to foster unity by installing him as leader of the Irish Party. His support for Healy was as divisive as it was constant. He may have promised Haldane, following the collapse of the St Patrick's scheme, that the bishops would stop agitating on single issues and 'go in with all the energy the country can command for Home Rule' but he took no action to further the cause of the Home Rule Party.[29]

The impetus for party unity, however, came neither from the clergy nor from the leadership of any of the party factions. In 1898 O'Brien founded a new grass-roots organisation, the United Irish League (UIL), to promote unity and act as successor to both the National League and Federation.[30] By 1900, the growth in the new movement was such that it threatened to supplant the party leadership. It also signalled a resurgence of popular interest in Home Rule. That, and the prospect of recapturing the halcyon days of the National League, forced the factions to compromise and in the party conference of January 1900 a breakthrough was made when Dillon and O'Brien accepted the leadership of Redmond.[31] It should be noted that Healy refused to sign the new party pledge and remained effectively an independent.

Logue was not enthused at the prospect of a united and reinvigorated national movement. His central difficulty remained with the party's leadership which, despite the reorganisation, remained the same. Logue's problem was not with Home Rule, nor with the United Irish League, but with his inability to trust Dillon, Redmond and O'Brien. His experiences to date had made him sceptical of any measure of self-government which could be wrung from Westminster and he felt that Catholic interests were not safe in Irish Party hands.

Despite his deep-seated mistrust of the party leadership, Logue seldom voiced his dissatisfaction in public. While other bishops associated freely with the party and the UIL (Patrick O'Donnell, for example, was Northern Treasurer), Logue expressed his disaffection in his continuing support for Healy. When, in January 1905, the party leadership appealed for a statement of endorsement from the bishops, he responded along with his colleagues. The bishops' statement called for the Irish people to rally round their representatives and give them 'the whole strength of the nation's support in their endeavour to secure ordinary civil rights for Irish Catholics in education and all other matters'.[32] In sending his own subscription to party funds Logue noted that, in the present circumstances of the country, it was vital to her interests 'spiritual and temporal, that she should be represented in the House of Commons by a strong party; united, independent, efficient'.[33] This was hardly a ringing endorsement and the sentiments expressed were clearly at odds with Logue's continuing sponsorship of Healy.[34]

A striking instance of open opposition to the leadership occurred in 1905 when Logue petitioned Redmond to leave the North Louth seat uncontested in the forthcoming general election. He was joined in this request by Walsh, and Redmond, unwilling to risk any ecclesiastical trouble, succumbed to the pressure.[35] Logue's intervention followed a meeting of the electors of Dundalk with Dillon, Devlin and Redmond in Dublin in December 1905. The electors had requested that no party candidate should be run against Healy but the notion was bitterly rejected by John Dillon and Joe Devlin.[36] On the eve of a party convention in Dublin, Redmond told Logue that, having anxiously considered his request, he had decided to leave Healy to run unopposed.[37] That Logue was now joined by Walsh in his campaign was significant. The dissatisfaction with the party's championing of Catholic causes and suspicion regarding the leadership was now being manifested rather openly in the continued support for Tim Healy by the two foremost Catholic clerics in Ireland.

It was not just the party that irritated Logue. In 1909 he launched a vociferous attack on the Irish Party's newest adjunct, the Ancient Order of Hibernians (AOH). Moribund since the 1880s, the order was rejuvenated in 1902 and was quickly brought under the control of the party with Devlin's election as president. Although the order received some political sanction in the form of support from individual bishops, such as O'Donnell, and from local clergy, most notably James McFadden in Donegal, the hierarchy remained cautious.[38] Just what the order was in political terms remains a subject for debate. It is perhaps more easily defined in terms of the functions it provided. Padraig Yeates has described it as an 'amalgam of benefit society, sectarian secret society and political voting machine'.[39]

Logue was unconcerned with the political function of the AOH. He declared in a pastoral in February 1909 that, as long as the order remained within the limits set by the Church on secret societies, he had no political quarrel with it. It was on moral and social grounds that he objected to it. He accused the Hibernians of representing a threat to the innocence and virtue of Catholic youth. He objected strongly to the culture of drink and dance halls on which he believed the order was based. He was also concerned that it sought to separate Irish youth from the good influences of their parents.[40] Logue followed up his pastoral in May with an extraordinarily vehement attack. He branded it a 'pest and a cruel tyranny' in certain areas in Ireland. He accused the AOH of press-ganging people to join by means of boycotting, threats, waylaying and beating. His concern was such that he forbade priests to give absolution to anyone guilty of such practices which he derided as a 'revival of old Ribbonism or the Molly Maguires'.[41]

One surprising casualty of Logue's inability to accommodate the emerging facets of Irish nationalism was Healy. By 1910, wrangling over the Liberals' reform budget had greatly strengthened the hand of the Irish Party. Their support for Asquith on the budget question and the collision course set between Commons and Lords over the issue had increased the chances of a third Home Rule Bill to virtual certainty. Despite the changing political fortunes for Home Rule, Logue remained loyally committed to Healy. In the election in January 1910, he was provoked to declare openly for him following allegations that he had backed the party's candidate, Richard Hazelton, MP for North Galway, for the seat.[42] In a letter to the electors of North Louth, he declared that he did not think it strictly in keeping with his position to take so prominent a part in a contested election as to nominate a candidate. 'Otherwise', he went on, 'I should willingly nominate Mr Healy'.[43]

The election itself proved a bitter affair with all the resources of the party being thrown behind Hazelton, as well as some clerical support. On 21 January, however, a delighted Logue telegraphed Walsh to tell him that Healy had retained the seat by 84 votes.[44] The re-elected MP was also surprised and much gratified to receive a congratulatory telegram, the following day, from the Archbishop of Dublin.[45] By the second election in December 1910, however, the euphoria had vanished. Healy was deprived of clerical backing on Logue's express instructions and he lost the seat.

Healy blamed Logue's sudden defection on his alliance with William O'Brien. O'Brien had become increasingly estranged from the party leadership and the split widened when Redmond and Dillon declared their support for Lloyd George's reform budget. Despite a warning from Logue that he should 'fight a lone hand' in Parliament, Healy found common cause with O'Brien on the issue of taxation.[46] In spite of the ominous signals emanating from *Ara Coeli*, Healy appeared on a platform with him at Dungarvan. He later commented to his brother Maurice that 'ecclesiastics, however well read and farsighted, sometimes as little understand the links and kinks in parliamentary politics as a layman would the direction of a monastery'.[47] Healy greeted Logue's withdrawal of support stoically and without rancour. He told his brother that he 'would have gone with O'Brien even if I knew that this was the consequence'.[48]

Logue, however, gave very different reasons for this last intervention in North Louth. He told Walsh in December 1910 that he had forbidden clerical involvement in the election after the bitterness aroused by events in January. It was largely due to the influence of Healy that no priest had ended up in court.[49] It must be noted that Logue felt no pleasure in ending Healy's hopes. He told Walsh before the election that it would be a kind of miracle if he was returned. 'He is completely alone', Logue noted sadly, 'his chief helpers keeping aloof while his opponents have flooded the constituency with their enemies'.[50]

Unexpectedly, however, Healy had the result overturned on appeal and it looked as if another divisive and bitter contest was on the cards. Logue was appalled. His sorrow for the demise of Healy was quickly transformed into concern for his own position and the clergy of Dundalk. In a letter to Walsh in February 1911 he complained that Healy's challenge had left him in an unpleasant fix. Another election campaign would likely get up a bitter feud that would last for a generation with priestly interference rendering their ministry useless among one section of the population. The whole matter left Logue feeling rather sorry for himself. 'Unhappily, I am all alone here', he lamented, 'and there is no one with whom I could take counsel'.[51]

This was, perhaps, more political isolation within the northern episcopacy, rather than any personal animosity among the bishops. The northern bishops remained close to the party and Logue's views were certainly at odds with those of some of his colleagues, especially Patrick O'Donnell in Raphoe. In the end, Healy spared the cardinal and did not stand again. He was subsequently elected for a seat in Cork and despite the events of 1910 the two men retained a cordial relationship, though it was never the same. Logue's severing of his only political tie in such a fashion was a miscalculation and could only increase his remoteness from the currents of Irish nationalism. He let his mistrust of O'Brien outweigh his respect for Healy and in doing so lost a valuable political contact as the prospects for Home Rule brightened.

Self-determination

Logue's disaffection from the Irish Party remained consistent and unabated. This, along with genuine interest, contributed to his admiration for the cultural nationalism of organisations such as the Gaelic League. A lifelong Irish speaker, Logue had been President of the Society for the Preservation of the Irish Language at Maynooth and, although he was never a member, he tried to give the Gaelic League a lift whenever he could.[52] He was also aware of the political value of the League. He told a branch meeting in Omeath that if the Irish language was allowed to die out, then the spirit of nationality would also die out. The revival of the Irish language and culture, he said, 'would be the first step in driving out the English'.[53] There was a certain amount of playing to the gallery here but Logue was prepared to back the League as a real alternative to the moral bankruptcy of the AOH. In condemning the Hibernians in 1909 he suggested that the League not only furnished 'an opportunity for improving the mind by interesting studies, but in their lighter exercise of music, song and the old modest Irish dances, supply the means of most enjoyable recreation'.[54]

This relationship, however, was not without tension. Logue did not appreciate the confrontational tactics of the League and its vociferous campaign for the Irish language. He told Walsh in 1899 that its criticism of political figures like Dillon for a lack of Gaelic credentials would cause nothing but mischief.[55] He had occasion to experience such tactics personally in 1909. At Maynooth, Logue had presided at the dismissal of Professor Michael O'Hickey for his constant criticism of the bishops and their attitude to Irish in Maynooth and the fledgling National University. O'Hickey refused to go quietly and fought his sacking for the next five years, though without success, taking his case to the Holy See.[56] The priest had spearheaded a campaign waged by the League newspaper *An Claidheamh Soluis* not only to have Irish made a compulsory subject for matriculation but to have Irish as the language of tuition at the university.[57] The paper had also criticised the decision to sack O'Hickey to such an extent that in January 1909, Logue issued a public dressing down to the League in the columns of the *Freeman*. He rejected angrily its temerity in commenting on the internal workings of Maynooth and refused to saddle the new university with preconditions on attendance by making Irish compulsory.[58] Despite this altercation, Logue retained much admiration for the League, which was evident in his strenuous denial in 1916 that its members had fomented the Rising.

Logue's disillusionment with the national movement was matched by his scepticism regarding any measure of reform wrung from Westminster, regardless of which party was in power. Even the long sought settlement of the University Question inspired little confidence. The National University, after all, like most 'gifts' from London, bore the 'brand of slavery impressed upon it'.[59] Neither was he impressed with the Irish Local Government Act of 1898, the only significant measure of self-government extended to Ireland before the 1920s. He complained to Thomas O'Dwyer, Bishop of Limerick, in February 1898 that the act was a sign of the growing anticlericalism abroad. He pointed to the exclusion of the clergy from participation in local government elections as further evidence of this. Such a bar on priests standing in elections existed nowhere else in Europe. 'I do not say that I would care to see clerics mixing in county councils', he went on, 'but I do not like to see them deprived of the right more than other citizens'.[60]

That is not to say, however, that Logue's perpetual disappointment masked a lack of political vision. Nor was he guilty of fault-finding for its own sake. He retained a fundamental belief that any measure of Home Rule would not be enough. Logue's ideal for Irish self-determination was provided during a visit to Canada for a eucharistic conference in 1910. On his return to Armagh in October he told an audience that they were a free people in Canada. 'They made their own laws and were ruled by their own ministry. They had created a spirit of freedom, liberality and mutual kindness that could exist under no other circumstances.' Moreover, the freedom experienced there had fostered a spirit of religious toleration. With more than a nod to the Unionist constituency in the north, Logue declared that no people were more devoted to the interests of the Empire than the people of Canada. If they had the same freedom in Ireland 'they would be just as loyal in this country, if they were not so already'.[61]

However, this was as far as Logue was prepared to go in conciliating Unionists. As political tension mounted in the north over what was perceived as the inexorable approach of a Home Rule Bill, he was outraged at nationalist attempts to placate Protestant opinion. In February 1911 he complained to Walsh about articles in the press in which Redmond emphasised how secular a Home Rule parliament would be. He observed that Redmond was going 'very far in playing to the nonconformist gallery' particularly in questioning the Pope's right to interfere in politics.[62] Logue repeated these concerns to Michael O'Riordan, Rector of the Irish College in Rome. 'I fear very much that if Home Rule be granted', he said, 'it will mean freedom for Irish Protestants and forge shackles for Irish Catholics'.[63]

Given Logue's uncompromising mood, it was no surprise that the Home Rule Bill, once unveiled, was a disappointment. It fell far short of his ideal of Dominion Home Rule and was really not much different from Gladstone's bill of 1893. It envisaged the establishment of a regional assembly with both upper and lower houses. As in 1893, Westminster retained authority over foreign relations along with customs and excise. Once again, the Liberal Government inserted clauses concerning religion. Clause 3 prohibited the state endowment of any one religion or the granting of privileges to one section of the people on religious grounds. On denominational education, the bill upheld the right of any child to attend a school receiving public money without attending the religious instruction available in that school.[64]

Despite Logue's vocal interventions in the run up to the bill, there was no episcopal statement on it, or on Home Rule as a whole. Indeed, Redmond was particularly concerned by the silence of the Archbishop of Dublin. He told Walsh in March 1912 that with his silence 'the national movement has been shorn of a great element of strength for some time'. The prevalent impression was that Walsh had 'been out of sympathy with the methods and policy of the Irish Party'. Redmond was sure, however, that the terms of the bill would be acceptable to him.[65] But Redmond could expect no endorsement or approbation from Walsh, who was as unimpressed as Logue. In his reply Walsh declared, 'it is some years since I have made up my mind to have nothing more to do with Irish politics and that nothing in the world could induce me to change my mind on the matter'.[66]

Logue took a leading role in scrutinising the bill along with the other members of the Standing Committee. Together with a Dublin solicitor, J. A. Murnaghan, they proceeded to analyse the clauses point by point. Logue was extremely sceptical. As in 1893, he remained convinced that the provisions of the bill simply did not go far enough in providing sufficient authority to enact real change. Murnaghan was asked to clarify if an Irish parliament could fund denominational education, provided all faiths were treated equally. It was his opinion that only the Imperial Parliament could reverse problematic educational and religious clauses in the bill. In practical terms, a Home Rule parliament could not, for example, reverse the prohibition laid down in the Universities Act on the public funding of theology in the National University.[67]

Logue complained to the Bishop of Raphoe, Patrick O'Donnell, that the safeguards for Protestants embodied in the bill would be 'so many fetters riveted to our limbs'.[68] He further protested, 'as far as religious interests are concerned, I would rather live under an Imperial parliament than under a Home Rule parliament. The former might be brought, sooner or later, to remove religious grievances; the latter simply cannot'.[69] Such comments, taken in isolation, have contributed greatly to the perception among historians that Logue was ideologically opposed to Home Rule.[70] Despite his misgivings he was concerned that the bill should pass. He remained anxious that the concessions to Protestants would be 'so many encroachments on our legitimate freedom' and that the safeguards would be pushed to extremes in order to prove 'our flowing liberality'. Nevertheless, his objections did not develop into outright rejection.[71]

Asquith's bill was introduced into the Commons on 11 April 1912 amid an increasingly bitter campaign of opposition from Unionists. Opposition to Home Rule coalesced around Ulster with the new Conservative Party leader, Andrew Bonar Law, more willing than his predecessor to exploit the climate of rebellion there. That the bill would pass the Commons was almost certain and the Parliament Act had ended the veto of the House of Lords. At a meeting at Blenheim in July 1912, however, Law declared that he could 'imagine no length of resistance to which Ulster can go in which I would not be prepared to support them'. He concluded darkly that there were things stronger than parliamentary majorities.[72]

In September 1912 thousands assembled in Belfast and across Ulster to sign a Solemn League and Covenant, pledging to resist Home Rule at all costs; in January 1913, Ulster Unionists formed and armed an army of popular resistance, the Ulster Volunteer Force. The passage of the bill progressed despite the growing rebellion in Ulster but, by 1913, the notion of exclusion had gained much currency at Westminster. Indeed, by March 1914, the Government made support for the bill contingent on the temporary exclusion of Ulster. Redmond was willing to support Lloyd George's county option scheme, the exclusion of six northern counties for a period of three years, as the price of peace.[73]

All that remained was to convince the national movement, including the bishops, to accept the scheme. To this end, the MP for South Down, Jeremiah MacVeagh, was despatched to *Ara Coeli* to gauge Logue's reaction. The party could already count on the support of party bishops such as Patrick O'Donnell in Raphoe and Charles McHugh in Derry, but the cardinal primate was an unknown quantity. Despite his generally poor opinion of the bill Logue was primarily concerned that it should be saved and gave a cautious assent to Redmond's acceptance.[74] Privately, however, he was extremely anxious. He told Walsh that the concessions made on the Home Rule Bill would be a bad business for the north. 'It will leave us more than ever under the heel of the Orangemen', he said and worried that partition, even temporary partition, would leave Unionists free to tamper with education.[75]

Logue's anxieties persisted, even when Home Rule was enacted in September 1914. Amid the euphoria and gratitude in Nationalist Ireland, he remained cautious. On his return from the conclave that elected Pope Benedict XV, Logue, almost alone among his colleagues, sounded a note of caution. He told the *Freeman's Journal*, 'I don't trust your politicians in England very much. They have an amending bill to bring in; what that will be I don't know.'[76] Walsh, with whom Logue had dined on his return from Rome, remained silent on the passing of the bill. He had flatly told Augustine Birrell, the Chief Secretary, that he could not support the measure.[77] There would be no episcopal endorsement of the Home Rule Act. The party leadership basked in the adulation of individual bishops, but received no approbation from the Archbishops of Armagh or Dublin.

Notes

1 Miller, *Church, State and Nation*, p. 11.
2 Aan de Wiel, *Catholic Church*, p. 43.
3 Logue to Walsh, 31 July 1890, Walsh Papers, DDA, box 362, folders 404/4–6, 405/1–2.
4 Logue to Walsh, 16 Aug. 1890, Walsh Papers, DDA, box 362, folders 404/4–6, 405/1–2.
5 Logue to Parnell, undated, Logue Papers, ADA, box 7, folder 1, 'Political'.
6 Healy, *Letters and Leaders*, p. 337.
7 Curtis, *Coercion and Conciliation*, p. 309.
8 Logue to Walsh, 28 Nov. 1890, Walsh Papers, DDA, box 362, folders 404/4–6, 405/1–2.
9 Logue to Walsh, 4 Dec. 1890, Walsh Papers, DDA, box 362, folders 404/4–6, 405/1–2.
10 Logue to Walsh, 27 Dec. 1890, Walsh Papers, DDA, box 362, folders 404/4–6, 405/1–2.
11 *Freeman's Journal*, 12 Jan. 1891.
12 Lenten pastoral, 5 Feb. 1891, Logue Papers, ADA, box 9, folder 6, 'Sermons and Pastorals'.
13 *National Press*, 11 Mar. 1891.
14 Croke to Walsh, 4 Dec. 1891, Walsh Papers, DDA, box 363, folder 405/3–6.
15 Croke to Logue, 8 July 1892, Logue Papers, ADA, box 3, folder 8, 'Irish Dioceses'.
16 Kirby to Logue, 15 Jan. 1891, Logue Papers, ADA, box 7, 'Irish College'.
17 Maume, *Long Gestation*, p. 15.

18 O'Day, *Home Rule*, p. 321.
19 Logue to Walsh, 10 May 1893, Walsh Papers, DDA, box 365, folder 365/2.
20 Logue to Walsh, 2 June 1893, Walsh Papers, DDA, box 365, folder 365/2.
21 Logue to Kirby, 23 June 1893, Kirby Papers, AICR, no. 129 (1893).
22 Logue to Kirby, 27 Sept. 1893, Kirby Papers, AICR, no. 196 (1893).
23 Logue to Walsh, 14 Dec. 1893, Walsh Papers, DDA, box 364, folder 407/1–4.
24 *Irish News*, 17 Nov. 1894.
25 Callanan, *T. M. Healy*, p. 431.
26 Maume, *Long Gestation*, p. 16.
27 Walsh to Logue, 5 July 1895, Logue Calendar, p. 187. The letter is missing from the 'Dublin Archdiocese' correspondence in box 3, ADA.
28 Miller, *Church, State and Nation*, p. 244.
29 Haldane to Balfour, 6 Mar. 1899, Balfour Papers, BL, MS 49724, fols 64–7.
30 Bull, 'United Irish League', p. 52.
31 *Ibid*, p. 54.
32 Miller, *Church, State and Nation*, p. 125.
33 *Ibid*.
34 Healy, *Letters and Leaders*, p. 451.
35 Miller, *Church, State and Nation*, p. 144.
36 Sheridan to Logue, 29 Dec. 1905, Logue Papers, ADA, box 7, folder 11, 'Political'.
37 Redmond to Logue, 2 Jan. 1906, Logue Papers, ADA, box 7, folder 2, 'Political'.
38 Miller, *Church, State and Nation*, p. 210.
39 Yeates, *Lockout*, p. 45.
40 *Irish Times*, 22 Feb. 1909.
41 *Ibid.*, 14 May 1909.
42 Miller, *Church, State and Nation*, p. 262.
43 Healy, *Letters and Leaders*, pp. 491–2.
44 Logue to Walsh, 21 Jan. 1910, Walsh Papers, DDA, box 382, folder 382/2.
45 Healy, *Letters and Leaders*, p. 492.
46 *Ibid.*, p. 498.
47 *Ibid*.
48 *Ibid.*, p. 502.
49 Logue to Walsh, 24 Feb. 1911,Walsh Papers, DDA, box 383, folder 376/5.
50 Logue to Walsh, 7 Dec. 1910, Walsh Papers, DDA, box 382, folder 382/6.
51 Logue to Walsh, 24 Feb. 1911, Walsh Papers, DDA, box 383, folder 376/5.
52 Logue to Walsh, 19 Oct. 1899, Walsh Papers, DDA, box 371, folder 364/3.
53 Unidentified newspaper clipping, 1899, Logue Papers, ADA, box 10, folder 9, 'Biography'.
54 *Irish Times*, 22 Feb. 1909.
55 Logue to Walsh, 19 Oct. 1899, Walsh Papers, DDA, box 371, folder 364/3.
56 Briody, 'From Carrickbeg to Rome', pp. 143–66.
57 *An Claidheamh Soluis*, 25 Jan. and 21 Aug. 1908.

58 *Freeman's Journal*, 23 Feb. 1909.
59 *ICD*, 1910, p. 478.
60 Logue to O'Dwyer, 23 Feb. 1898, O'Dwyer Papers, LDA, file N.
61 *Irish Times*, 26 Oct. 1910.
62 Logue to Walsh, 11 Feb. 1911, Walsh Papers, DDA, box 383, folder 376/5.
63 Logue to O'Riordan, 24 Feb. 1911, O'Riordan Papers, AICR, no. 43 (1911).
64 O'Day, *Irish Home Rule*, pp. 322–3.
65 Redmond to Walsh, 7 Mar. 1912, Walsh Papers, DDA, box 384, folder 377/1.
66 Walsh to Redmond, 20 Mar. 1912, Walsh Papers, DDA, box 384, folder 377/1.
67 Murnaghan to O'Donnell, 9 and 14 Nov. 1912, O'Donnell Papers, ADA, box 3, 'Government of Ireland Bill'.
68 Logue to O'Donnell, 5 Nov. 1912, O'Donnell Papers, ADA, box 3, 'Government of Ireland Bill'.
69 Logue to O'Donnell, 6 Dec. 1912, O'Donnell Papers, ADA, box 3, 'Government of Ireland Bill'.
70 See Phoenix, *Northern Nationalism*, p. 141, among others.
71 Logue to O'Donnell, 20 Dec. 1912, O'Donnell Papers, ADA, box 9, folder 3, 'Patrick Cardinal O'Donnell'.
72 O'Day, *Irish Home Rule*, p. 253.
73 Miller, *Church, State and Nation*, p. 303.
74 *Ibid.*
75 Logue to Walsh, 13 Mar. 1914, Walsh Papers, DDA, box 386, folder 384/4.
76 *Freeman's Journal*, 30 Sept. 1914.
77 Walsh to Birrell, 15 Feb. 1914, Walsh Papers, DDA, box 386, folder 384/4.

6

England's extremity

It is a mistake to view Ireland's response to the outbreak of the First World War in 1914 in pro- or anti-British terms. There was a very real sense that this was Ireland's war, as the issues of participation and the enactment of Home Rule merged in the general euphoria of Nationalist Ireland. As Jeffery has pointed out, this was a war for big words. It was a war for the freedom of small nations, for King, Country, Democracy, Duty and Liberty.[1] There was a widespread conviction among nationalists that now was the time for Europe's newest small nation to take to the international stage. In September, Patrick O'Donnell declared that 'in the day of small nations, success has crowned our age-long struggle at an opportune, if not indeed, a Providential moment. Ireland, as a whole, has now the chance of taking her part in moulding the destinies of nations.'[2]

With the enactment of Home Rule, John Dillon felt justified in talking of the 'union of two democracies' of Britain and Ireland in the coming struggle in Europe despite the postponement of the Home Rule Act for the duration of the war.[3] Not only was the war a chance for Ireland to demonstrate her new status as a nation, there was still much to be fought for in terms of the final Irish settlement. When Redmond pledged the National Volunteers for the defence of Ireland, Carson offered the services of the UVF at the front. As Fitzpatrick has argued, for Redmond, Irish involvement in the war promised the reward of early Home Rule; while Carson saw an opportunity to strengthen Ulster's case for exclusion 'by demonstrating that its loyalism was more than a rhetorical figment'.[4] Thus, on 20 September at Woodenbridge, County Wicklow, Redmond told Irish Nationalists that they should take care that Irish valour proved itself on the fields of battle – 'not only in Ireland itself, but wherever the firing line extends, in defence of right, of freedom and religion in this war'.[5]

Throughout Ireland, nationalist fervour mingled with anger at the tactics employed by the Germans. Patriotism and moral outrage combined to produce not only justification for the war but a moral obligation to enlist.[6] In 1914, for example, Tom Kettle, former MP for East Tyrone, was in Belgium buying weapons for the National Volunteers. Incensed by German shelling of Reims Cathedral he promptly turned the rifles over to the Belgian Government 'to protect the rights of small nations'.[7] This same anger was evident in a speech given by Charles McHugh, Bishop of Derry. He declared that the Irish people, one and all, were with the arms of England. Germany was a power 'that would set at nought the very foundation upon which civilisation rests'.[8]

The outbreak of hostilities provided a welcome respite for the British Government. By the summer of 1914, two opposing volunteer armies faced each other over the approach of Home Rule. The rebellion in Ulster had gathered pace and the UVF had blossomed into a formidable fighting force. As Fitzpatrick has pointed out, with nearly a hundred thousand men, an experienced officer corps and forty thousand rifles and carbines, 'the Ulster Volunteer Force was a far more impressive striking force than the British army in Ireland'.[9] Nationalists at first derided the new army, with even Logue trying to diminish the threat. Between the quality of the rifles and the skill of the gunmen, he did not think there would be much danger.[10] Others found the prospect of an Orangeman with even an old rifle a far less ridiculous spectacle than a nationalist without one. Thus, in November 1913, a volunteer movement had been founded in Dublin. The prospect of bands of even badly armed nationalists drilling in Ireland caused some alarm among the bishops. The Volunteers were not a creation of the Irish Party or the Church, having their origin in the initiative of a loose affiliation of Gaelic Leaguers. What was hidden was the influence in the new body of the Irish Republican Brotherhood (IRB).

Elements within the hierarchy, bishops close to the Irish Party such as Patrick O'Donnell, moved to assist Redmond's assertion of control.[11] The subsequent split in 1914 into National and Irish Volunteers caused outrage and incredulity. The *Freeman's Journal* found it amazing that anyone would not wish to submit to the authority of the triumphant leaders of Ireland at such a critical juncture for the country.[12] After Redmond's Woodenbridge speech, the volunteer movements, north and south, began a period of enlistment en masse and the political tension in Ireland, along with the prospect of violence, suddenly dissipated. Indeed, Patrick Callan has asserted that the volunteer armies in Ireland provided forty-five per cent of the total Irish enlistment by 1918.[13]

Given that, by September 1914, thousands of Irish were participating in a general European conflict there was remarkably little discussion of the war among the bishops. Indeed, in the run-up to the conflict, the hierarchy had had little time to pay attention to national events at all as the bishops, particularly Walsh, were embroiled in the bitter labour dispute which had wracked Dublin for most of the previous year. Like his colleagues, Logue was alarmed at the strike and suspicious of the unions. 'They are not working in the interests of the men', he told Walsh, 'but using the unfortunate men for the purpose of propagating and establishing their socialist and syndicalist principles'. He found the civil unrest disturbing and the plight of the families of the strikers distressing. However, there was no small sense of betrayal in his assertion that 'this unfortunate business is a greater back set to Home Rule than all the vapourings of Sir Edward Carson'.[14]

The bishops were further distracted from the outbreak of war by the sudden death of Pius X on 20 August 1914. In a letter to the clergy of Ireland, Logue lamented the passing of the Pope. Evident in the statement, was the fact that, in contrast to most of nationalist Ireland, he viewed the coming war with great apprehension. 'The lamented death of the Sovereign Pontiff', he said, 'at a moment when the dark cloud of a destructive war hangs over Europe, tends to deepen the gloom and intensity of sorrow with which the passing away of the saintly Pontiff would at any time overwhelm his afflicted children'.[15] It was only on his return from the Conclave which elected Benedict XV that Logue commented on the conflict in Europe. His reluctance to issue a statement has been portrayed by some as ambivalence towards the war but this was certainly not the case.[16] His refusal to join in the patriotic fervour which greeted the outbreak of war was symptomatic of Logue's revulsion at the prospect of conflict. For him, war meant 'the mother's longing for the son whose sight shall never glad her eyes, the widow's tears, the orphan's helplessness'. These evils, he declared, 'furnish a striking practical lesson to those enthusiasts who, at a safe distance and unacquainted with its realities, contemplate war with a light heart'.[17]

On his way back from Rome, Logue gave an interview to a journalist at Plymouth. Exactly what was said was matter of some controversy. The interview, which appeared in the *Freeman's Journal* and other newspapers, quoted Logue as rather enthusiastically supporting the war effort. There was no more loyal country than Ireland, he apparently said, and there could be nothing but horror at the barbarities of Germany. The bombardment of Reims Cathedral had aroused the indignation of every civilised being outside that country. 'All men with the slightest appreciation of art, whatever their religion', he went on, 'must cry aloud for reparation against people who proved even worse than the Hun'.[18] The following day, however, Logue disputed these reports. He told the *Freeman* that he had only denounced the German bombardment of the cathedral. 'This gentleman', he said, referring to the journalist at Plymouth, 'gave his own version of the conversation and attributed to me things I didn't say at all'. Logue said he had seen various versions of his remarks in numerous papers, none of which were accurate.[19]

Aan de Wiel has stated that Logue supported the Empire and the Allied cause but felt constrained from giving any material help because of his disaffection with the British Government.[20] In reality, however, Logue refrained from any overt political comment on the war for almost its entirety. His resentment at the Government was sustained and played little part in his overall attitude to the conflict. The fact of vast numbers of Irish Catholics serving in the British armed forces was never a political problem for Logue but a spiritual one. By 1915, the number of Irish Catholics serving on the various fronts and in the army camps had risen considerably.[21] Logue's moral aversion to the suffering caused by war had long equipped him with a deep affinity for those in the armed forces and concern for their spiritual welfare. He did not pass moral judgement on enlistment but retained a fundamental belief that, having volunteered to risk their lives for the state, the least Irish soldiers or sailors could expect in return was that their immortal souls should not be imperilled.

The issue of army chaplains, therefore, played a central part in Logue's response to the outbreak of war. In 1900, for example, the poor provision of Catholic chaplains in the navy during the South African War, prompted him to denounce Catholic parents who allowed their children to join. They were guilty, he said, 'of the most grave violation of their most sacred duty'.[22] Logue returned to the same theme in a pastoral in 1902, declaring the naval authorities' failure to provide chaplains was a poor return for those willing to risk death for the welfare of the state. They should not, in addition, be required to endanger their eternal salvation.[23] This notion of a fair transaction permeated Logue's call in 1914 for the Government to increase the number of Catholic chaplains which the *Freeman's Journal* had put at just twelve.[24] Speaking in October 1914, he demanded that the practice of confining Catholic military chaplains to hospital and rear area work should cease and that they be allowed to accompany Irish troops to the front. Logue also expressed confusion as to his role in appointing chaplains. He told his audience in Dundalk that he had been given no authority to nominate or appoint chaplains by the War Office.[25]

Later, in a letter to the *Irish Catholic*, Logue explained that he had been contacted by a number of priests seeking positions with the military but that he could not appoint them. He included an extract from a letter issued by the War Office explaining that responsibility for chaplains had been given to Francis Cardinal Bourne, Archbishop of Westminster. However, the War Office did think it was desirable that the head of the Irish Church should nominate chaplains for Irish soldiers. Logue took this request to mean the appointment of chaplains for soldiers *in* Ireland, for which there was no real need as the local parish priest could easily serve at local army camps. He went on to bitterly criticise the Government's insensitivity to the spiritual needs of Catholics who, he said, could hardly be expected to fight when their immortal souls were endangered by being deprived of the sacraments.[26]

In one sense, Logue may have been deliberately obtuse. Bourne's quick move to position himself as the supreme authority over Catholic army chaplains had caused much resentment in the Irish Church. It had the effect of reigniting old rivalries between the hierarchies in England and Ireland. As in previous years, the Irish bishops reacted badly to any situation which implied subservience to Westminster. The concern among the bishops for the spiritual welfare of Irish soldiers and sailors was, however, keenly felt. In October, they issued a joint pastoral calling on the Government to increase the places for Catholic chaplains in the army and the navy. Irish fighting men, they declared, were entitled to the solace provided by the last rites.[27]

The statements issued by Logue and his episcopal colleagues on the issue had the desired effect. In November, H. J. Tennant, Under-secretary for War, wrote to John Redmond to clarify the situation regarding the numbers and appointment of chaplains. It had been decided at the War Office that every Irish regiment which was predominantly Catholic should have a Catholic chaplain. The number of chaplaincies had been increased from 14 to 30. Tennant also clarified the process for nominations. Chaplains would now be appointed in Ireland by the General Officer Commanding in consultation with Cardinal Logue. The letter revealed that eight such nominations had already been carried out.[28] Despite the improving situation, Logue was still unsatisfied and attacked the Government again in his Lenten pastoral in February 1915 for failing to increase the number of chaplains in the navy.[29]

In fact, the bishops had already begun moves to address this particular want. In March, the Bishop of Waterford, Richard Sheehan, was deputed to travel with Redmond to London for a conference with Admiralty officials and Cardinal Bourne. Sheehan had high hopes for the outcome, but he confessed to Michael O'Riordan, Rector of the Irish College, that he felt it 'most unfortunate that the care of Irish sailors should be left in the hands of English bishops'.[30] The following month, Sheehan reported that the conference had gone well and that the Admiralty had been very kind. The places for Catholic chaplains would be increased, particularly among the naval squadrons in the North Sea, the Mediterranean and the Dardanelles. The attitude of the English hierarchy, however, still rankled. As usual, Sheehan told O'Riordan, the English bishops were taking all the credit.[31]

Despite their initiative on naval chaplains and their appeals for chaplains for the army, an impression existed in some quarters that the hierarchy was not doing enough. In April, Captain Patrick Butler of the Royal Irish Regiment in Dublin wrote to Walsh to protest at the 'aloofness' of the Irish Church. Not only was there no encouragement for Irish soldiers heard at masses, but the bishops remained silent on what Butler viewed as the essential justice of the war. 'The Irish soldiers', he told the archbishop, 'are not outcasts, pariahs, men of no account. They are heroes, next to martyrs, men worthy of esteem and honour.'[32] Logue, however, was fully committed to the spiritual welfare of soldiers and continued to press for improvement on the chaplaincy issue. Speaking at the Maynooth Union in June 1915 he condemned what he saw as the *ad hoc* and cavalier attitude with which the War Office treated the spiritual needs of Irish Catholic soldiers. 'Catholic chaplains were not recognised', he said, 'they have no official position; they have no Chaplain General; they have no regular organisation for the permanent supervision of the religious interests of their people'.[33]

Though bitterly critical of the Government, Logue was less than effective when it came to the nomination process in Ireland. In July 1915, Father John Mulderry, a priest from Dublin, told Walsh that he had been waiting for three months to be appointed as a military chaplain. He had applied to Logue as per the instructions issued in November 1914 but his eventual reply was unhelpful. The cardinal informed him that he had been asked to appoint a few chaplains at the beginning but his association with 'that business' had now ceased. Soon after, however, Mulderry did receive a hurried letter from *Ara Coeli* confirming a position in the military.[34]

There was, perhaps, a degree of petulance in Logue's refusal to have his own role in the nomination process clarified. However, he was not the only bishop alienated by the attitude of the English hierarchy. In May 1915, Bourne had received papal sanction for his position as ecclesiastical superior of all Catholic military chaplains. The Bishop of Waterford, Richard Sheehan, was of the opinion that the decision of the Holy See had rather tied the hands of the bishops by anointing Bourne, effectively, with sole authority to treat with the Admiralty and the War Office.[35] Logue was disillusioned. Before the conference at the Admiralty he told O'Donnell in Raphoe that there was no point in convening the Standing Committee on the chaplaincy issue. 'It is pretty clear that the government pay very little attention to the bishops', he said, 'and I think they pay just as little to the representations of Mr Redmond'. Logue believed the Government felt it had the country stalemated by keeping Home Rule hanging in the balance, 'and so far as our interests go they seem quite indifferent to them, providing they get plenty recruits'.[36]

Eventually, word of a chronic shortage of chaplains began to filter back to Ireland. In August 1915, Father L. Stafford wrote to Walsh about conditions in the Mediterranean. On the hospital ship *Andiana*, he had the care of nearly 3,000 men. The navy was being very kind in providing facilities for him to hear confessions and say mass. Despite the privations, Stafford summed up his position as 'happy and hot'.[37] In July 1915, Sheehan complained to O'Riordan that Bourne was not being effective in providing chaplains. The Government was willing to appoint but the cardinal was unable to secure any priests.[38] Confirmation of a crisis arrived in September in an appeal to the Irish bishops from Cardinal Bourne to nominate twenty-five priests immediately. There were already 270 serving with the armed forces and in the camps but this was simply not enough.[39]

Leonard has argued that the apparent failure of the Irish bishops to appoint chaplains indicated their reluctance to act as recruiting sergeants.[40] This is not strictly true. There was a certain amount of reluctance among the bishops to place the Church at the head of the campaign for voluntary enlistment. Walsh, in particular, consistently refused to cooperate in the recruitment campaign by denying the military the use of churches and church property to hold meetings or even hang recruitment posters.[41] Moreover, he refused to say requiem masses for the war dead in Dublin's pro-cathedral, though there were some exceptions.[42] The issue of chaplains, however, was fundamentally different. The question of recruitment had little bearing on the problem. There were already thousands of Irish Catholics fighting with the British army and navy and the bishops remained willing to appoint, provided they had volunteers. There is little evidence that any bishop actively discouraged applications for chaplaincies or refused to appoint once a volunteer had come forward. Even Walsh gave full support to serving chaplains and enjoyed their confidence.[43] The bishops responded to Bourne's appeal with a joint pastoral issued on 12 October. They reiterated their deep concern for the 'spiritual wants of our Catholic sailors and soldiers at the front'. They would welcome applications from zealous priests for immediate service as military chaplains.[44] Applications from the secular clergy could be made through their local ordinary. Clergy from religious orders should apply to their superiors.

Bourne, however, continued to cause considerable resentment among the Irish Bishops. In January 1916, the Rector of the Irish College, Michael O'Riordan, told Logue that Cardinal Bourne had been lobbying strongly at the Vatican to have total authority over chaplains in both England and Ireland vested in him. The Bishop of Southwark, Peter Amigo, told Benedict in the course of an audience that the Irish hierarchy would not recognise such authority.[45] Despite this simmering rift, the bishops used their October meeting to organise a more formal response to the issue of chaplains. The Bishop of Ross, Dennis Kelly, had been deputed to examine the need for chaplains. He reported in January 1916 that there was still a great need for priests and that that need was growing daily. In a letter sent to every bishop he appealed for volunteers to come forward. Names could be forwarded to Cardinal Logue.[46] Just as Logue had begun to accept responsibility for the nomination of chaplains and the bishops become more proactive, problems again surfaced from Rome.

At the end of January, Robert Browne, Bishop of Cloyne, reported that Bourne's meddling at the Vatican had produced the suggestion from the Holy See of a restructuring of the chain if command regarding chaplains. It was envisaged that Logue and the Archbishop of Westminster should jointly nominate a chaplain-general. Browne concluded that this position, by necessity, would be filled by an Englishman, probably drawn from Bourne's entourage. The new man 'would practically act as the mouth of Cardinal Bourne' and Browne warned that they should be careful not to endanger 'their rightful claims'.[47] John Hagan, the Vice-Rector of the Irish College, told O'Donnell that 'in keeping with his usual sanctimonious dodging' the Archbishop of Westminster was doing his utmost to blame the shortage of chaplains on the Irish. He warned that subservience to Westminster on this issue would be the thin end of the wedge.[48] Logue had written to the Holy See to put the Irish bishops' case in 1915, and he did so again on 10 February 1916.[49] He denied that the Irish bishops were in any way responsible for the shortage of chaplains and pointed out that they were working with Bourne to solve the problem.[50]

This was quite true. On 3 February 1916, Bourne had contacted Logue to appeal for help and enclosed a detailed report on the shortfall in the number of chaplains by Father William Murphy. Bourne pointed out that there were, in all branches of the armed services, a total of 400 serving Catholic chaplains. Some 270 of these had been supplied by the Catholic hierarchy in England. 'Can your Eminence', Bourne pleaded, 'in your charity obtain more help from Ireland which so far has given less than sixty?'[51] If Logue was not moved by Bourne's appeal, he was by Murphy's report which detailed, among other emergencies, a shortfall of some twenty chaplains for the Dardanelles.[52]

His response was swift. In his Lenten pastoral on 6 February he asked for volunteers to fill these vacancies at once. Ignoring the rift with Westminster, he recommended that nominations be sent directly to Bourne in London.[53] By March the situation had improved greatly. Murphy, now operating as a central liaison at the Curragh army camp, reported to the bishops that he had processed applications from 27 priests following Logue's appeal with another three pending. There were still vacancies for a total of forty-four chaplains – thirty in England and another fourteen at the various fronts.[54] Dennis Kelly, Bishop of Ross, also noted an improvement in his report to the bishops at the end of March 1916. He put the number of Irish chaplains at a more respectable 118. Of these, 72 had come from the secular clergy while 46 had volunteered from the religious orders. The Jesuits had supplied the largest number from the regular clergy with a total of thirteen. Logue's last appeal had secured the nomination of thirty-six new chaplains.[55] The willingness of the bishops to appoint chaplains stemmed not only from the spiritual crisis faced by Irish Catholic soldiers and sailors. There were also those within the hierarchy who had relatives serving in the forward areas. Frank Browne, for example, nephew of the Bishop of Cloyne, was a Jesuit chaplain attached to the Irish Guards on the Western Front and served at the Somme, Messines, Ypres and Arras.[56] Such links served to make conditions faced by members of the armed forces seem not so remote.

The improving situation regarding chaplains in Ireland was undermined somewhat by continuing tension between the Archbishop of Westminster and the Irish hierarchy. In 1916, the British Government moved to formalise the structure of Catholic chaplaincies with the appointment of Monsignor William Keating as chaplain-general. Rather than soothing dissension, Keating's appointment served to increase the division between the two hierarchies. In September Logue wrote to the *Irish Catholic* warning that the number of chaplains at the front was woefully short of what was required. Relying on figures supplied to him by Kelly, he appealed for a further thirty volunteers to meet the urgent need.

'It would be sad indeed', he said, 'while we read in the daily papers of the imperishable glory which Irish Catholic soldiers have won for their country, to feel that anything in our power had been left undone to secure for them the blessing compared with which all earthly . . . interests are but transient shadows'.[57]

A week later, Keating wrote to contradict Logue's appeal. He denied that the shortage was as bad as the Cardinal had made out and that there certainly was no shortage of chaplains at the front.[58] This was not the picture painted in a letter to the press from France by Father M. H. Bolger at the end of October. 'We have not nearly enough priests out here', he said, 'we cannot do more than half of what night be done for the fine fellows who look to us for spiritual help and whose need is greater and more urgent than any one I know'.[59] Where Bourne had fully acknowledged the want of Catholic chaplains, Keating seemed to regard appeals for more as a slight on his management. Perhaps he and the cardinal had a certain justification for feeling some proprietorship over military chaplains. It was the English hierarchy who maintained the closest contact with the troops. Bourne had personally inspected the Sixteenth (Irish) Division before it embarked for France and in October 1917, he had visited them in the trenches.[60]

Keating again clashed with Logue in 1917 over the number of vacancies. Quoting from a letter he had received from the War Office, the cardinal appealed for volunteers to fill ninety-three vacancies in France and a further sixty in Salonika.[61] Keating wrote, once again, to quibble with the numbers. He argued that the shortage in France was not as bad as Logue had made out and put the number of chaplains required for Salonika at only ten.[62] Questions were being asked in other quarters regarding Keating's management of chaplaincies. In May 1917, Father E. M. Morgan (BEF) wrote seeking Walsh's help in having the chaplain-general removed for failing to provide adequate chaplains for soldiers in forward areas. Replying on Walsh's behalf, however, his secretary, Michael Curran, declared that the archbishop had no responsibility for army arrangements and saw no reason to interfere now.[63] More criticism came from the Bishop of Auckland, Henry Cleary, in July. He complained bitterly to Walsh over the performance of both Keating and Cardinal Bourne, describing it as a 'lamentable failure' to supply an adequate number of chaplains for the front. Cleary accused Keating of mismanaging chaplains to such an extent that the two largest military hospitals in England had been left without cover for two periods of six and seven weeks. The military camps in England were overcrowded with chaplains while the front was being starved of them. The bishop went on to tell Walsh that he had compiled a dossier of his complaints and was in the process of forwarding it to the authorities at the Holy See.[64]

In spite of the efforts of the Irish bishops, some of them very public, the impression persisted that they were still not doing enough on the question of Catholic chaplains. At the end of 1916, a memorial signed by 140 Irish Catholics with relatives serving in the armed forces was received by the hierarchy. The signatories included influential members of the laity such as Sir John Ross and Sir Henry Bellingham, along with MPs and professionals. They respectfully concluded that the appeals by Cardinal Logue, however welcome, were not having the desired effect. They pointed out that the barriers to the appointment of chaplains which had existed in the armed forces in 1914, and about which the bishops had complained, had now been overcome. Still, they pointed out, there was a lack of volunteers and this they laid at the door of the bishops.[65]

In June, the signatories contacted the bishops again and their secretary, Nicholas Synott, summarised the progress thus far. He detailed that in February 1916 the Bishop of Kildare, Patrick Foley, had been confident of meeting the demands for priests for the front. Following the original appeal, Synott revealed that this expectation had not been realised and, moreover, the response from the hierarchy had been disappointing. Out of twenty-nine bishops and archbishops in Ireland, only three had directly replied to the memorial. Synott was at pains to point out that it was not the intention of the signatories to apportion blame. But they were certain that the solution to the chaplaincy problem lay with the Irish bishops. In April 1917 there were 3,227 priests in Ireland and yet 100 vacant posts had yet to be filled. Robert Browne had told Synott in January 1917 that everything that could be done was being done to meet the demand. The sincerity of the bishops in tackling the issue, he argued, could be seen the fact that students at Maynooth who volunteered for military service were being ordained a year early. Synott insisted, however, that this was not enough. The bishops' efforts had only netted ten new chaplains for 1917 and the appeal issued by Logue on 20 March had met with little success.[66]

By April, however, Logue had had enough. In a letter to Synott he angrily denied that the Irish bishops required any prodding to undertake the care of the spiritual welfare of Irish soldiers and sailors. They had made every effort possible on the question. He criticised the signatories and their memorial for creating the impression that there were no Irish chaplains serving abroad. He also accused them of maliciously putting their memorial in the hands of the British envoy in Rome.[67] Logue's rancour was perhaps fuelled by more unwelcome interference from the Vatican. In March he had received a proposal from Cardinal de Lai, Prefect of the Sacred Congregation of the Council, suggesting the creation of a joint English and Irish episcopal board to oversee the appointment of chaplains. A representative of each of the two Cardinals, Bourne and Logue, or they themselves, would meet and jointly present nominations to the War Office. Logue did not see how he could participate, either personally or by delegate, in this 'hybrid council'.[68]

The rivalry between the Irish and English hierarchies was ancient and the bishops reacted viscerally to interference from Bourne on the chaplaincy issue. The fear that the political dominance of London would become reflected in the ecclesiastical domination of the Irish Church was real and constant. This served to muddy the waters around the nomination of chaplains and led to a considerable degree of foot-dragging on the part of the bishops, Logue included. Nevertheless, it would be a mistake to assign the shortage of chaplains solely to the attitude of the bishops and their willingness, or not, to appoint. Like the British army in Ireland, the Catholic Church was reliant on a system of voluntary recruitment. Callan has shown that there was a steady and significant decline in enlistment after the initial influx in 1914 and a virtual collapse after the Easter Rising. By February 1915, the level of Catholic recruits numbered 23,677 but by August 1916, this had drastically declined to just 3,775.[69] A similar drop in the number of volunteers for chaplaincies is visible in the aftermath of the Rising. In March 1916, for example, there were thirty-six volunteers compared with only ten in June 1917.

By 1915, Irish nationalist support for the war was ebbing. The initial enthusiasm and rapture at Home Rule dissipated as the realisation grew that this would not be a short war. The Government had not helped the situation. The appointment of such Unionist *bêtes noires* as Edward Carson to the coalition cabinet was greeted with dismay. As Miller has pointed out, 'the spirit of friendliness to Irish nationalism which Redmond hoped support for the war would garner in the government did not materialise'.[70] Such ennui, however, was not universal. Preaching at a recruitment rally in December 1915, Father R. Doherty, a curate in Dublin's pro-cathedral, declared that he was in no way disgracing himself in appearing on this platform, as some might accuse him. He was proud to be there. 'They might say, "Oh, Father, you should be a missioner of peace!"' He declared that he would never disgrace his collar or cloth to be a missioner of peace to the savage Hun![71] These were, perhaps, the kind of sentiments which Captain Butler sought to elicit from Walsh and the other bishops in his letter in April. But, after their initial support for enlistment, the bishops failed to give any moral or political support for the war effort, beyond the provisions of chaplains. Walsh was particularly steadfast in his refusal to have the pro-cathedral or his office associated with the war, war dead or recruitment. There were, however, exceptions. A requiem mass was held for Captain Willie Redmond who was universally mourned after his death in 1916. Masses were again held for the 400 lives lost following the sinking of the *Leinster* in the Irish Sea in 1918.

The choice made by priests to volunteer for chaplaincies or not, was, in the end, a personal one. It was a complex combination of politics, faith, spiritual dedication and even fear of the risk to life and limb. The bishops could in no way order them to serve. Such ecclesiastical conscription was simply not feasible. There is evidence that events in Ireland could have some direct effect on serving chaplains. In April 1917, Walsh received notice from Army GHQ in Parkgate, Dublin, of the imminent return from France of Father Christopher Heron. On St Patrick's Day Heron had preached in the Avenue Hoche in Paris to a mixed congregation of British and Irish soldiers. In the course of his sermon he declared, among other things, that England had committed worse excesses against Ireland than the Germans had in Belgium. Protests were raised in the church and Father Heron was in the process of being deported by order of the Cardinal Archbishop of Paris.[72]

Despite a slow start and ecclesiastical politics notwithstanding, Logue maintained a consistent commitment to Irish Catholic servicemen. This continued regardless of political events in Ireland and the shifting direction of public opinion and his impassioned pleas for chaplains reflected a deep concern for their spiritual welfare. In his statements to the press, Logue painted a picture of Catholic souls either in imminent and mortal peril or a state of 'spiritual destitution'.[73] He did not pronounce on the morality of enlistment but was convinced that Catholic chaplains were performing a service of absolute good. His refusal to question the morality of enlistment was complemented by the fact that he never impugned the honour of Irish soldiers nor diminished the validity of their sacrifices.

The prospect of soldiers and sailors facing death without the sacraments filled him with horror. He told the *Irish Catholic* in 1917 that he wished he were a few years younger so he might, at least, do 'one man's share to prevent a soul from perishing'.[74] This genuine compassion was very much in evidence in his reception of Irish Canadian soldiers in Armagh in 1917. The regiment had landed in Ireland at the beginning of January, but their reception had been clouded by the events of Easter

Week. Daniel Cohalan, Bishop of Cork, had refused to attend a banquet in their honour in the city. Walsh refused to allow the pro-cathedral to be used for a mass for the soldiers and they were hastily despatched to Armagh to avoid the appearance of a public snub.[75] Logue, however, received the men courteously, saying high mass for the regiment in the cathedral in Armagh. During his sermon he praised the dedication of the soldiers present. 'When the cry went out from the centre of the Empire', he told them, 'they had nobly responded and had come in their hundreds, not alone offering themselves to defend the honour and interests of the country'.[76]

Aan de Wiel has pointed to this service as evidence of Logue's British and Imperial sympathies.[77] It is more likely that his reception of the Canadian troops was undertaken with little or no consideration for politics at all. Logue had links with Canada, having attended a eucharistic conference there in 1910 and would have been careful not to deliver a snub to the hierarchy. He consistently avoided irritating the hierarchies of other countries, England excepted. He retained a great affection for Canada and admired the system of government there. More than anything, perhaps, it was a reflection of Logue's inability to send soldiers to face the prospect of death with harsh words, boycott or disapproval. This compassion for the soldier at the front remained undiminished even after the cessation of hostilities in 1918. The apparent unwillingness or inability on the part of the British Government to share this respect for the sacrifices of Irish Catholics in the war, or deem them as valid as those of Ulstermen, left Logue with a bitter sense of betrayal.

Notes

1 Jeffery, *Ireland and the Great War*, p. 11.
2 *Freeman's Journal*, 22 Sept. 1914.
3 *Ibid.*, 21 Sept. 1914.
4 Fitzpatrick, 'Logic of Collective Sacrifice', p. 1028.
5 *Freeman's Journal*, 21 Sept. 1914.
6 Jeffery, *Ireland and the Great War*, p. 11.
7 Yeates, *Lockout*, p. 572.
8 Miller, *Church, State and Nation*, p. 310.
9 Fitzpatrick, 'Logic of Collective Sacrifice', p. 1027.
10 Miller, *Church, State and Nation*, p. 295.
11 *Ibid.*, p. 306.
12 *Freeman's Journal*, 25 Sept. 1914.
13 Callan, 'Recruitment', p. 52.

14 Logue to Walsh, 16 Nov. 1914, Walsh Papers, DDA, box 385, folder 377/8.

15 *ICD*, 1915, p. 532.

16 Aan de Wiel, *Catholic Church*, p. 42.

17 *Freeman's Journal*, 26 Feb. 1900.

18 *Ibid.*, 29 Sept. 1914.

19 *Ibid.*, 30 Sept. 1914.

20 Aan de Wiel, *Catholic Church*, p. 53.

21 See Callan, 'Recruitment', p. 53.

22 *Freeman's Journal*, 26 Feb. 1900.

23 *Ibid.*, 10 Feb. 1902.

24 *Ibid.*, 18 Sept. 1914.

25 *ICD*, 1915, p. 543.

26 *Irish Catholic*, 24 Oct. 1914.

27 *Freeman's Journal*, 13 Oct. 1914.

28 *ICD*, 1915, p. 546.

29 *ICD*, 1916, p. 503.

30 Sheehan to O'Riordan, 15 Mar. 1915, O'Riordan Papers, AICR, no. 42 (1915).

31 Sheehan to O'Riordan, 16 Apr. 1915, O'Riordan Papers, AICR, no. 58 (1915).

32 Butler to Walsh, 7 April 1915, Walsh Papers, DDA, box 387, folder 378/5.

33 *ICD*, 1916, p. 506.

34 Mulderry to Walsh, 6 July 1915, Walsh Papers, DDA, box 387, folder 378/5.

35 Sheehan to O'Riordan, 15 Mar. 1915, O'Riordan Papers, AICR, no. 42 (1915).

36 Logue to O'Donnell, 11 Mar. 1915, O'Donnell Papers, ADA, box 9, folder 3, 'Patrick Cardinal O'Donnell'.

37 Stafford to Walsh, 2 Aug. 1915, Walsh Papers, DDA, box 387, folder 378/5.

38 Sheehan to O'Riordan, 13 July 1915, O'Riordan Papers, AICR, no. 98 (1915).

39 Bourne to the Irish bishops, 16 Sept. 1915, Walsh Papers, DDA, box 387, folder 378/5.

40 Leonard, 'Catholic chaplaincy', p. 5.

41 J. W. Dane to Walsh, 6 Oct. 1915, Walsh Papers, DDA, box 387, folder 378/5.

42 Bellingham to Walsh, 22 Oct. 1916, Walsh Papers, DDA, box 388, folder 385/6.

43 Morrissey, *William Walsh*, p. 306.

44 *ICD*, 1916, p. 532.

45 O'Riordan to Logue, 23 Jan. 1916, Logue Papers, ADA, box 2, folder 3, 'Army Chaplains'.

46 Kelly to the hierarchy, 27 Jan. 1916, Logue Papers, ADA, box 2, folder 3, 'Army Chaplains'.

47 Browne to Logue, 2 Feb. 1916, Logue Papers, ADA, box 2, folder 3, 'Army Chaplains'.

48 Hagan to O'Donnell, 16 Jan. 1916, O'Donnell Papers, ADA, box 6 'Irish College'.

49 Sheehan to O'Riordan, 13 July 1915, O'Riordan Papers, AICR, no. 98 (1915).

50 Logue to Benedict, 10 Feb 1916, Logue Papers, ADA, box 2, folder 3, 'Army Chaplains'. (Translation).

51 Bourne to Logue, 3 Feb. 1916, Logue Papers, ADA, box 2, folder 3, 'Army chaplains'.
52 Murphy's report, 31 Jan. 1916, Logue Papers, ADA, box 2, folder 3, 'Army chaplains'.
53 *ICD*, 1917, p. 503.
54 Murphy's report, 6 Mar. 1916, Logue Papers, ADA, box 2, folder 3, 'Army chaplains'.
55 Kelly's report, 29 Mar. 1916, Logue Papers, ADA, box 2, folder 3, 'Army chaplains'.
56 See O'Donnell, *Father Browne*.
57 *Irish Catholic*, 25 Sept. 1916.
58 *Ibid.*, 9 Oct. 1916.
59 *Ibid.*, 21 Oct. 1916.
60 Denman, 'Catholic Irish soldier', p. 361.
61 *Irish Catholic*, 11 Sept. 1917.
62 *Ibid.*, 23 Oct. 1917.
63 Morgan to Walsh, 26 May 1917, Walsh Papers, DDA, box 389, folder 379/5.
64 Cleary to Walsh, 20 July 1917, Walsh Papers, DDA, box 389, folder 379/5.
65 Memorial to the bishops, 1916, Logue Papers, ADA, box 2, folder 3 'Army Chaplains'.
66 Memorial to the Irish bishops, 1 June 1917, Walsh Papers, DDA, box 389, folder 385/8.
67 Memorial to the Irish bishops, 1 June 1917, Walsh Papers, DDA, box 389, folder 385/8.
68 Logue to Walsh, 8 Mar. 1917, Walsh Papers, DDA, box 389, folder 385/8.
69 Callan, 'Recruitment', p. 54.
70 Miller, *Church, State and Nation*, p. 314.
71 *Irish Independent*, 6 Dec. 1915.
72 Fitzpatrick to Walsh, 16 Apr. 1917, Walsh Papers, DDA, box 389, folder 379/3.
73 *ICD*, 1918, p. 512.
74 *Irish Catholic*, 11 Sept. 1917.
75 Curran Memoirs, Ó Ceallaigh Papers, NLI, MS 27728(2), p. 183.
76 Drysdale, *Canada to London*, p. 14.
77 Aan de Wiel, *Catholic Church*, p. 54.

7

Sinn Féin ascendant

Blood sacrifices

Historians have long since divined the signs and portents encompassed in the events of April and May 1916. It has often been chronicled how the seizure of buildings in Dublin by elements of the Irish Volunteers, the proclamation of an Irish republic, the short war of attrition followed by surrender and execution, led to a seismic shift in Irish political aspirations. What has sometimes been lost amid the heavy symbolism of Pearse's blood sacrifice and the aura of resurrection surrounding the Easter Rising was the fact that it was a military disaster. The destruction of much of the centre of Dublin caused incredulity and outrage in Ireland. It was only afterwards that this anger transferred to the British Government following its harsh response to the uprising. Like other acts of violence in the past, the Rising provoked disunity and disagreement among the bishops. In the immediate aftermath of the rebellion, anger at the insurgents vied equally with resentment at the Government's draconian reaction. On 2 May 1916, Logue had had the foresight to head off any unwelcome intervention from the Vatican with a telegram stating only: 'Insurrection happily terminated. Insurgents have surrendered unconditionally. Hope peace soon re-established.'[1] That left the bishops free to grapple with events in Ireland on their own.

Despite some verbal skirmishes with the authorities over accusations of clerical involvement in the Rising, the bishops were, as a body, rather paralysed.[2] The Standing Committee met on 22 June 1916 but remained deadlocked as to how to proceed. Walsh was absent but Logue reported that the meeting could not agree on even the most innocuous of actions. It was impossible, for example, to organise a relief effort for those left destitute by the shelling in Dublin for fear of 'incurring an imputation of favouring, in any way, the authors of the unfortunate attempt'. In the end nothing was done. The bishops confined themselves to issuing a protest against accusations of complicity in the rebellion levelled against the junior clergy and Logue was rather put out that they left the wording and delivery to him. Much to his surprise, Ireland's Military Governor, General Sir John Maxwell, appeared at Maynooth and sought an urgent meeting on the activities of the younger priests. Logue told him that the complaints made against the clergy were groundless. 'I also spoke pretty freely of the mistake the authorities are making', he told Walsh, 'in keeping the country in a state of excitement by their wholesale arrests.[3] Logue did indeed speak freely. Father Patrice Flynn, a member of a French clerical goodwill and fact-finding mission who was at Maynooth recorded that Logue had told the general bluntly, 'you put your foot in it!' By executing the rebel leaders they authorities had made martyrs out of them. 'Since then', Logue went on, 'the small Sinn Féin group has considerably increased, the majority is in favour of them'.[4]

Logue carried out the charge placed on him by his colleagues on 23 June in an address to the Maynooth Union. He had been placed in a difficult situation, had little time to prepare and thus chose his language carefully. He rejected the accusations against the junior clergy as 'suspicions founded on the most futile grounds'. He said he did not believe there was any sympathy among the junior clergy for the insurgency. Moreover, not one in five hundred of the Irish Volunteers were involved or 'ever foresaw what their inner body was driving at – the organisation of a rebellion'. Neither could he believe that members from such organisations as the Gaelic League or GAA took part in the Rising. There were no grounds, therefore, for the wholesale arrests and deportations which were blighting the country. The entire affair, he said, had been mismanaged by the authorities. 'This was the greatest folly any government could have been guilty of', he declared. 'They should have let the matter die out like a bad dream and it was a dream – so painful that it was not likely to be repeated – without going to these extreme measures.'[5]

Logue's speech was a delicate balancing act. His attempt to be critical of the Government yet refrain from inflammatory language had produced a rather tortuous affair which was riddled with inconsistencies. His denial, for example, that the Gaelic League was involved was surprising since he was familiar with the organisation and the prominence in it of men such as Patrick Pearse and Eoin MacNeil. What dictated Logue's response, above all, was his aversion to conflict. For him, the Rising was a disaster and he was as repulsed by the violence on the streets of Dublin as he was by the slaughter in Flanders. This, perhaps more than anything, formed the basis for his negative reaction to republicanism. He was able to articulate his feelings when, in July 1916, Colonel Maurice Moore, Inspector-General of the Irish Volunteers, circulated a petition seeking clemency for Sir Roger Casement. Logue signed the petition along with most of his colleagues but his reply perfectly illustrated his attitude to the Rising. He told Moore he had agreed to sign the petition 'from motives of mercy and charity and not from any sympathy whatever in the unfortunate course taken. There has already been enough of human life sacrificed by that unfortunate rebellion.'[6]

Logue, along with most of his colleagues, reacted negatively to the Government's attempts at a political settlement in the summer of 1916. Rumours of exclusion and partition had reached *Ara Coeli* via the MP for South Down, Jeremiah MacVeagh. Logue warned Patrick O'Donnell that the bishops needed to be on their guard otherwise 'they may be held up and go down as the destroyers of the country'.[7] Fulfilling all of his fears, Lloyd George's June proposals involved the immediate enactment of Home Rule but with the exclusion of six Ulster counties. Logue declared that it would be 'infinitely better to remain as we are for fifty years to come under English rule than to accept these proposals'.[8] The bishops, with the exception of O'Donnell, condemned the scheme.[9]

Logue's opposition to the prospect of partition continued at the bishops' meeting in October. Deadlock remained over a suitable response to both the growing republican movement and the spectre of partition. Three motions were tabled. The first two, dealing with a call for an end to martial law and warning the Government not to extend the Military Service Act to Ireland, passed more or less unanimously. The third, however, proved the sticking point. The motion called for Irish politicians to commit to the pursuit of strictly constitutional means. It was attacked by Logue together with the Bishop of Limerick, Thomas O'Dwyer, and the Bishop of Derry, Charles McHugh, as seeming to lend approbation to the policy being pursued by Redmond.[10] Walsh also opposed it and wished to introduce a further motion calling for the release of political internees.[11] As in June, no statement was issued.

Towards the end of the year there was a growing drift on the part of individual prelates towards the republican movement. Walsh, along with Michael Fogarty, the Bishop of Killaloe, proved particularly receptive to the overtures of Sinn Féin. In August, the Archbishop of Dublin had been consulted by the Lord Mayor, Laurence Ginnell, on the launch of a new political party. All involved, Ginnell reported, were of the opinion that an interview with Walsh was most desirable.[12] The archbishop, however,

declined. He believed that the time was not opportune because the Irish
Party had not yet been discredited enough in the eyes of the people.[13] It
was not surprising that republicans should gravitate towards Walsh. He
had ever been one of the most politically forthright of the episcopate and
had been in close contact with republicans in the aftermath of the Rising.
In July 1916, for example, he received complaints from the prisoner Henry
Dixon regarding the provision of religious services in the internment
camp at Frongoch.[14] Through Walsh's influence, a chaplain was provided
in Father Stafford, late of the *SS Andiana*, though the prisoners were
reluctant to accept him at first because he 'wore khaki'.[15]

An opportunity to test the mood of the nation arose in January 1917
with a by-election called in North Roscommon. George Plunkett, papal
count and father of the executed Joseph Plunkett, was persuaded to stand
on a republican platform. The republican movement had yet to coalesce
into a coherent and organised political party but this proved immaterial
to the election as Plunkett won easily. Further victories for republicans followed in May, July and August. The by-election in May 1917 in South
Longford was significant because it swung on the overt interference of the
Archbishop of Dublin. The republican candidate was Joe McGuiness, a
political prisoner and the son of a prominent Longford family. John
Dillon took personal charge of the Irish Party's campaign in support of
their candidate, Patrick McKenna.[16] The election was closely fought but
Dillon believed he had all the resources necessary in place.[17]

The issue of partition, however, was seldom far away. In March, the
Prime Minister seemed to declare a permanent commitment to partition
by stating that 'those in the North East are as alien in blood, in religious
faith, in tradition, in outlook from the rest of Ireland as the inhabitants of
Fife or Aberdeen'.[18] On the eve of the election, Walsh wrote to the *Evening
Herald* declaring, 'I am fairly satisfied that the mischief has been done and
that the country has been sold'. The text of his comments appeared on a
Sinn Féin election leaflet above the slogan 'McGuiness will not sell
Ireland!'[19] McGuiness won by just thirty-seven votes and in all likelihood,
as Laffan has argued, but for this timely intervention would have been
beaten.[20] This was the first time a republican candidate had received moral
sanction from the Church. South Longford was significant in another
respect, in that it witnessed the emergence of Father Michael O'Flanagan,
a curate from Roscommon, as Sinn Féin's clerical mouthpiece. 'Mercurial,
dynamic and inconsistent', O'Flanagan provided the public face of the
growing involvement of priests in the republican movement's electoral
machine.[21]

The bishops met at Maynooth in June 1917 and issued their first statement in over a year. It was not quite the *nihil obstat*, the ecclesiastical seal
of approval to mark a publication as free from doctrinal or moral error,
envisaged by Miller.[22] The statement was a cautious one and, in trying to
grapple with the political changes in Ireland, it trod a fine line between
opponents of the new republican movement and those who sought to
accommodate it. The bishops noted only what they referred to as 'forms
of government that are popular at the moment'. They suggested such
forms of Government had been 'associated with the worst kind of civil
tyranny and religious persecution' and admonished that 'it is well to test
ideals by what is just as well as by what is practicable'.[23] Logue's opinions
were very much represented in the statement. He was ever nervous of
democracy unrestrained. On a visit to Washington in 1908 he had
told President Roosevelt that 'there was no tyranny like the tyranny of a
republic'. He recalled that the President had agreed.[24]

As the year progressed, however, several bishops and a sizeable portion
of the clergy edged closer to the republican movement. Despite the militancy evident at the funeral of the republican hunger-striker Thomas
Ashe in September 1917, the clergy had a strong presence. Indeed, the
Irish Catholic Directory noted that 'the most unusual feature of a procession of this kind was the large body of priests who took part in it, a
hundred and twenty of them marching behind the honour guard of
Volunteers and immediately in front of the hearse'.[25] It was the most
public association yet seen between the clergy and republicans. It also
signalled that that the pro-cathedral was open to dead republicans but
remained closed to war dead. The Bishop of Killaloe, Michael Fogarty,
reflecting the intense public bitterness over Ashe's death, bestowed on
the dead Volunteer and all the Irish dead the status of martyrs. 'Their
deaths', he said, 'will sanctify them in the memory of Ireland and
surround their heartless torturers with inextinguishable hatred and
ignominy'.[26]

Logue's politics did not mean he was automatically predisposed to
reject the republican movement. His disaffection with the Irish Party had
been exacerbated to an extreme by the encroachment of partition. He
believed that Home Rule would not provide the necessary framework to
enact real change and, therefore, favoured dominion status. In many
respects, Logue's politics were close to those of Walsh. However, the overt
militancy and the potential for physical force inherent in the republican
movement caused Logue to reject it. Where Walsh saw a new and vibrant
political force in Irish nationalism, Logue saw the possibility of a repeat of

the disaster of Easter Week. He simply did not believe that a republic was achievable, let alone desirable.

Logue's denunciation of republicanism in November 1917 has led to accusations by some historians that he was hopelessly out of touch with the political reality in Ireland.[27] This was simply not the case. Logue was well aware of the political direction not only of the country but of the clergy and chose to meet the challenge head-on. In a pastoral letter to the clergy of the archdiocese issued on 25 November, he warned against the lure of the republican dream. 'An agitation has sprung up and is spreading among our people', he said, 'which, ill-considered and utopian, cannot fail, if persevered in, to entail present suffering, disorganisation and danger and is sure to end in future disaster, defeat and collapse'. No one could hope to realise the dream of a republic, he argued, 'either by an appeal to the potentates of Europe seated at a peace conference or an appeal to force by hurling an unarmed people against an empire'.[28]

For someone unused to political controversy, or independent action, Logue's November pastoral was a bold departure. He had put himself in the way of the prevailing political winds of the country and potentially isolated himself from a considerable section of the clergy. His opinions, however, according to Walsh's then secretary, Michael Curran, were shared by at least two-thirds of his episcopal colleagues.[29] Reaction to the pastoral was mixed. The *Irish Catholic* described Logue's pastoral as possessing a 'characteristic intermingling of shrewd Irish common sense and Irish piety'.[30] Eamon de Valera, however, was forthright in reply. Speaking to an audience at a concert in Roscommon, he asked in what way was the struggle for democracy utopian and immoral? Was it immoral for the Belgians to resist the occupation of the Germans? 'Sinn Féiners', he said, 'have a definite policy and the people of Ireland are determined to make it a success; that is, to make English rule absolutely impossible in Ireland'.[31]

Logue retained a personal antipathy towards de Valera that was never resolved. The reasons for his bitterness were never stated but lay, perhaps, in the often described 'aura of 1916' which surrounded the latter. This aura, which attracted so many, repelled Logue. Neither was he impressed with de Valera's overt Catholicity and the theatre of his being escorted to and from political platforms by a 'sombre bodyguard of priests'.[32] Logue resisted all attempts to persuade him from his dark view of the future president. The day after the pastoral, the Irish Attorney General, James O'Connor, wrote to assure him that de Valera was 'a high minded and sincere Catholic and that he does not want physical force'.[33] Such opinions had no effect and Logue remained suspicious of de Valera throughout the remainder of his office.

The effect which the cardinal's pronouncement had in the three by-election defeats for Sinn Féin in early 1918 is unclear. The Irish Party took Redmond's old seat in Waterford easily enough but by-elections in South Armagh and East Tyrone, both within Logue's archdiocese, were a different matter. The avowed disapproval emanating from *Ara Coeli* caused some priests to shy away from overt support for Sinn Féin; others did so regardless. For his part, Logue received the Irish Party candidate in South Armagh, Patrick Donnelly, but he also met with Count Plunkett. He refused to grant an audience to de Valera.[34] That the Irish Party was able to carry both northern seats was perhaps due more to the efficiency of their party machine than Logue's interference. The accusation, however, levelled by Coogan that the cardinal conspired with the Hibernians and the Orangemen to defeat the Sinn Féin candidates is simply without foundation.[35]

Concern over the drift towards radical politics evident in Ireland meant that Logue grasped at the prospect of a negotiated settlement of the Irish Question. In June 1917 Lloyd George convened a convention, chaired by Sir Horace Plunkett, with the aim of securing an agreement among Irish political parties, Sinn Féin excluded. For Logue, the Irish Convention represented an avenue of escape from the advance of republicanism and he was, at least initially, enthusiastic for the scheme. The problem was who to send. Logue discussed the issue of clerical delegates with Walsh in June 1917 and recommended that they should be selected by a free vote of the assembled hierarchy.[36] Interestingly, neither man favoured sending the Bishop of Raphoe, Patrick O'Donnell, who had equivocated on the issue of partition. Although initially supportive of the Convention, Walsh took no part in the election at the bishops' meeting. The refusal of Sinn Féin to attend and the final format convinced him that the conference would simply be a device of the Government.[37] In the end O'Donnell was sent along with the Archbishop of Cashel, John Harty, and the Bishop of Down and Connor, Joseph MacRory.

The Irish Convention opened in July 1917 and sat until March 1918, and despite some initial problems, the bishops threw themselves, heart and soul, into it.[38] In their final report they declared firmly for full dominion status. In a statement full of the language of separation, they recommended a sovereign, independent parliament for Ireland with power co-equal to that of Westminster. They demanded full fiscal autonomy and the power to raise military and police forces. Reconciliation between

England and Ireland would remain difficult 'unless it can be shown that the British people sincerely believe in liberty for its own sake'.[39] Their report declared that no settlement would be possible until it could be shown that 'the supposed military interests of great states shall not override the rights of small nationalities'.[40] One of the concerns expressed by the bishops was that an Irish parliament should have the power to deny the British Government the right to impose conscription on Ireland.[41]

In many respects, the Convention represented the last gasp of constitutionalism in the Irish Question. The deadlock apparent by the spring of 1918 moved Logue to issue an impassioned plea in his Lenten pastoral. Should the Convention fail, he warned, 'their failure will throw the country back for a length of time . . . into the old rounds of alternate outbreak and repression'.[42] Walsh was less concerned by the imminent failure of the Convention and his pastoral merely noted that a crisis in public affairs had been reached. The archbishop declared the rather begrudging hope that 'a policy, for the adoption of which the people of Ireland are in no way responsible, may work out for good'.[43] The political divergence between Armagh and Dublin was evident in the pastorals. Logue, despite his misgivings, still looked to London to provide a settlement while Walsh had abandoned that hope altogether and embraced the separatism of Sinn Féin.

Passive resistance

In spite of their diverging political opinions, Logue and Walsh together forged a remarkable degree of unanimity among the bishops in response to the threat of conscription. The outcome of the Convention had been anxiously awaited not just by Logue but also by Lloyd George. In the spring of 1918, the peace on the Eastern Front between Russia and Germany had freed enough resources to enable the Germans to launch a massive offensive against the Allies in the west. The British came under intense pressure and the Government looked to Ireland to provide the necessary resources of manpower to meet the German threat.

The feasibility and logistics of conscription were discussed at Cabinet meetings at the end of March. It was estimated that Ireland had an untapped reservoir of 150,000 men of recruitment age, and more if the age limit was increased to fifty.[44] Conscription was deemed a necessity because of the virtual collapse of the voluntary recruitment system in Ireland.[45] The Government had decided to postpone the extension of the Military Service Act until the final report of the Convention in the hope that a settlement might ease its introduction.[46] However, as the Convention had 'dissolved onto nothingness', to use Tim Healy's evocative phrase, it was decided to press ahead regardless.[47] Both the GOC in Ireland, Sir Bryan Mahon, and the Inspector-General of the RIC, General Byrne, agreed that conscription could be enforced. However, such a move would likely be opposed by the combined forces of Irish nationalism and the Catholic Church. In their assessment, Byrne and Mahon floated the idea that prior to the introduction of the Act, known political troublemakers should be 'got out of the way'. Everyone suspected of posing a problem, irrespective of who they were, should be arrested at the first sign of trouble.[48]

There were, however, dissenting voices. On the same day the Cabinet read the assessment from the generals, the Chief Secretary, H. E. Duke, forwarded a memorandum warning against conscription. He told Lloyd George that it would be impossible to enforce in such a way that would materially help the war effort.[49] Ireland's Lord Chief Justice, Sir James Campbell, also sounded a note of caution. He warned that conscription could only be introduced at the cost of tremendous bloodshed. The whole clergy, he told the Prime Minister, from the bishops down, would take the field against the Government.[50] Lloyd George remained undaunted. At a Cabinet meeting on 27 March 1918 he proposed combining the extension of the Military Service Act with an immediate measure of Home Rule. Ulster, of course, would be excluded. In the meantime, the Government's plans should remain absolutely secret.[51] On 29 March, however, Mahon wrote to tell the Cabinet that the imminent introduction of conscription was common knowledge on the streets of Dublin. He suggested that it might be useful to enlist the help of the bishops. 'If Cardinal Logue and the hierarchy of the Roman Catholic Church denounce futile resistance which might lead to bloodshed', he proposed, 'opposition would be diminished'. Mahon volunteered to communicate directly with Logue but it was felt in the Cabinet that no contact should be made at this stage.[52]

It is doubtful whether Logue would have been amenable to such an initiative. Despite his aversion to violence, his mistrust of and disillusionment with the Government had deepened as the war progressed. In February 1918, he had used his Lenten pastoral to criticise Britain's rejection of the Pope's peace appeal which had been issued the previous year. Rejection was bad enough, but it had emerged that a deal had been struck among the Allied powers to exclude the Holy See from any future peace conference. The agreement had been negotiated on the Italian entry into the war in 1915 but only came to light following the revolution in Russia and its disclosure by the Bolsheviks.[53] Logue condemned the exclusion of 'the greatest moral power in Christendom' on the say of 'wretched Italian politicians'.[54]

When the Military Service Act was eventually extended to Ireland in April 1918, the bishops' response was swift but measured. The statement issued by the Standing Committee on 9 April condemned the Government 'with all the responsibility that attaches to our office'. The bishops also articulated a sense of betrayal at the attitude emanating from Westminster. 'Had the government given Ireland the benefit', they went on, 'of the principles which it had declared to be at stake in the war . . . there would be no occasion for forced levies from her now'.[55] Logue called a general meeting of the hierarchy for the following week, telling Walsh on 13 April, 'I find the whole country expects action by the bishops'.[56]

The news of imminent conscription plunged Ireland into crisis. The Irish Party withdrew from Westminster uttering words of rebellion. The party rejected the Government's offer of immediate Home Rule, choosing instead to mount a campaign of opposition to conscription from Ireland. This aura of crisis was suffused with the probability of violence. No one had any illusions that the Volunteers would confine themselves to mere protest.[57] Given Logue's concerns over the prospect of another rebellion, the sudden lurch towards violent confrontation throughout the country was alarming. Thus, when the bishops met on 18 April 1918, he had no qualms about putting the Church at the forefront of the anti-conscription campaign. What form that campaign would take, however, was yet to be decided.

One of the few accounts of the inner workings of the hierarchy during this period has been provided by Michael Curran. As Walsh's secretary, he had a unique insight into the bishops' deliberations and divisions as, by his own admission, the archbishop frequently shared his thoughts with him. However, Curran's account must be approached with caution. He was a republican and bitter Anglophobe and his memoirs make no pretence at objectivity. He was a priest who delighted in his privileged position, in conspiracies and being 'in the know'. He emphasised the republican credentials of bishops like Walsh while deriding the actions and views of others. Curran retained a remarkable antipathy towards Logue. Every good story needs a villain, or a turncoat, and he cast the cardinal frequently as both. What is also remarkable about Curran's views was his unquestioning approval of republican violence. His zealous politics, however, would eventually get him into trouble.

Curran has recalled that after the meeting of the Standing Committee on 9 April 1918, Walsh was astonished by the vehemence of some of his episcopal colleagues in opposing conscription. He recounted that Logue was greatly perplexed by the attitude of the bishops. The cardinal, according to Curran, 'consoled himself by his own conviction that the clergy would be exempted if conscription was foolishly introduced'. With their exclusion, the bishops would not be called in to lead the opposition.[58] It seems utterly inconsistent, however, that Logue would have dismissed the crisis in such a fashion. There may have been more truth in Curran's assertion that Walsh was worried lest Logue's caution should blunt the thrust of the bishops' protest at the forthcoming general meeting. On the morning of 18 April, the date set for the meeting, Eamon de Valera called to meet Walsh. The archbishop refused to see him but Curran took the opportunity to relay the details of the forthcoming meeting and some of Walsh's privately expressed concerns over his 'less courageous' colleagues.[59] It was Curran's recollection that it was he who suggested a deputation to Maynooth from politicians then meeting in the Mansion House.

The conference had been convened in the hope of providing a united nationalist opposition to conscription. Those present included John Dillon, now leader of the Irish Party following Redmond's death at the time of the Convention, Labour's William O'Brien, Tim Healy, Eamon de Valera and Arthur Griffith. Although not present at the meeting himself, Curran later wrote that Walsh related the events of the day on his return. The Archbishop of Dublin had led Logue from point to point away from his notion of passive resistance, which was abandoned because nobody knew what it meant. At the end of the meeting Logue remarked that 'I think this is the worst day's business the bishops ever did'.[60] It was Curran's belief that Walsh wanted to avoid a pronouncement which would reflect badly on Sinn Féin or the Volunteers. This was perhaps the case but what emerged from the meeting was hardly a clarion call to arms.

If, as was the case, Logue had wanted above all to prevent a fresh outbreak of violence, then the anti-conscription declaration drafted by O'Donnell at the meeting went a long way towards addressing his concerns. The Military Service Act was condemned as 'oppressive and inhuman' but the bishops declared that resistance must be conducted 'by all means that are consonant with the law of God'. The people were reminded that there was 'a higher Power which controls the affairs of men. They have in their hands a means of conciliating that Power by strict adherence to the Divine law.' With such an appeal to piety, Logue had no qualms about putting the Church at the centre of the opposition movement. There was also an anti-conscription pledge, which would be taken at churches, denying 'the right of the British government to enforce compulsory service in this country'. Those swearing fealty were bound 'to resist conscription by the most effective means at our disposal'.[61] That the bishops, who had thus far been divided on republicanism, could agree on such a course of action was a testimony to the compromise brokered by Walsh and Logue.

Curran's recollections have prompted Aan de Wiel to conclude that the whole conscription debate had gone against Logue's wishes, but this was not the case.[62] The bishops' statement and the anti-conscription campaign contained something for everyone. Logue's anxieties over violence and his preference for a campaign of passive resistance were soothed somewhat by the appeal made to keep all agitation within God's law. Republicans could be satisfied with the terms of the pledge which gave militants room for manoeuvre in the term 'most effective means at our disposal'. In the end, Curran's depiction has been calculated to show Logue in the worst possible light in order to emphasise the influence of William Walsh. However, despite the cardinal's commitment to non-violence he did not display the callous indifference to conscription attributed to him by Curran. Healy recalled that when arguing for passive resistance he told de Valera, 'when I talk about passive resistance, I don't mean we are to lie down and let people walk over us'.[63]

As for being led by the clever Archbishop of Dublin, Curran's account takes no consideration of the long collaboration and friendship between Logue and Walsh. Aan de Wiel makes much of the cardinal's imagined displeasure at the presence of de Valera but ignores the fact that Logue was also in the presence of his closest ecclesiastical colleague in Walsh and his most consistent political ally in Tim Healy. Logue had always been willing to take counsel from the Archbishop of Dublin and Walsh had no need for duplicity. Curran recalled that Walsh took a 'certain malicious pleasure' at Logue's discomfiture at the meeting.[64] This is perhaps more unflattering to the Archbishop of Dublin than to Logue. This portrayal of Walsh sniggering behind the back of one his oldest clerical partners seems altogether out of character and at odds with what was, despite differing political opinions, a consistently respectful and courteous relationship between the two men.

The Mansion House meeting and subsequent conference at Maynooth represented the last clerical-nationalist alliance. It was Sinn Féin, however, that emerged with clerical blessing bestowed on it. As Laffan has pointed out, 'in the eyes of many cautious and moderate nationalists, the party's close association with the Catholic Church made it seem more respectable and less dangerous'.[65] Shielded by the ambiguities of the anti-conscription declaration, the Volunteers took to planning military resistance. Amid these feverish preparations, Logue stuck doggedly to his insistence on non-violence. He told an audience at confirmations in Coalisland that people should be guided by the direction they received from their bishops. He reiterated the appeal for agitation to be kept within the law of God.[66]

Clerical opposition to conscription caused great anxiety in the British Cabinet. On 16 April 1918, Duke warned Lloyd George that even 15,000 extra troops would not be enough to enforce the Act.[67] General Byrne was also nervous. Lord French told the Cabinet that the Inspector-General feared that the bishops would induce young Catholic police officers not to enforce the conscription act.[68] Lloyd George was particularly resentful of the attitude of the Church. Tim Healy told his brother Maurice that the Prime Minister's 'nonconformist conscience' had been aroused and this was very much in evidence in a meeting with Belfast trade unionists on 7 May.[69] The deputation had been organised to protest at the proposal to link Home Rule with conscription. Lloyd George appealed for their understanding and support now that 'the supremacy of parliament had been challenged by the Catholic hierarchy'. It was most important, there-fore 'that they should render him every assistance in their power to defeat this challenge'.[70]

The attitude of the Church was also being viewed with considerable anxiety on the other side of the Atlantic. In a memorandum to the Foreign Office in January 1918, the Assistant Military Attaché in Washington, Arthur C. Murray, had warned how events in Ireland were playing badly in the United States. The imminent failure of the Convention had caused concern among all shades of American opinion. Murray argued that nearly all Americans were Home Rulers either because of where they came from or from outright sympathy with the nationalist cause. 'It must be remembered', he concluded, 'that anything calculated to impair the belief in Great Britain on the part of the large percentage of the American forces might gravely weaken the American war effort'.[71]

The introduction of conscription in Ireland was, therefore, viewed with dismay. Murray told the British Ambassador, Lord Reading, in April that it would have a serious effect on public opinion in the United States. America had lost faith in the implementation of Home Rule and he bit-terly criticised the ham-fisted approach taken by the British Government which could only lead to trouble. 'Violence', Murray went on, 'leading to martyrdom is most to be feared in its effects here'. It was his opinion that Home Rule should be enacted without delay but conscription withheld until the new system of Government had time to take effect.[72] Reading passed on Murray's assessment to the Chief Secretary who told the Cabinet on 16 April that immediate Home Rule would meet with great approval in the United States.[73]

Before any action was taken, however, the Government moved to put Byrne and Mahon's recommendations into practice and get prominent republicans out of the way. The pretext for what became known as the 'German Plot' was found in the actual landing of a German spy in County Clare in 1918 and on 17 and 18 May Sinn Féin members were rounded up in a campaign of mass arrests. When the Government published its evidence of a conspiracy between Sinn Féiners and Germany it proved rather flimsy and was universally ridiculed. For the Irish Party, however, the arrests were disastrous. Dillon, who had opposed conscription as vociferously as anyone, was outraged. He 'had shared platforms and attended committee meetings with de Valera and yet he and his colleagues were left unscathed, unmartyred, as if they were beneath Lloyd George's contempt'.[74]

As the conscription crisis continued into the summer of 1918, Logue remained fretful of the threat of violence. He told O'Donnell in July that he had angrily rejected an invitation from the Chief Secretary to nominate a bishop to sit on a proposed education commission because it was obvious that Sir Edward Carson was bossing the show here. Along with his continued resentment towards the Government, Logue was primarily concerned with avoiding bloodshed. 'If we could induce our people to keep quiet', he said, 'and bear patiently, giving no opportunity for active measures of repression, the present regime of coercion will end, like its predecessors, in ghastly failure'.[75]

The threat of conscription receded as the summer progressed, but in August Logue appeared to embark on what, for him, was an extraordinary political gambit. On 3 August he was handed a letter from Cardinal Amette, Archbishop of Paris, appealing for Irish volunteers for service in labour battalions in the French army. The idea had not originated in France but was the brainchild of Captain J. Stuart Hay, an officer at the British Ministry of Information. The proposal had obvious attractions for the Government. It was now accepted that there was no chance of implementing conscription in Ireland and Hay's plan presented a way of harnessing the untapped reservoir of Irish manpower. The Irish were deemed more likely to serve France than Britain but would help the war effort nonetheless. The Catholic bishops were crucial to the plan. Hay's scheme was seen as an opportunity for them to save face and throw their weight behind the Allied cause. Such a course would wean the Church away from the republican movement as enlistment for France was preached from every altar in Ireland.[76] Even allowing for that section of the hierarchy which remained nervous of Sinn Féin, Hay's plan was remarkably optimistic. The level of support it received from the Government was also remarkable. Hay reported that his plan had the approval of the Prime Minister; his Private Secretary, William Sutherland; the new Chief Secretary, Edward Shortt; and the Adjutant General at the War Office, Sir Nevil Macready.[77]

Just how or when Captain Hay's confidential report on his activities found its way to *Ara Coeli* remains unclear. Nevertheless, it reveals the level of subterfuge and conspiracy involved in executing the plan. In July 1918, having received official approval for his scheme from Dublin Castle, Hay stopped in London before travelling on to Paris and Cardinal Amette. He discussed his journey with Sutherland and Cardinal Bourne's secretary, Monsignor Jackman, before leaving for France. It was decided that Hay should carry Amette's appeal, subject to Government approval, personally to Logue. Hay met with both Amette and the French Prime Minister, Georges Clemenceau, at the end of July. Clemenceau was interested in the scheme but Amette required some persuading before issuing an appeal.[78] Hay then travelled to Ireland via London, where the appeal was scrutinised and approved, and met with Logue in Carlingford. It was important that the impression be given that he had come hotfoot from Paris with Amette's letter.

Amette's appeal was based on the historic links between Ireland and France. His country was the victim of violent and unjust aggression and required all the men at its disposal to fight the invader. But France had urgent need of workers in the ports, transport and auxiliary tasks. Could these not be found in Ireland? Amette pleaded for Irish help against the barbarities of German aggression. Volunteers would be trained in France and be coalesced into a single brigade. 'Time is essential', he went on, 'you are wanted at once, the French government pledges its word to you. Come at once before it is too late. Join the democratic nations of the earth in the fight against tyranny.'[79]

Hay reported that Logue received him extremely warmly and was enthusiastic for the scheme. His first thought was to have the bishops issue the appeal immediately through the newspapers but he was worried about the attitude of the British Government and that travel restrictions under the Defence of Realm Act (DORA) would make the movement of volunteers impossible.[80] In his reply, Logue acknowledged the historic link between Ireland and France but told Amette that 'if the opposition of the British government could be overcome a successful effort to meet the needs mentioned in the appeal could be met'. The cardinal did, however, sound a note of caution. He told Amette that the British had recently attempted to introduce compulsory military service in Ireland and 'an appeal now could be considered an ecclesiastical ruse to promote conscription'.[81]

Although cautious in his approach to the scheme Logue's enthusiasm, according to Hay, was unmistakable and the plan, at least on the surface, had its attraction. Logue had historic links with France, having been a professor at the Irish College in Paris. Moreover, the cause of France was a worthy one. Before the war there had been considerable concern at the enactment of laws in France designed to separate Church and State. Pius X had been especially critical of their impact on Catholic education in a papal letter in 1907.[82] After 1914, however, 'the Church had been re-established in the French trenches' and the French Government was keen to emphasise this point to an Irish audience.[83] To this end an ecclesiastical deputation had been despatched to Dublin after the Rising in 1916 on a good will mission. Logue viewed the struggle of France as worthy of praise and was sure the days of religious persecution in the country were over.[84] One of the French clerics, Monsignor Touchet, Bishop of Orléans, thanked the Irish in the course of a speech in Maynooth for the numbers who had joined in the Allied cause. 'Some people ask me whether', he said, 'after the war, France will remember that act of filial heroism. For me, I cannot hesitate to believe that France will remember.'[85]

Perhaps it was the prospect of this promise of the patronage of a grateful France after the war which prompted Logue's approval of Hay's scheme. There was the added attraction that none of the volunteers, according to Amette's letter, would be going into frontline service. The most extraordinary aspect of his reaction was that he committed the hierarchy's support to the scheme without consulting his episcopal colleagues. Hay reported that Logue viewed the proposals as 'the salvation of Ireland'. It would have the benefit of 'getting rid of the disloyal element' and gave the hope that the Irish Question would be settled at the inevitable post war peace conference.[86] For someone of Logue's innate caution, his support for the Hay plan was an uncharacteristic gamble. His approval was undiminished even when Hay revealed that the British Government was the real author of the scheme and not the Archbishop of Paris. In June the cardinal had refused to take part in a recruitment conference with Ireland's Viceroy, Lord French.[87] To back Hay's scheme, then, appears a somewhat strange choice.

Having succeeded in his mission by securing Logue's backing, however, Hay found that support was diminishing in the Government. He recorded that bitter opposition to the scheme was emanating from the Chief of the Imperial General Staff, Field Marshal Sir Henry Wilson, who deemed Hay a disgrace and threatened to have him arrested.[88] The policy was thought to be anti-Ulster and Hay recalled that 'it seemed to me that the government were now afraid of their own actions because of Ulster opposition and I gathered at the time that I had to be sacrificed'.[89] The instrument of Hay's demise proved to be his referral to an army medical board where he was designated category C2, unfit for foreign duty. He had sought sanctuary by applying to Dublin Castle for a job but was refused. By degrees, Hay discovered that the Government's policy had been dramatically reversed. He had expected to be back with Logue on 17 August 1918 bearing assurances from the French Government. Instead, on 24 August, he received a letter from the Irish Under-Secretary, Samuel Watt, informing him that Logue's reply had been delivered.

Despite being under official censure, Hay remained remarkably committed to his scheme and concerned that Logue would suspect a plot against him. He advised Watt to send the cardinal a note, postmarked from France, telling him that the plan had the support of the most highly placed officials in England, but was meeting with opposition 'in certain well known quarters'. Hay submitted two letters for consideration but whether, as his report concluded, they reached their destination he could not say.[90] In fact, Logue received a letter dated 1 September 1918 and postmarked from Versailles, as per Hay's advice. It stated that the scheme was still under discussion but the process would be a long one. He would be advised of future developments, provided a secure means of communication could be found.[91]

The whole episode of the Hay plan has retained an unreal and dreamlike quality. There is scant evidence that the scheme existed at all and this emanated from the captain, though the idea was mentioned in French Intelligence reports.[92] At a British Cabinet meeting in June 1918 it was recorded that the Government had no objection to Irish recruitment into the French army, but it would prefer a scheme of individual enlistment rather than some kind of Irish brigade.[93] There is no evidence that the bishops knew of the plan and Logue discussed it in none of his correspondence. Even the letter to Amette was drafted by Hay, though Logue was a capable French speaker. The scheme, therefore, remains a historical curiosity and if it existed at all was an uncharacteristically swashbuckling political gambit from a prelate unused to such adventures.

In August 1918, the Government had an opportunity to measure Logue's mood. The occasion was a confidential letter sent to *Ara Coeli* by

Sir Horace Plunkett. Plunkett criticised the bishops as the chief obstacle to a settlement in Ireland. He further denounced the hierarchy for failing to lend their full support to the Allied war effort.[94] Logue was furious. He vehemently denied that the Church was in any way responsible for the failure to establish self-government in Ireland. The more insurmountable obstacle was the 'insincerity, bad faith and, what someone has called, the political strategy of the present British Ministry'. Logue condemned the determination of the Government 'to subordinate the interests of four fifths of the people of Ireland to the interests and prejudices of a small minority in the north east corner of Ulster'. The Government had kept Home Rule dangling before their eyes and cast it aside when its purpose was served. Now that America was committed to the war 'beyond the possibility of retreat or slackening' it was no longer necessary to keep up pretences.

Logue declared that it was a complete misrepresentation of the motives and actions of the bishops to accuse the Church of not supporting the Allies. Neither indifference to the Allied cause nor sympathy for Prussian militarism, as Plunkett had suggested, had anything to do with their attitude to conscription. 'Both in the past and recently', Logue continued, 'we have suffered too much from Prussian methods to have any sympathy with them'. No bishop, as far as he could ascertain, had ever said anything to discourage enlistment. Logue interpreted Plunkett's letter as an invitation for him to pronounce or make public policy for the bishops. This he had no authority to do and had never done so in the past. 'I might express my personal views freely enough', he said, 'but I have never made such a pronouncement except in consultation with and in union with my colleagues of the episcopate'.[95]

Logue's letter represented one of his few statements on the war, though it was never published. It was, perhaps, a typical response to criticism of the Church from outside. But Logue's resentment at the Government, especially over its support for Unionists, was palpable. Given the bitterness of his reply to Plunkett, and his avowal that he would never act alone, his alleged participation in the Hay plan is all the more remarkable. Logue's letter was dated 9 August 1918 and he received Captain Hay at Carlingford the following day.[96]

The end of hostilities in Europe in November 1918 greatly increased the perception in Ireland that partition was imminent. The Home Rule Act of 1914 had been suspended until the end of the war and there was a general certainty that, if it was implemented, Ulster would be excluded. Wartime emergency legislation enacted after the Rising remained in force. The opinion expressed in the Cabinet was that Ireland was passing through the 'most critical phase of Irish history' and without the Defence of the Realm Act would be ungovernable.[97] The aura of oppression and the threat of partition benefited Sinn Féin, as did the increase in the size of the electorate following the Representation of the People Act as many first-time voters gravitated towards the republican movement. In the north, however, the bishops were preoccupied with partition.

On the day of the armistice, Logue wrote to Patrick O'Donnell on the need for some sort of episcopal action in the forthcoming election. He told the Bishop of Raphoe that he had received letters from a number of persons asking that the bishops intervene and prevent the nationalist vote being split. 'If there be contests in Ulster', he said, 'you may have two members in Donegal, Devlin may possibly carry West Belfast; but all the other seats in Ulster will infallibly go to the Carsonists. This will be a pretty result of our divisions!'[98] The very real and imminent threat of partition meant that there would be no anti-republican declarations on this occasion. The northern bishops met in Maynooth to discuss the elections and on 26 November issued a statement calling on the Lord Mayor of Dublin urgently to convene a conference to 'take in hand and have settled the greatest difficulty this election presents'. They called on Dillon and de Valera to apportion eight marginal seats between them fairly, the strength of the vote deciding candidates for each constituency.[99] Sinn Féin had narrowly voted to accept the bishops' proposal but Dillon dragged his feet.[100]

The reluctance of the Irish Party provoked Logue into sending a furious letter to the *Freeman's Journal* on 28 November. He declared that no one could ever accuse him of supporting the Sinn Féin policy as he had never concealed his views on its futility. 'But now there is no question of rival policies', he went on, 'but of saving the country from inevitable calamity'. Logue made it perfectly clear that if there were any 'pettifogging difficulties' raised in opposition to the settlement, he would consider it his duty 'to advise the people to go straight to work and vote for the Sinn Féin candidate in all the constituencies in which division would endanger seats'.[101] Logue's threat was enough to bully the Irish Party to the table in the Mansion House. It was a striking reversal of his position the previous year. His aversion to republicanism had, at least temporarily, been outweighed by his anxiety over partition. Despite the threats from *Ara Coeli*, the politicians remained deadlocked over Sinn Féin insistence that, if elected, the Irish Party candidates should not take up their seats. An exasperated Logue telegraphed Walsh to seek his intervention on 3 December but without result.[102]

Logue had no choice but to arbitrate, but the whole affair left him exhausted. He told the Bishop of Down and Connor, Joseph MacRory, that he had 'not had a moment's peace since I put my finger in the ugly pie'. His telephone, telegraph and post were kept busy with complaints from Sinn Féin. 'Neither side is carrying out the agreement honestly', he complained, 'and it is likely to end in the Carsonites getting the seats'.[103] Michael Farrell has described the electoral pact as 'rather sordid', but Logue's intervention, though slightly ham-fisted, was an honest attempt to maximise the nationalist vote against partition.[104] In the end, despite considerable confusion over names on ballot papers, the agreement worked as well as could be expected. The one glaring flaw in the whole pact was East Down. Logue had apportioned the constituency to Sinn Féin but the UIL candidate failed to withdraw. The nationalist vote was split and a Unionist candidate took the seat. Logue was furious. He told Walsh on 29 December, 'I find East Down has gone to Carson through the treachery of the National Party. They are likely to hear more about it.'[105]

If Logue's intervention in the general election in Ulster indicated his acceptance of Sinn Féin as a party to do business with, other bishops were more forthright in their support. In private, Walsh had refused attempts by Irish Party candidates to elicit his support, and prior to the election he openly declared for Sinn Féin.[106] Three of his suffragans, Brownrigg in Ossory, Codd in Ferns and Foley in Kildare, publicly declared for the Irish Party. The archbishop responded with a letter to the press, feeling compelled to correct any misconception which the other bishops' letters might inspire about which way he would vote.[107] The Bishop of Killaloe, Michael Fogarty, gave notice in the press of a donation to the Sinn Féin election fund along with his best wishes for the coming election. 'The country is sick of the House of Commons', he said, 'with its plutocratic record of oppression, corruption and chicanery. I am not afraid of abstention.'[108] It is uncertain whether these declarations had any real effect on the outcome of the election. In the end, the die had been cast against the Irish Party in previous months. At the election, Sinn Féin won 73 seats in total, sweeping away the old political order. There would be few Irish members going to Westminster as Sinn Féin looked to Dublin, having secured what many in the party interpreted as a mandate for revolution.

Notes

1 Curran Memoirs, Ó Ceallaigh Papers, NLI, MS 27712(1), p. 392.
2 See O'Dwyer's condemnation of General Maxwell, *ICD*, 1917, p. 514.

3 Logue to Walsh, 23 June 1916, Walsh Papers, DDA, box 388, folder 385/1.
4 Aan de Wiel, *Catholic Church*, p. 100.
5 *ICD*, 1917, pp. 517–18.
6 *Ibid.*, p. 521.
7 Logue to O'Donnell, 7 June 1916, O'Donnell Papers, ADA, box 9, folder 3, 'Patrick Cardinal O'Donnell'.
8 *ICD*, 1917, p. 517.
9 Laffan, *Resurrection of Ireland*, p. 59.
10 Miller, *Church, State and Nation*, p. 346.
11 Curran Memoirs, Ó Ceallaigh Papers, NLI, MS 27728(1), p. 171.
12 Ginnell to Walsh, 14 Aug. 1916, Walsh Papers, DDA, box 388, folder 385/6.
13 Morrissey, *William Walsh*, p. 296.
14 Dixon to Walsh, 12 July 1916, Walsh Papers, DDA, box 388, folder 385/6.
15 Morrissey, *William Walsh*, p. 297.
16 Maume, *Long Gestation*, p. 195.
17 Lyons, *Ireland Since the Famine*, p. 383.
18 Morrissey, *William Walsh*, p. 299.
19 Handbill, Walsh Papers, DDA, box 389, folder 385/8.
20 Laffan, *Resurrection of Ireland*, p. 102.
21 *Ibid.*, p. 78.
22 Miller, *Church, State and Nation*, p. 391.
23 *ICD*, 1918, p. 538.
24 Hopkinson, ed., *Sturgis Diaries*, 5 Apr. 1921, p. 153.
25 *ICD*, 1918, p. 538q.
26 *Ibid.*, p. 538d.
27 Aan de Wiel, *Catholic Church*, p. 148.
28 *ICD*, 1918, p. 538.
29 Curran Memoirs, Ó Ceallaigh Papers, NLI, MS 27728(2), p. 236.
30 *Irish Catholic*, 1 Dec. 1917.
31 Coogan, *Long Fellow*, p. 103.
32 Laffan, *Resurrection of Ireland*, p. 199.
33 O'Connor to Logue, 26 Nov. 1917, Logue Papers, ADA, box 7, folder 6, 'Political'.
34 Miller, *Church, State and Nation*, p. 400.
35 Coogan, *Long Fellow*, p. 102.
36 Logue to Walsh, 12 June 1917, Walsh Papers, DDA, box 389, folder 385/8.
37 Curran Memoirs, Ó Ceallaigh Papers, NLI, MS 27728(2), pp. 208–9.
38 Plunkett to O'Donnell, 18 Jul. 1917, Logue Papers, ADA, box 6, folder 7, 'Irish Convention'.
39 *Report and Proceedings of the Irish Convention*, Cd 9019, p. 32.
40 *Ibid.*, p. 38.
41 *Ibid.*, p. 32.
42 *ICD*, 1919, p. 501.

43 *Ibid.*, p. 502.
44 Cabinet Conclusion, 25 Mar. 1918, TNA, CAB 23/5, WC 372.
45 Callan, 'Recruitment', p. 42.
46 Cabinet Conclusions, 26 Mar. 1918, TNA, CAB 23/5, WC 373.
47 Healy, *Letters and Leaders*, p. 594.
48 Cabinet Conclusions, 27 Mar. 1918, TNA, CAB 23/5, WC 374.
49 Duke to Lloyd George, 27 Mar. 1918, TNA, CAB 23/5, WC 375.
50 Campbell to Lloyd George, 28 Mar. 1918, TNA, CAB 23/5, WC 376.
51 Cabinet Conclusions, 27 Mar. 1918, TNA CAB 23/5, WC 375.
52 Mahon to Lloyd George, 29 Mar. 1918, TNA CAB 23/5, WC 377.
53 Mgr. Cyril Fay to Cardinal Gibbons, 23 Jan 1918, Elibank Papers, NLS, MS 8805, fols 175–80. The letter was retained by the British Military Attaché in Washington.
54 *ICD*, 1919, p. 501.
55 *ICD*, 1919, p. 534.
56 Logue to Walsh, 13 Apr. 1918, Walsh Papers, DDA, box 390, folder 379/6.
57 Laffan, *Resurrection of Ireland*, p. 135.
58 Curran Memoirs, Ó Ceallaigh Papers, NLI, MS 27728(2), p. 253.
59 *Ibid.*, p. 254.
60 *Ibid.*, p. 264.
61 *ICD*, 1919, pp. 534–5.
62 Aan de Wiel, *Catholic Church*, p. 319.
63 Miller, *Church, State and Nation*, p. 405.
64 Curran Memoirs, Ó Ceallaigh Papers, NLI, MS 27728(2), p. 263.
65 Laffan, *Resurrection of Ireland*, p. 140.
66 *Irish Catholic*, 22 April 1918.
67 Duke to Lloyd George, 16 Apr. 1918, TNA, CAB 23/6, WC 392.
68 French to Lloyd George, 23 Apr. 1918, TNA, CAB 23/6, WC 397.
69 Healy, *Letters and Leaders*, p. 597.
70 Cabinet Conclusions, 7 May 1918, TNA, CAB 23/6, WC 406.
71 Murray to the Foreign Office, 17 Jan. 1918, Elibank Papers, NLS, MS 8805, fol. 163.
72 Murray to Reading, 15 Apr. 1918, Elibank Papers, NLS, MS 8805, fols 255–8.
73 Duke to Lloyd George, 16 April 1918, TNA, CAB 23/6, WC 392.
74 Laffan, *Resurrection of Ireland*, pp. 143–5.
75 Logue to O'Donnell, 20 Jul. 1918, O'Donnell Papers, ADA, box 9, folder 3, 'Patrick Cardinal O'Donnell'.
76 Hay to Logue, undated, Logue Papers, ADA, box 8, folder 3, 'European Bishops'.
77 Hay's Report, Logue Papers, ADA, box 7, folder 10, p. 5.
78 *Ibid.*, p. 2.
79 Amette to Logue, 3 Aug. 1918, Logue Papers, ADA, box 8, folder 3, 'European Bishops' (Translation).

80 Hay's Report, Logue Papers, ADA, box 7, folder 10, p. 2.
81 Logue to Amette, Undated, Logue Papers, ADA, box 8, folder 3, 'European Bishops' (Translation).
82 *Irish Times*, 12 Jan. 1907.
83 Shane Leslie to O'Riordan, 25 Mar. 1916, O'Riordan Papers, AICR, no. 47 (1916).
84 *Irish Times*, 11 Oct. 1916.
85 *Ibid.*
86 Hay's Report, Logue Papers, ADA, box 7, folder 10, p. 3.
87 Curran Memoirs, Ó Ceallaigh Papers, NLI, MS 27712(1), p. 395.
88 Hay's Report, Logue Papers, ADA, box 7, folder 10, p. 4.
89 *Ibid.*
90 *Ibid.*, p. 5.
91 Hay to Logue, 1 Sept. 1918, Logue Papers, ADA, box 7, folder 11.
92 Aan de Wiel, *Catholic Church*, pp. 315–24.
93 Cabinet Conclusions, 19 June 1918, TNA, CAB 23/6, WC 433.
94 Plunkett to Logue, 6 Aug. 1918, Elibank Papers, NLS, MS 8806, fols 185–8.
95 Logue to Plunkett, 9 Aug. 1918, Elibank Papers, NLS, MS 8806, fols 197–8.
96 Hay's Report, Logue Papers, ADA, box 7, folder 10, p. 3.
97 Long to Lloyd George, 21 Nov. 1918, TNA, CAB 23/8, WC 505.
98 Logue to O'Donnell, 11 Nov. 1918, O'Donnell Papers, ADA, box 9, folder 3, 'Patrick Cardinal O'Donnell'.
99 Curran Memoirs, Ó Ceallaigh Papers, NLI, MS 27712(1), p. 433.
100 Laffan, *Resurrection of Ireland*, p. 161.
101 *Freeman's Journal*, 28 Nov. 1918.
102 Logue to Walsh, 3 Dec. 1918, Walsh Papers, DDA, box 390, folder 379/6.
103 Logue to MacRory, 9 Dec. 1918, Logue Papers, ADA, box 3, folder 8, 'Irish Dioceses'.
104 Farrell, *Orange State*, p. 21.
105 Logue to Walsh, 29 Dec. 1918, Walsh Papers, DDA, box 390, folder 379/6.
106 Boland to Walsh, 23 Nov. 1918, Walsh Papers, DDA, box 390, folder 386/1.
107 Morrissey, *William Walsh*, p. 317.
108 Curran Memoirs, Ó Ceallaigh Papers, NLI, MS 27712(1), p. 443.

8

Revolution and collapse

Resistance

The first Dáil which met in Dublin on 21 January 1919 had something of an air of unreality. Only twenty-seven members took part, the remainder being in prison or on the run. The proceedings were dismissed by some as a charade and it was certainly the case, as Lyons has suggested, that the new parliament was convened as much for foreign consumption as it was for Irishmen.[1] Indeed, one of the Dáil's first acts was to organise a delegation to the Paris peace conference. The new Government was surrounded by an aura of insurrection. Hopkinson has argued that the preponderance of militants, such as Cathal Brugha, in the new Government locked the republican movement into a commitment to the ideal of 1916. Moreover, the arrests during the conscription crisis and after meant that, for the period after the general election, the republican movement was dominated by the proponents of physical force.[2]

Logue had lost none of his anxieties regarding republicans but by 1919 his essential political pragmatism was very much in evidence. In his Lenten pastoral published in February, he made reference to the new states emerging in Europe from the ruins of the Russian, German and Austrian empires. 'To Catholics', he wrote, 'it is a matter of indifference what forms these new governments may take'. Benedict XV had decreed that that Church was averse to no form of government provided it was 'legitimately and peacefully established and not in conflict with the law of God from whom all authority comes'. As Logue cautiously circled the new Government in Dublin, his overriding concern remained that conflict should be avoided. Although not a republican, Logue was still committed to the idea of self-determination. There was a real sense of betrayal that the sanction for nationalism extended from the Paris peace conference to the rest of Europe did not apply to Ireland. The country, he said, was being 'deprived of what is emphatically proclaimed to be the birthright of every free nation – full and adequate control of its internal affairs'.[3]

By 1919, the bishops were increasingly adopting the language of separation. Their pastorals were filled with the notions currently in vogue across Europe: democracy, self-determination and freedom. There was also frustration that the emergency legislation enacted after the Rising was still in force. In his March letter, Logue complained that 'we are not ruled by the ordinary law, but are subject to a drastic military code under which actions, otherwise trivial or harmless, become grave offences and are pitilessly punished'.[4] For the bishops as a body, however, anger at the British Government and declarations regarding the nationhood of Ireland did not translate into outright support for the Dáil and the republican movement.

A major factor in this reticence was the promise of violence which surrounded the establishment of Dáil Éireann. The bishops were aware that Irish Volunteers had been conducting raids for weapons since the days of the Irish Convention. James O'Connor, the Attorney General, told Logue in 1917 that Volunteers were stealing rifles and importing gelignite from Glasgow.[5] However, the tenor of such raids changed in 1919. There was a sharp reaction to the deaths of two police officers killed in an arms raid at Soloheadbeg, County Tipperary, on the day the Dáil was convened. Monsignor Arthur Ryan, the county's vicar-general, condemned the killings as cold-blooded murder. The same sentiments were expressed by the Archbishop of Cashel, John Harty.[6] Michael O'Riordan was even more forthright. 'I am puzzling myself to find the secret or occasion for the tragedy near Tipperary', he told Patrick O'Donnell, 'it is inexpressibly sickening. If the people discover the murderers, they should, for their honour, [catch] and lynch them.'[7]

The bishops touched on the growing conflict in their June statement. They laid the blame for acts of violence, which they had to deplore, firmly on the Government for its tyrannical rule in Ireland and its denial of the country's national rights. They did, however, ask that the 'faithful should not allow any provocation to make them overstep the law of God'.[8] The events in Soloheadbeg, however, did not occur in isolation. In September 1919, an arms raid took place on an army parade at a Methodist church at Fermoy in County Cork resulting in the death of a British soldier. At the subsequent inquest the jury held that the Volunteers, now the Irish Republican Army, had not intended to kill the soldier. They declared the arms raid a regular act of war and refused to bring in a verdict of murder. Following the result, infuriated troops broke barracks and attacked property belonging to the jurors.[9] Fermoy set the pattern of attack and reprisal that would characterise the coming conflict.

However, it was one thing to accuse the Government of tyranny and partiality but quite another to endorse a campaign of assassination against the police. Thus, when the bishops met on 22 October 1919, they responded to the escalating violence as they always had – with division and dissent. Walsh was absent from the meeting due to illness but his secretary, Michael Curran, has recorded that 'a proposal to issue a statement denouncing the murder of policemen found the general body against the publication on the grounds that political capital would be made out of it by the enemies of Ireland'.[10] More likely, however, as Keogh has argued, the bishops remained deadlocked by the fear of lending moral sanction to either side in the growing conflict.[11] In his address to the Maynooth Union on 23 October, Logue studiously avoided any comment on the deteriorating situation throughout the country. Curran rather spitefully observed that the cardinal 'realised that priests and laymen resented his unfortunate political declarations'.[12] This was not the first time, however, that the bishops had foregone issuing a statement in deference to a delicate political situation.

The British Government responded to the republican campaign with force, internment and suppression. In September 1919 Sinn Féin was banned in Cork and the proscription then extended throughout Ireland with Dáil suffering the same fate. Restrictions were placed on newspapers and public meetings, while curfews were enforced in many areas. The harshness of the British response however, provoked certain members of the hierarchy to break ranks and publicly side with Dáil Éireann. In November, through the medium of Cardinal O'Connell in New York, Walsh made a very public donation to the Dáil. He told O'Connell he was anxious to contribute to the national fund, but any newspaper that published details of his action would be suppressed and, thus, he was relying on the American press. He pointed out that, valuable as his contribution was, public knowledge that he had contributed at all was even more important.[13] Walsh was joined in this public display of solidarity by Michael Fogarty, Bishop of Killaloe, who became treasurer of the Dáil loan scheme.[14]

Walsh's action, however, was as much prompted by resentment at the British Government as it was by sympathy with the republican movement. It was certainly not an extension of moral or episcopal approval to insurrection, as Michael Curran was about to find out. On 9 December 1919 he gave an interview to the *Daily Mail* wherein he represented Walsh's subscription to the Dáil loan as support for total separation. When asked about the killing of policemen, Curran equivocated. He attempted to differentiate between political killings and those committed by criminals. As Morrissey has pointed out, Curran had blundered into the essential dilemma inherent in physical force nationalism. Killing was wrong and must not be condoned; but to condemn the killing of soldiers and police was to appear to take sides with an unwanted and oppressive Government. On the day that Curran's interview appeared, Logue met with Walsh in Dublin and the decision was taken that he had to go.[15] Curran subsequently left Dublin to take up a post as Vice-Rector of the Irish College in Rome. A promotion, perhaps, but the move retained some element of disgrace nonetheless. It certainly conveyed the displeasure of the archbishop, although the two remained on good terms. For the Irish bishops, however, Curran's appointment was to have far reaching consequences. In the Rector, John Hagan, who had replaced Michael O'Riordan, Curran found a priest of like mind and political outlook, and the two set about placing the Irish College firmly at the disposal of the republican movement.

Walsh was soon given an opportunity to pronounce for himself on the IRA campaign. On 19 December the Lord Lieutenant, Lord French, narrowly escaped assassination in a republican ambush at Ashtown in County Dublin. The attempt on such a high profile target represented the extent to which the war was changing tempo. Republicans, as Townshend has argued, had an instinctive grasp of guerrilla strategy and the effectiveness of propaganda over military might. The attack at Ashtown galvanised the authorities into committing the British army to the fray to augment the floundering RIC. The army would soon become 'virtually a supplementary department of the administration' despite the absence of martial law.[16]

Walsh could not ignore the attack which had happened virtually on his own doorstep but the statement which he issued was a rather masterful negotiation of the physical force dilemma. As Michael Curran rightly pointed out, 'the archbishop was very careful that it would not be used as an opportunity for denouncing the popular movement'.[17] Nevertheless, Walsh's statement was unequivocal in its condemnation of the ambush. He compared the attempt on the life of the Viceroy to the Phoenix Park murders of 1882. Such an act, he said, 'calls for the melancholy protest of every Irishman who loves his country and hopes to see the present coercive government brought to end'. The archbishop cleverly wove pointed criticism of the Irish administration into his condemnations but there was no mistaking his moral disapproval of the IRA campaign. 'Surely there is no one in Ireland', he wrote, 'in such ignorance of the moral law as not to know that murder . . . is one of the most appalling crimes in the whole catalogue of guilt'. Such acts could not effect redress for the misgovernment of Ireland.[18]

A week earlier Logue had been provoked into issuing a blunt rejection of criticism of the bishops in the press that the hierarchy remained silent when their flocks were killing policemen. In a letter published on 14 December, he described Ireland as being in a miserable position with repression on one side and 'restive opposition' on the other. The great majority of the Irish people, Logue said, 'felt nothing but horror at murder, whether they supported Sinn Féin or not'. He argued that the bishops had never hesitated to condemn murders. But even if they did, he said, crime would be beyond their control 'while the state of things which gives an opportunity and some pretext for crime continues'.[19] In spite of his revulsion at conflict and his suspicions regarding the republican movement, Logue's position was not that far removed from that of Walsh. Both laid final blame for the disturbed state of the country at the door of the British Government. The statements issued from Armagh and Dublin gave the hierarchy a course which skirted the political divisions among the bishops. There were aspects of the current conflict upon which a degree of unity might be forged and might circumvent the differences on Ireland's political future. As Logue pointed out in a letter to the *Irish Catholic*, on 10 January 1920 'the wish to have an end put to misgovernment . . . gives no grounds to infer that there is any sympathy with or want of reprobation of the unfortunate crimes to which misgovernment leads'.[20]

Thus, when the bishops met at the end of January 1920, the central theme of their statement was the abject failure of British policy in Ireland. They blamed the Government's disregard of the country's national feeling for the current disorder. They demanded that Ireland be accorded the same rights as any other civilised nation and the same rights extended by the Paris peace conference to the rest of Europe. The bishops declared that the only way to restore friendly relations between Britain and Ireland was for British politicians to 'allow an undivided Ireland to choose her own form of government'. On the question of violence, the hierarchy issued no specific condemnation but appealed to their flocks to abstain from 'deeds of bloodshed and outrage calculated to bring on themselves and their country shame, and the anger of heaven'.[21]

This was not quite active encouragement of the republican movement but neither was it an outright condemnation. Political divisions still remained among the bishops. Thomas O'Doherty, Bishop of Clonfert, told John Hagan in Rome that the bishops' statement had passed unanimously in place of one which would not have passed at all.[22] Keogh has argued, quoting a 'confidential source', that Logue was dissatisfied with its final wording.[23] However, there was little evidence of this, or any obvious divergence, among the archbishops when their Lenten pastorals were published in February. Logue was obviously preoccupied with the events of the First World War. He condemned the current Irish administration as a 'military regime rivalling in severity even that of countries under the most pitiless of autocratic government'. The same kind of repression had occurred when the Germans occupied Belgium and had raised a 'wild cry' of protest. On political violence, however, Logue was more forthright than his colleagues had been in January. 'It is not only our duty', he said, 'but in our interest to unite in a determined effort to discourage and root out lawlessness and crime from our midst'.[24]

In his pastoral, the Archbishop of Dublin condemned the British Government's denial of the right of Irish people constitutionally to seek redress for their grievances. Under such circumstances, he went on, it was 'impossible to expect that they can rest content with such a state of things'. Thomas Gilmartin, who had replaced John Healy as Archbishop of Tuam, was more critical of IRA violence. People had a right, he said, to change the government if they were being misgoverned. Any action, however, must be kept within the moral law as expressed in the Ten Commandments. 'The end, no matter how noble', Gilmartin said, 'does not justify immoral means'. In Cashel, John Harty declared that the Irish people were living under a government which had proven an abject failure. Coercion and crime went hand in hand and peaceful citizens were being made victims of this vicious circle.[25]

The archbishops at least could unite around their condemnation of British policy in Ireland and also appeals for restraint. But they continued to send a mixed message to their flocks. Ireland was in the grip of tyranny and was being denied justice on the question of independence. There was no move, however, to legitimise rebellion against such tyranny and, despite their resentment and outrage against the Irish administration, the bishops, as a body, withheld their moral sanction from the Dáil. The obvious alarm in the hierarchy belied the fact that by February 1920 the IRA campaign was still relatively confined and the response of the Government not as harsh as would be seen in later months. Nevertheless, the violence had already surpassed anything witnessed by the bishops in their long careers.

Periods of conflict in Ireland had seldom passed without taking on a Roman dimension. In contrast to the comparative neutrality practised by Tobias Kirby, John Hagan's term as Rector pushed the Irish College in an altogether different direction. Aided by Michael Curran as Vice-Rector, Hagan transformed the role of the college to reflect his republican politics. In many respects, the Irish College began to function almost as an outpost for the Dáil's fledgling Foreign Service. Hagan often took his Anglophobia to extremes and remained obsessed with real or imagined British intrigue at the Vatican. His suspicion of English influence was as constant as his long held antipathy towards Logue. In 1914, for example, while Vice-Rector, he complained to the Bishop of Raphoe over British efforts against Home Rule in Rome. 'What a pity', he told O'Donnell, 'that we have not in Ireland an energetic Cardinal who would make himself felt here and prevent the Irish from being walked on by anyone who cares to come along'.[26] Logue did not return Hagan's dislike. In fact, the cardinal had recommended him to succeed Michael O'Riordan as Rector. He told Walsh 'I think the Vice Rector, Doctor Hagan, would be a good and efficient Rector. He is a good man and a clever man.' The only drawback Logue could see was that Hagan was 'a good deal infected with the chitchat and gossip which goes on in Rome'. He expressed the hope, vain as it turned out, that responsibility would render him more prudent and reserved. The cardinal did not think, however, the new Rector would get on well with the English colony in Rome.[27]

Hagan embarked on his political offensive by arranging an audience with Benedict XV for Seán T. Ó Ceallaigh and providing him with an aggressive statement on conditions in Ireland. The statement unapologetically defended the IRA campaign. 'As long as human nature is human nature', he wrote, 'individuals or sections of the community can hardly be restrained if in vengeance for savage acts they take the law into their own hands and wreak the vengeance that is within their grasp'. Ó Ceallaigh was aghast and redrafted a more moderate statement to place before the Pope. He painted a picture of a Catholic nation enslaved by a Protestant power and applauded the neutral stance of the Holy See thus far in the conflict. Benedict proved sympathetic to Ireland's claim for self-determination but was critical of the republican movement. 'Ireland has every right to its independence', he said, 'but remember my words, be careful of the methods you use. I think you should not shoot police and I think you should consider the question of ambushes.'[28] It is worth noting that Curran omits the Pope's admonishment from his memoirs, noting only that Ó Ceallaigh cleverly deflected any hint of criticism.[29]

At the end of May 1920 a sizeable portion of the Irish hierarchy travelled to Rome for the ceremony of beatification for the Irish martyr, Oliver Plunkett. Curran recalled that the impending visit of Cardinal Logue left Hagan distinctly nervous. The Rector was anxious lest any dissenting voices be heard criticising the republican movement. He begged Michael Fogarty, Bishop of Killaloe, to accompany the bishops' delegation to counter the prospect of negativity from the cardinal.[30] In the end, the event passed off without incident to everyone's satisfaction. Even the presence of representatives from Dáil Éireann caused no friction.[31] Benedict refrained from any controversy when he dealt with Ireland in a reply to an address from the Irish prelates. 'The present hour', he told them, 'is indeed one in which Ireland needs altogether peculiar help from on high that she may be enabled to attain the goal of her just aspirations without the violation of a single duty'.[32] As yet, the Holy See was inclined not to interfere in the Irish conflict.

Attrition

By the summer of 1920 the war in Ireland had entered a new phase. Republican attacks upon the police had escalated and the response of Crown forces had become more robust. As the IRA campaign grew more sophisticated and organised, changes were made in the Irish administration. General H. H. Tudor was placed in overall command of the police in Ireland while Hamar Greenwood replaced Sir Ian Macpherson as Chief Secretary. To fill the gaps in the ranks of the police caused by the republican campaign, Tudor began to recruit demobbed soldiers in England. In July the administration established an elite gendarmerie recruited from ex-army officers to bolster the RIC. Both the new Auxiliary Division (RIC) and the so-called 'Black and Tans', as the English recruits were dubbed, would, through a consistent lack of discipline, play a pivotal role in intensifying the bitterness of the conflict.

The bishops met in June 1920 and again failed to reach consensus on a statement. In April the Standing Committee had unified around the issue of political prisoners and conditions in Irish and British prisons but at their meeting on 22 June, politics again proved the stumbling block.[33] Speaking at the silver jubilee of the Maynooth Union, Logue hinted at the political divisions among the bishops. They were, however, united in their condemnation of violence. Implicit in his statement was a reminder to the clergy that they answered to a higher authority than Dáil Éireann.[34] Earlier Logue had renewed his attack on the administration. At the end of 1919, the British Government had introduced the Government of Ireland Bill to almost universal dismay. Unveiled in February 1920, the bill provided for the establishment of two Home Rule parliaments in Ireland, one in Dublin and the other in Belfast. It was not only the prospect of partition but the limited and ineffectual powers granted to both parliaments that caused resentment.[35]

Logue was scathing. He told O'Donnell in March 1920 that 'the so-called Home Rule Bill is hopeless'. He believed that the whole thing had been guided and directed by Sir Edward Carson and that if the Ulster Unionists succeeded in this 'they will be satisfied and trouble little about what will come after'. The whole matter had left him extremely bitter. Logue told O'Donnell that he had received letters and telegrams from England asking him to join in conciliation efforts. 'I told them I could not touch their movement in the present state of things', he said, 'the government is merely playing with the feelings of the people'.[36] Logue retained the belief that the only acceptable solution to the Irish Question lay in the provision of dominion status for the whole island. He took the opportunity of the publication of the Government of Ireland Bill in February to say as much in an interview with an American journalist. Denouncing the proposed partition of Ireland, Logue derided the scheme because 'it settles nothing, is worse than useless and does not make for tranquillity'. He was convinced that a satisfactory measure of Home Rule applied to the whole of Ireland would meet with general acceptance. He simply could not conceive of any settlement which left Ireland outside the British Empire. 'Personally, not being a Sinn Féiner', he said, 'I believe a republic is out of the question'.[37] The timing of Logue's comments was not insignificant. His remarks were carried in the Hearst newspapers in New York and appeared at the same time as de Valera arrived there on a speaking and fundraising tour. The cardinal's old antagonism toward the President of the republic remained undiminished.

There is little doubt that Logue was deeply affected by the bloodshed in Ireland. Miller has stated that in July 1920 he was found by the Irish Under-Secretary, James MacMahon, weeping over an account of the death of a district commissioner of the RIC in County Cork.[38] In no sense did he view the IRA campaign as legitimate or valid or as a war of independence. He told a congregation in Armagh Cathedral on 4 July that republicans could never expect to regenerate the country by crime and bloodshed, or 'any conduct which would bring God's curse upon them'.[39] Logue was similarly repelled, however, by the actions of Crown forces. When MacMahon attempted to enlist his help in quelling the IRA campaign, the cardinal asked, 'what is the good of attempting the impossible when the government provides the excuse for those men to commit such outrages'?[40] In the same way as the IRA campaign of violence precluded support for Sinn Féin on Logue's part, the activities and reprisals conducted by Crown forces precluded support for the Government.

On 30 September 1920, MacMahon delivered a letter to *Ara Coeli* from the Chief Secretary. Greenwood alleged that the IRA were using police officers' attendance at weekly mass as a cover to launch attacks on them and their barracks. He wanted Logue to issue a rescript absolving Catholic RIC officers from the obligation of attending Sunday mass. He believed such a notice would be better coming from the Church as it was 'certain to be represented as dictated by sectarian prejudices' if it came from Dublin Castle.[41] Logue was unimpressed by the appeal and refused to be drawn to side publicly with the administration. He told the Chief Secretary that he had overestimated the extent of his ecclesiastical authority. He had no power to interfere in the arrangements in any other diocese and he had 'never attempted to assume any such authority'. Catholic policemen, he went on, knew well their obligations and their duties governing attendance at mass in times of danger. Logue refused to issue any such order in the archdiocese because it was relatively free from strife save for that caused by the very same Crown forces he was being urged to protect. He angrily told Greenwood that these, who were supposedly the guardians of law and order, 'under the name of reprisals, set the pace in lawlessness and disorder'. Logue raged that 'in their terrible outbursts innocent people are done to death sometimes in the most savage manner'.[42]

Despite his own moral and political difficulties with the Irish administration, Logue maintained steady contact with officials from Dublin Castle. On 2 August 1920 he again met with MacMahon and pushed, once more, the belief that a settlement could be found in a formula involving Dominion Home Rule. MacMahon told his colleagues that Logue had practically pledged the support of the Irish Church to the idea and it was widely held in the Castle that the country would support such a scheme if only Lloyd George would act on it.[43] Walsh had publicly aligned himself with Sinn Féin and had had little contact with the Irish administration. He was reluctant to provide any suggestion of a way forward in terms of a settlement. In reply to an article which appeared in the press arguing for repeal of the Act of Union, the archbishop declared that any attempt to suggest a settlement would simply furnish the Government with the excuse to throw more dust in the eyes of the Irish people. 'Are they prepared to give Ireland independence', he demanded, 'in favour of which the electorate declared so clearly and emphatically at the General Election?'[44] Logue's willingness to work with Dublin Castle to find a political settlement was symptomatic of his growing desperation to stop the violence. The sentiments were shared by the Archbishop of Tuam, Thomas Gilmartin, who cast a plague on both the IRA and the British Government for the state of Ireland. He told an audience in Athenry on 20 September 1920, 'for some time past this poor country has been the theatre of misgovernment, injustice, terrorism; one wrong leading to another and all making a lurid chapter of crime, counter-crime and brutal retaliation'.[45]

The Government's autumn offensive pushed the IRA into forming Active Service Units, or flying columns, of full-time guerrillas who engaged the police and army in rural areas. There was no let-up in the campaign against the RIC in the towns and cities. The police, and to a lesser extent the army, reacted with reprisal. On 20 September 1920, for example, following the shooting dead of three police officers in and around the capital, police broke barracks and went on a spree of looting and burning in the seaside town of Balbriggan. In all, forty-nine properties were burned and two prominent Sinn Féin members were bayoneted to death. Townshend has argued that the English recruits to the RIC lacked discipline and that the command structure was insufficient to curb excesses. There was, however, tacit approval in certain quarters of the practice of counter-terror.[46]

In this climate of escalating violence and crisis the bishops needed unanimity of purpose when they met in Maynooth on 10 October 1920. What emerged from their general meeting was an impassioned condemnation of British policy in Ireland, north and south. The IRA did not escape the anger of the assembled hierarchy but the bishops reserved the worst of their wrath for the Irish administration and the policy of reprisals. They accused the Government of terrorism and partiality. Reprisals were branded 'the indiscriminate vengeance of savages, deliberately wreaked on a whole town or countryside without any complicity in crime'.[47] It was a powerful statement which gave full vent to the moral revulsion and bitter resentment felt by the bishops for the cycle of retaliatory violence. They established a publicity committee to aid in disseminating their statements during the conflict and appointed the Bishop of Clonfert, Thomas O'Doherty, as secretary. The pastoral was translated into French and Italian and distributed to both the peace conference at Versailles and the Vatican.[48]

In their statement, the bishops also took on the thorny moral and theological issue of republican hunger-strikes. Members of the hierarchy had reacted with outrage to the death of Thomas Ashe in 1917 during forced feeding by prison officers. In some respects, however, the manner of this death had absolved the bishops from pronouncing on the morality of hunger-strikes. The plight of Terence MacSwiney in 1920, however, forced them to confront the issue. The Lord Mayor of Cork had spent most of the month of August on the run but was arrested at a meeting of Cork No. 1 Brigade of the IRA at the City Hall by British soldiers. From the moment of his arrest, MacSwiney embarked on his hunger-strike.[49] For the Church, there was an obvious moral dilemma in the fact of a Catholic starving himself to death in pursuit of a political goal. Suicide was wrong and carried the penalty of excommunication and the denial of the burial rites of the Church. However, MacSwiney's hunger-strike became more than a mere tactic. His slow suicide became an act of defiance and it assumed a religious element which gripped Catholic Ireland. He was transferred to Brixton Prison where he was attended throughout his fast by Father Dominic O'Connor who acted as intermediary and confessor.

Costello has argued that the presence of a priest at the side of a hunger-striker, with the permission of the Church, was a visible sign that the hierarchy had extended their moral sanction to the action.[50] Whether influenced by the popular support for MacSwiney or convinced of the essential justice of his cause, the Irish bishops declared that the hunger-strike was sacrificial and not suicidal.[51] The news dismayed officials at Dublin Castle. Mark Sturgis recorded angrily only that the hierarchy had sided with MacSwiney – 'damn them!'[52] In their pastoral the bishops branded the continuing imprisonment of MacSwiney as cruel and destructive of peace. They praised MacSwiney and his comrades on hunger-strike. These men, they said, 'think nothing of their lives if they can do anything for Ireland in the sad plight to which the rule of the stranger has reduced them'.[53] MacSwiney died on 25 October 1920. At what amounted to a state funeral in Cork, Bishop Cohalan remarked that 'periodically, the memory of a martyr's death will remind a young generation of the fundamental question of the freedom of Ireland'.[54]

A stark indication of how far the conflict had intensified occurred on Sunday 21 November 1920. Members of the Dublin Brigade Active Service Unit shot dead twelve alleged British spies. That afternoon, officers of the Auxiliary Division entered Croke Park where a football match was taking place. They opened fire on the crowd, killing twelve people. The deaths in Dublin caused a collective shudder across Ireland. The killing of the 'Cairo

Gang' that morning proved, as Keogh has pointed out, that the IRA could match the ruthlessness of Crown forces.[55] Logue was deeply affected by the violence of what became known as 'Bloody Sunday'. A week later he issued a pastoral letter to the archdiocese unequivocally condemning the actions of the IRA as cold-blooded murder. 'No object could excuse them', he said, 'no motive could justify them; no heart, unless hardened and steeled against pity, would tolerate their cruelty'. Patriotism, he went on, was a noble virtue but it must be kept within the law of God. 'Otherwise', he warned, 'it degenerates into blind reckless passion inspired not by love of country, but by Satan, who was a murderer from the beginning'.[56] Logue reacted with equal revulsion to the shootings in Croke Park which he called an 'indiscriminate massacre of inoffensive victims'. If a balance were struck on the day, however, between the deeds of the morning and the deeds of the afternoon, he believed it should be given against the forces of the Crown. 'All Ireland', he concluded, 'was groaning under this competition of murders'.[57]

To his astonishment and horror, however, Logue found that his impassioned and articulate statement had been reported only in part by newspapers in Europe. Much was made of his condemnation of the IRA. There was little or no mention of his criticism of British forces. The omission was highlighted by Seán T. Ó Ceallaigh in a letter to the Bishop of Down and Connor, Joseph MacRory, from Rome. He complained that the publication of only the first half of Logue's pastoral in the *Osservatore Romano* had produced a very bad effect.[58] He made a similar complaint to Hagan stating, 'that last letter from our friend in Armagh has done us, I believe, considerable harm'.[59]

On 10 December Logue enclosed the full text of his pastoral along with a letter of protest to the editor of the *Osservatore* in a note to Hagan.[60] Fortunately, the bishops' Publicity Committee swung into action when the *Osservatore* delayed printing a retraction. In February 1921 they issued a public letter denouncing the treatment meted out to the cardinal. 'This incident has been noted and discussed in the Irish press', they said, 'and had produced a most painful impression on the minds of our faithful people'. They accused the *Osservatore* of suppressing the truth and being complicit in a campaign waged by English diplomats who were 'pressing the Holy See to condemn the Irish movement'. Meantime, they went on, 'a campaign of slander and misrepresentation is pursued by British propaganda which now, as during the war, is shameless in its mendacity'.[61]

Pressure for some kind of papal intervention was mounting at Rome. According to John Hagan, demands for a statement were being made by

Cardinal Rafael Merry del Val of the Holy Office. The Rector was sure the cardinal was the 'devil of the piece' and that he wished to remind Irish Catholics that there was such a thing as the Fifth Commandment.[62] However, no statement appeared. Curran later told the Bishop of Raphoe, Patrick O'Donnell, that the threat of a pronouncement had given them the fright of their lives.[63] According to both Hagan and his Vice-Rector, papal intervention had only been postponed and the threat that Benedict would once again entangle the Vatican in Irish affairs remained a real one.

It was not, however, from Rome that clerical condemnation of the IRA emanated at the end of 1920. December proved to be one of the bloodiest and destructive months of the war to date. A week after the killings in Dublin an Auxiliary patrol was ambushed by the IRA's West Cork Brigade at Kilmichael. The flying column, led by Tom Barry, killed 16 policemen. Townshend has stated that all of West Cork trembled in anticipation of the reprisals which would follow. It was the Government, however, which provided the response with the introduction of martial law.[64] Whatever discipline existed within the army did not extend to the police. Following an attack outside Victoria Barracks in Cork on 11 December, police officers broke barracks and looted and burned a sizeable portion of the city centre. This was by far the most spectacular act of counter-terror yet witnessed and the whole country reeled in shock.[65] Exasperated at the cycle of killing and blow and counter-blow, the Bishop of Cork, Daniel Cohalan, issued a remarkable condemnation of the violence on 12 December.

In a public letter he denounced kidnapping, arson and ambushes as being patently contrary to the law of God. 'Anyone who shall', he said, 'within the diocese of Cork, organise or take part in an ambush or a kidnapping or otherwise shall be guilty of murder shall incur, by that very fact, the censure of excommunication'.[66] Despite the bombshell quality of Cohalan's letter, the threat of excommunication for acts of violence was not altogether novel. On 5 December the Bishop of Galway, Thomas O'Dea, had cut off from the Church's communion anyone guilty of murdering or otherwise assaulting a priest.[67] Nevertheless, Cohalan's declaration represented an unprecedented attack on the methodology of the IRA. Keogh has pointed out that the statement applied to Crown forces and the IRA alike, but this was not how it was interpreted by those within the republican movement.[68] Séan T. Ó Ceallaigh was outraged at the bishop's intervention. He told Hagan, 'I would like to have a chance of telling that man to his face what a cowardly slave and traitor to Ireland this last pronouncement proves him to be!'[69]

The Commandant of the IRA's West Cork Brigade, Tom Barry, recalled that the threat of excommunication affected his volunteers deeply. 'Let nobody minimise', he said, 'the gravity of such a decree in a Catholic country'. Barry has recorded that, like many other flying columns, the West Cork Brigade enjoyed a working relationship with the local clergy. Prior to the ambush at Kilmichael, for example, the brigade was given the last rites by Father O'Connell, the parish priest at Ballina. Barry has noted that the decree had little practical effect. All of his unit continued to fight and most priests continued to administer the sacraments. The IRA practised their religion as before.[70] The bishops made no comment on Cohalan's outburst. Mark Sturgis recorded the event in his diary with obvious expectancy that the decree would be followed up.[71] No action was forthcoming, a fact which *The Times* greeted with incredulity. It condemned the 'impossible and incredible neutrality of the general body of the Irish bishops' in the wake of Cohalan's pronouncement.[72]

'A Truce of God'

Despite their reticence to join with Cohalan in a condemnation of the national movement, the crescendo of violence at the end of 1920 marked a watershed for the hierarchy. There was a sense of growing impatience with both sides in the conflict and the bishops began to increase the pressure for a truce. The first initiative undertaken by the Church was during the visit to Ireland by Patrick Clune. The Archbishop of Perth met many in the episcopacy and Dublin Castle officials. The Bishop of Killaloe, Michael Fogarty, facilitated meetings with Sinn Féin leaders. It had been suggested by the Under-Secretary, James MacMahon, that both sides in the conflict should pause or 'rest on their oars' and this idea was pushed hard by Clune. Sturgis recorded wryly that the suggestion was that the IRA should stop assassination and the army and police should stop raiding 'and, incidentally, looting, burning and shooting'.[73] Nothing came from the meetings but officials at the Castle maintained contact with the bishops, especially Logue, in the hope of brokering a ceasefire.

In their Lenten pastorals of 1921, the archbishops continued the moral pressure by denouncing the activities of both sides in the conflict. On 6 February Logue issued a forceful condemnation of both the Irish administration and the IRA. He described British policy in Ireland as 'repression pure and simple' the likes of which had not been known in Ireland since the days of Cromwell. The barbarity of Crown forces, he said, rivalled that practised by the Turks and the Bolsheviks. He was equally scathing, however, of the actions of the IRA, particularly on the issue of guerrilla warfare. 'Lying in wait', he said, 'and shooting policemen and soldiers is not an act of war. It is plain murder and will entail the punishment for murder here and, if not repented of and atoned for, will entail terrible punishment in the hereafter.'[74]

Thomas Gilmartin, who had previously called for a 'Truce of God' in a letter to the press, was as forthright in his condemnation of the IRA as Logue.[75] Speaking in Tuam in January 1921, the archbishop declared that, in the present circumstances, armed resistance to the existing government was unlawful and those Irishmen in secret societies risked excommunication.[76] He now argued in his Lenten pastoral that those who favoured the policy of armed insurrection 'had certainly got no mandate for their course of action from the Irish people'. John Harty in Cashel declared that he could not condone acts of violence 'committed with a view to national justice'. The Archbishop of Dublin was less forthright in his remarks but used what would be his last Lenten pastoral to urge the Irish to turn away from violence. 'Let it be the subject of our earnest daily prayer', Walsh urged, 'that our people may be strengthened to withstand every influence that would drive them . . . into courses forbidden by the law of God'.[77]

The changing mood of the bishops was viewed with alarm in Rome by Michael Curran. On 17 January 1921, he told Walsh of 'a certain confusion' that had arisen in the Vatican regarding the attitude of the Irish bishops to the national movement. He complained that their views on English tyranny were well known but pointed out that 'Anglophiles seize on the contradictory or opposed views or actions . . . of certain bishops or trade on the silence or reserve of others'. It was also being widely reported in Rome that Ireland would settle for dominion status as a solution to the current conflict.[78]

Despite reluctance on the part of the Government to negotiate directly with Sinn Féin, there were channels of communication between the two sides. In January 1921 a meeting took place in London between Edward Carson, James O'Connor, the Irish Attorney General, and Father Michael O'Flanagan. Carson was willing to discuss eventual Irish unity under the Council of Ireland as laid down in the Government of Ireland Act but refused to countenance Dominion Home Rule for all Ireland. He was willing, however, to offer safeguards for Catholics in Northern Ireland. O'Flanagan did his best to convince the meeting that Sinn Féin offered no threat to Protestants but had to admit that he had no authority to speak on behalf of the republican movement. O'Connor later told Dublin's coadjutor, Edward Byrne, that the chief stumbling block regarding peace was the fact that the Government had no one on the republican side with which to do business. Carson declared that the administration desired peace above all else but had no one to talk to.[79]

Carson's viewpoint hardly seemed plausible given that Irish and English jails were stuffed full of republicans, including many who were regarded as part of the Sinn Féin leadership. In Ireland, Dublin Castle officials concentrated their efforts on the hierarchy in the hope of finding a settlement. On 5 April 1921, Logue and Gilmartin were received at the Lord Lieutenant's residence in Phoenix Park. Mark Sturgis was particularly impressed by the cardinal. 'He is a wonderful old man', he wrote, 'and talked about all the world and the revolutionary spirit'. A second meeting took place on 15 April and Sturgis was surprised to find himself being mercilessly teased by Logue. 'The old cardinal was very pleasant', he noted in his diary, 'and asked me with a prying finger stuck under my ribs did I wear a tin waistcoat'.[80] It was all jolly stuff but rather useless in terms of brokering a ceasefire. It is fair to say that the officials at Dublin Castle had picked the two clerics with perhaps the least influence over the republican movement.

At the end of April 1921 further tentative steps were taken towards a truce with the arrival in Ireland of Lord Derby. The initiative took everyone by surprise, though it was hardly a secret. Derby was an influential Tory and former Minister for War who had been persuaded by English Catholics to act as an honest broker in the conflict.[81] He intended to meet with Logue and senior figures in the republican movement. Prior to his visit, a Liverpool priest, Father James Hughes, had met with Logue at *Ara Coeli* and found the cardinal 'willing to do anything to assist in bringing about peace'.[82] According to Lord Longford, Derby had less success in his meeting with de Valera who viewed him as little more than a political scout and 'talked to him no more freely than he would a pressman'.[83]

De Valera had been concerned that Logue might undermine the republican demand in his meeting with Derby. With the Bishop of Dromore, Edward Mulhern, acting as intermediary, the president attempted to advise Logue on how to proceed with the meeting. In a rather thinly coded response, however, the cardinal made it clear that he needed no such advice. De Valera commented to Michael Collins that 'the old man up north has given them his views. I would like to use bad language but I won't.'[84] Derby, however, had obviously impressed Logue. Speaking in Clonore in County Tyrone on 28 April, he told an audience that if Ireland would only renounce the campaign of assassination, it could obtain everything that was necessary. He also declared that 'they would never win a republic as long as England had a single soldier'. The newspaper of the IRA, the *Irish Bulletin*, stopped short, but only just, of attributing the cardinal's comments to senility.[85]

The pressure for a ceasefire, however, continued. In May 1921 the long dreaded pronouncement from Benedict XV arrived but hardly deserved the trepidation felt by Hagan and Curran earlier in the year. The Pope was careful to take neither side in the conflict, voicing only his deep concern over events there and praising the steadfast Catholicity of Ireland. In a blanket denunciation of the violence he condemned a conflict wherein 'property and homes are being ruthlessly and disgracefully laid waste, when villages and farms are being set ablaze, when neither sacred places nor sacred persons are spared'.[86] Overall, it was a statement of profound regret rather than condemnation and represented something of a coup for the republic's consular services in Rome. It was the first time in a generation that Irish nationalism had been addressed by the Holy See without censure.[87]

Logue's impatience with the lack of progress on a ceasefire was evident in his address to a congregation in Cookstown. Those who had the destinies of the country in their hands, he said, were trusting more to force than to justice. He continued his attack on the Irish administration, describing it as a 'regime of coercion and repression'. He urged the people to place their trust in God for deliverance rather than the politicians.[88] Similar sentiments were expressed at the bishops' meeting in June. This was the first meeting without William Walsh who had died on 9 April. There was little in the June statement to indicate that his death had had any effect on the bishops' attitude to the conflict or to the republican movement. Issued on 22 June, the bishops' expressed their united revulsion at the condition of Ireland. They utterly rejected the Government of Ireland Act and the creation of a parliament in the north and demanded that the British Government treat with the Irish as equals.[89]

However, Government overtures to the republican movement were already being made. At the state opening of the Belfast Parliament King George V issued what was, in effect, a peace appeal on behalf of the administration.[90] On 24 June Lloyd George invited de Valera to join him and Sir Edward Carson in London for a conference 'to end the ruinous conflict which as for centuries divided Ireland and embittered the relations of the people of these two Islands'.[91] De Valera did not respond directly but set about convening a Sinn Féin conference to discuss a ceasefire, but only as a prelude to negotiations. Despite the moral pressure on both sides and the apparent willingness to 'rest on their oars', a ceasefire was not a forgone conclusion. Townshend has pointed out that there were those in the military government who were reluctant to abandon the gains made against the IRA since January. A truce now, it was argued, would give republicans time to recover and rearm and would also cripple intelligence resources. At the conference at Dublin's Mansion House on 4 July, however, both sides agreed the terms of a ceasefire.[92]

Dermot Keogh has argued that the Anglo-Irish War radicalised the bishops. 'If the moral balance tilted in this period', he has stated, 'it was perceived to weigh finally in favour of Sinn Féin – and that despite the excesses of the IRA'.[93] To a certain extent, this was true. There was a perceptible shift towards a more radical political position after 1918 which was exacerbated by the war in Ireland. However, it was more a case of the moral balance tilting against the British Government rather than towards Sinn Féin. The bishops, and Logue in particular, were appalled at the excesses of Crown forces, partition and the abandonment of the 'Big Words' of the First World War in the case of Ireland. The adoption of notions of self-determination, independence and separation by the hierarchy as a whole did not translate into bestowing moral sanction or political legitimacy on Dáil Éireann and the republican movement. Likewise, the IRA campaign was not viewed as a national struggle or a war of independence, despite the many condemnations of British tyranny.

The Anglo-Irish War deepened the political divergence between Armagh and Dublin. Walsh was willing to subscribe to and support the new republic while Logue could not. Such tension, however, did not erupt into bitterness or open hostility. Despite their differing opinions, the attitude of the two men to the war and the issue of violence remained remarkably similar. In fact, the only evidence of a strain in their relationship was a lack of correspondence between the two after 1918. However, Walsh's death, in some respects, provided an opportunity for Logue to stamp his own politics on the direction of the hierarchy. This became very much evident during the negotiations which began in July 1921 and in the Church's attitude to the resulting treaty.

New departures

The cessation of hostilities in Ireland afforded the bishops the opportunity to extend their moral sanction to the national movement. Sinn Féin and Dáil Éireann were no longer regarded as dangerous revolutionary organisations but had become, in the eventual absence of violence, the duly elected representatives of the Irish people. It was not only gratitude for the truce of 1921 which prompted the hierarchy to back the national movement. There was also a degree of political pragmatism. Sinn Féin was now effectively the only representation available for Catholic Ireland.

Logue had recognised this fact much earlier. In February 1921, despite his condemnations of the IRA and his continuing suspicions regarding the republican movement, he had been willing to cooperate with the Dáil in relief efforts. The Irish White Cross was officially launched on 16 February to gather and distribute funds for the relief of families left destitute by the war in the south and the anti-Catholic pogroms in the north. Logue accepted a nomination for the presidency of the organisation declaring, 'I cordially approve of the White Cross association and shall be glad to give it any assistance I can'.[94] The presence of such leading figures in the republican movement as Michael Collins and Arthur Griffith in the list of trustees did not deter the cardinal from undertaking the work with the same zeal he had displayed with the Mansion House Relief Committee forty years earlier.

The archbishops had high expectations when the plenipotentiaries left for London in July 1921. The beginning of negotiations coincided with a Catholic Congress in Dublin and the two events offered the prospect of hope for both politics and religion. Speaking in Thurles, the Archbishop of Cashel, John Harty, declared that Ireland had passed through its Calvary but Easter was coming. Logue, too, was buoyed by what he saw as a real chance for not just political but spiritual renewal. He told an audience in Omeath, 'I believe that when we get over our present troubles . . . there will be a revival in Ireland of this old religious spirit'.[95] The mood of optimism persisted at the bishops' meeting in October. They offered their heartfelt support to the negotiators in London and called for 'a peace which will satisfy the national rights and aspirations of the Irish people . . . free from the hateful spirit of partition'.[96] However, they refrained from speculating on what form a settlement would take or declaring what would be most acceptable to the hierarchy.

There was growing unease among republicans as the negotiations progressed in London. In November 1921, Séan T. Ó Ceallaigh warned Hagan, 'I am told the whole history of the present conference has been a story of continued surrenders on the part of ours while they have nothing so far from the enemy but promises'.[97] The undercurrents of dissension in the national movement were also remarked upon by members of the hierarchy. In October, Abraham Brownrigg, Bishop of Ossory, voiced his foreboding regarding the future. 'If I read the signs of the times in the country aright', he told the new Archbishop of Dublin, Edward Byrne, 'it seems to me in the not too distant future, grave necessity will arise for a closer harmony and union among the whole body of the bishops than ever before. The fight and struggle will be under conditions different from those of old times.'[98]

The culmination of the negotiations was unveiled on 6 December 1921. Ireland would have dominion status on the Canadian model with full fiscal and legislative autonomy. The country would remain within the British Commonwealth and retain an oath of allegiance to the British Crown. A provisional government would be established to oversee the implementation of the Treaty and draft a constitution. Partition was addressed in the creation of a boundary commission to examine the borders of the new states. Ulster would hold a referendum to determine whether the north would come into the new Irish Free State. Five days earlier one of the delegates to London, George Gavan Duffy, told John Hagan that 'crisis has succeeded crisis until we find ourselves at the most crucial stage of all, and though we may be along way from settlement, I fancy that the next move will lie rather with Dáil Éireann than with us'.[99]

As the Dáil debates on the Treaty began and dissenting voices raised the real prospect of rejection, Logue moved quickly to place the moral weight of the hierarchy behind the proposed settlement. In a telegram to Byrne on 9 December he warned, 'It is fatal to leave the destiny of the country in the hands of two or three crochets'.[100] He convened a meeting of the hierarchy in Dublin for 12 December. Overall, the Treaty met with universal acceptance among the hierarchy. The Archbishop of Tuam, Thomas Gilmartin, told the *Freeman's Journal* that he was very satisfied with the terms and that 'the negotiators deserve the profound thanks of both nations'.[101] Even those bishops who had been closest to the republican movement approved the terms on offer. The Bishop of Killaloe, Michael Fogarty, declared on 6 December that 'the Treaty is worth the bitter price paid for it. Ireland is now free to live her own life without interference from outside. The men who made it will be immortal.'[102] Dennis Hallinan in Limerick said he had such perfect confidence in the plenipotentiaries that 'as they are satisfied with the settlement, so am I'.[103] Before the bishops convened in Dublin, Logue told the press, 'there is little doubt as to the attitude of the bishops towards the agreement. I believe the feeling in the country is anxious for peace and all are anxious that the agreement should be confirmed.'[104]

The statement issued from the December meeting was a measured one which refrained from hectoring the Dáil on the subject of acceptance of the Treaty. The bishops praised the patriotism, ability and honesty of purpose of the plenipotentiaries. 'Now Dáil Éireann have the responsibility of deciding the destiny of Ireland in the approaching deliberations', they said, 'in the course of which they will be sure to have before their minds the best interests of the country and the wishes of the people to whom they and we happily belong'.[105] The statement was one of implicit trust and confidence in the Dáil. The plea to ratify the Treaty was a mild one and the TDs were, more or less, left free to vote their conscience.

For many of the bishops, however, the statement did not go far enough. As the debates in the Dáil dragged on into the New Year several moved to back the Treaty more forcibly. Speaking on 31 December, Hallinan argued that Ireland was now getting substantially what she had suffered and fought for. Some accidentals were still wanting, he said, but these could be resolved 'through the natural use and peaceful evolution of what we are getting'. He warned that rejection would lead to a renewal of war in which Ireland, 'distracted and divided, would suffer disastrous defeat and be placed once more, bleeding and broken, at the feet and mercy of England'. He urged those in the Dáil to reflect the views being expressed across the country and ratify the Treaty.[106]

The archbishops, too, issued statements backing ratification. Speaking in Armagh Cathedral on 1 January 1922, Logue declared that the settlement gave everything substantial which was necessary for the welfare and progress of the country. The only alternative to acceptance was a return to coercion and oppression. He prayed that Almighty God would preserve them from the disaster that rejection of the Treaty would bring.[107] The Treaty was finally ratified in the Dáil by the narrow margin of sixty-four votes to fifty-seven on 7 January 1922. In one of his last acts, Benedict forwarded his congratulations to both King George and the deputies in the Dáil.[108] Logue contacted Byrne on 21 January informing him of news from Rome that the Pope had died. On the following day, he departed for the conclave to elect a successor.[109]

The ending of the Dáil debates did not settle the disputes or ease the divisions within the republican movement on acceptance of the Treaty. On 13 January, de Valera explained the republican position in a long and rather rambling letter to John Hagan at the Irish College. He compared the two sides in the debate to a party crossing a desert. Some stopped at an oasis and would go no further but some went on. 'They divided', he went on, 'sorrowfully, but without recriminations. I conceived it my duty to be with the hardier spirits – the pioneer party.'[110] The President was unclear on just how the divisions on the Treaty could be resolved without recriminations. For his part, Hagan resented the march stolen on the Irish

College by the bishops' unflinching support for the Treaty. The arrival of Logue in Rome for the conclave caused him further anxiety. In February, he complained bitterly to the Bishop of Raphoe that Logue was promoting the Treaty at the Holy See. 'I am sorry to say', he told O'Donnell, 'he went in for cultivating the union of hearts and how very well off we are under the order of things'. The Rector thought such a position was premature. He was also unhappy that the Provisional Government had begun lobbying at the Vatican for recognition and a permanent presence with the arrival there of George Gavan Duffy. Hagan found this extremely irksome. 'Duffy', he told O'Donnell, 'has the brain of a sparrow and the outlook of a Maori'.[111]

The Rector, however, had drastically underestimated the level of backing for the Treaty among the Irish bishops. In their Lenten pastorals, the archbishops were united in their alarm that dissent continued following the ratification. Logue forwarded his pastoral from Rome on 26 February and declared he had been deeply pained to hear 'that the benefits of the settlement are endangered and the return of real peace impeded by divisions among our own people'. Edward Byrne in Dublin issued a forceful endorsement of the Treaty, declaring that it offered, instead of an alien government, 'an Irish government which will have knowledge of our people's needs and may be expected to take a real interest in solving the many problems that concern our people's well-being'.[112] In the hope of healing some of the political divisions over the Treaty, Byrne invited both factions to attend a conference in the Mansion House.

Logue was sceptical about the chances for the conference. He told Byrne on 5 April that he had 'no confidence in the conference with the Valera [*sic*] Party. They would wrangle for days about their shadowy republic and their obligations to it'. For the cardinal, republican dissent validated his long held suspicion and distrust of de Valera. 'Judging by the past', he told Byrne, 'I believe that if an agreement were come to, these people would not keep it. The people should be warned solemnly not to let what they have won be filched away from them.'[113] It is difficult to know which past experiences Logue was referring to. Any dealings he had had with de Valera and Sinn Féin, and these were fleeting, had turned out more or less satisfactorily. His dislike of the President was never fully explained but Logue often felt the need to articulate it, now more than ever. His attitude towards the proposed Mansion House conference changed, however, as the divergence in the republican movement took an alarming turn.

On 14 April 1922, a detachment of IRA volunteers led by Rory O'Connor seized and occupied the Four Courts in Dublin in defiance of the Treaty and the Provisional Government. A more conciliatory Logue contacted Byrne on 15 April to acknowledge that a sigh of relief had gone through the country at the news of the impending meeting in Dublin. He earnestly hoped that an agreement could be reached. Despite all that was at stake, however, and the evidently deteriorating situation in the country, Logue was unable to shake his old animosities. Even if a settlement could be effected, he said, 'I fear it will be hard to keep de Valera and his party from wriggling out of every agreement reached. This has been the experience of all past conferences.'[114]

When the meeting got under way, Byrne's hastily scribbled minutes recorded the gulf between the politicians and the growing bitterness of the division. The archbishop's appeal had been founded on the hope that the conference would not involve interference with political beliefs or dictate those beliefs. Both factions had become entrenched and their intransigence was clearly evident in angry exchanges between those present. Cathal Brugha refused to recognise the Provisional Government or the Irish Free State as legitimate. Arthur Griffith accused the IRA garrison in the Four Courts of repudiating Dáil Éireann. He declared that he could not sit and talk with mutineers. Michael Collins, however, was more conciliatory and offered the idea of an appeal to the Irish people in the form of a referendum.[115]

In spite of the wrangling and divisions throughout the republican movement, the Provisional Government proceeded with the task of drafting a constitution for the Irish Free State. The bishops had been involved from the outset and Logue was keen to enhance the input of the hierarchy. He had seen preliminary drafts in March 1922 but, as he confessed to the Bishop of Dromore, Edward Mulhern, he could not make much of them. Logue, however, knew what he did not want. 'Those engaged in drawing up the constitution', he told Mulhern, 'should remember that it is being drawn up for a Catholic country, not for a soviet of Russia'. Care must be taken, he went on, that a pagan constitution was not foisted upon them.

To this end, Logue made the decision that the bishops should have a final say on the shape of the new constitution. 'It must be submitted to the bishops', he said, 'and a committee of theologians aided by lawyers should examine it and see that it is in accordance with the principles of Christianity'. Logue was adamant that, though they sought no special treatment, the areas in which he believed Catholics had been disadvantaged in the past should now be put right. This included state funding of religious education. Moreover, it was his fundamental belief that the state should proactively pursue a Christian agenda. It should undertake to guard and protect public morals and punish those who opposed them. The sanctity, unity and stability of Christian marriage must be enshrined in any new constitution. If an unchristian constitution were sprung on them at the last moment, 'without careful examination and consolidation, we shall certainly not advise our flock to vote for it'.[116]

For someone convinced that politics could not and should not be separated from religion, the framing of the constitution offered Logue an opportunity to finesse a Christian agenda upon a Government in serious jeopardy. He put the bishops at the centre of shaping the new Irish Free State and ensured that his own agenda – public morality, education and Christian marriage – became that of the Government. In this way, Logue restored some of the political influence which the Church had lost since 1916. Although the republican movement cherished its clerical supporters and activists, the dominance of Sinn Féin had been achieved largely despite the bishops. Now the Church was again an integral part of the political process in Ireland, perhaps even more so than during the era of Home Rule. Given the threats to its very existence, the open rebellion of O'Connor and the hectoring dissent of de Valera, the Provisional Government simply could not afford to have the constitution vetoed by the bishops.

On 24 March, Logue was informed that his recommendations, or demands, had been wholly accepted by the bishops' committee working on the constitution. The Bishop of Clogher, Patrick McKenna, told him, 'yours was a very wise decision because the wording of some of the clauses will need very careful reading to keep them within the proper limits'. He also enclosed a summary of the principles which would be included in the constitution. Marriage, as the basis of family life, would be under the special protection of the state. All attacks on the purity, health and sacredness of family life would be forbidden. Divorce was ruled out as the state was required to recognise the inviolable sanctity of the marital bond. Religious teaching was to be obligatory for all children under the age of eighteen. Under the constitution, there was no established Church. Liberty of conscience and religion was guaranteed to all citizens. The bishops' committee, however, while acknowledging this clause and allowing freedom of dissent to individuals, considered it their duty to uphold the basic Christian ideals of parental authority, family life, religious education and private property.[117]

Logue was concerned over the increasing tension and climate of lawlessness in the country as sections of the IRA moved once again to a war footing. He told O'Donnell on 8 April, 'at present, owing to the action of the Valera [*sic*] Party, the interests of the country are likely to go to ruin'. He deplored the ominous mutterings of insurrection emanating from the IRA. 'The people of Ireland', he said, 'were to be deprived of the liberty of declaring their will by free election. The country is to be placed under an armed dictatorship. English tyranny pales before the present tyranny.'[118] At the meeting of the Standing Committee on 26 April 1922, the bishops met the threat of civil war head on. They issued a strident and definitive statement on the legitimacy of Dáil Éireann as the rightful Government of Ireland. 'As to the organ of supreme authority in this country at present', they said, 'in practice there can be no doubt as long as the Dáil and the Provisional Government act in unison as they have hitherto done'. They denounced the IRA as espousing principles which were contrary to the law of God, especially 'the claim that the army, or part of it, can without any authority from the nation, declare itself independent of all civil authority'. The prospect of an IRA coup filled them with alarm and horror. 'What is this', they said, 'but to murder the free soul of Ireland and what national crime could be more shameful and wicked?'[119]

Although the bishops provided a unified front there were some concerns in the hierarchy over the overt political alignment of the Church behind the Provisional Government. On 8 April the Archbishop of Cashel, John Harty, wrote to the Archbishop of Dublin regarding the impending meeting at Maynooth to urge caution. He believed that the bishops should push the idea of a free vote in any referendum rather than issue a ringing endorsement of the treaty. If the bishops, he told Byrne, 'were to take sides in the political issue I am of the opinion that their meeting would do more harm than good'. Harty believed that if they were of the same mind, he and Byrne could carry their views.[120] However, the strident support for the Provisional Government showed the extent to which Logue's views, and those of like-minded bishops, dominated in the hierarchy. De Valera, who had remained outside the IRA deliberations, remarked only that it was a pity that the hierarchy had not showed similar support for the Dáil during the Anglo-Irish War.[121]

At their June meeting, the bishops once again backed the Provisional Government. They called upon 'this Christian nation, in the name of the manhood of Ireland, to insist boldly on that organised government which the people unmistakably demand and without which Ireland must rush headlong into the abyss'.[122] The election for the Dáil, on the unspoken issue of the treaty, took place on 16 June, the day the constitution of the Free State was published. The result was a resounding triumph for pro-Treaty candidates. Republicans managed to win only twenty-two per cent of the vote.[123] With its mandate secure, the Provisional Government took decisive action against the rebels in the army and shelling of the Four Courts garrison began on 28 June 1922.

Notes

1 Lyons, *Ireland Since the Famine*, p. 402.

2 Hopkinson, *War of Independence*, p. 38.

3 Lenten pastoral, 20 Feb. 1919, Logue Papers, ADA, box 9, folder 6, 'Sermons and pastorals'.

4 *Ibid.*

5 O'Connor to Logue, 26 Nov. 1917, Logue Papers, ADA, box 7, folder 6, 'Political'.

6 Keogh, *The Vatican, the Bishops and Irish Politics*, p. 24.

7 O'Riordan to O'Donnell, 10 Feb. 1919, O'Donnell Papers, ADA, box 6, folder 1, 'Irish College'.

8 *ICD*, 1920, pp. 517–19.

9 Townshend, *British Campaign*, p. 31.

10 Curran Memoirs, Ó Ceallaigh Papers, NLI, MS 27712(2), p. 562.

11 Keogh, *The Vatican, the Bishops and Irish Politics*, p. 26.

12 Curran Memoirs, Ó Ceallaigh Papers, NLI, MS 27712(2), p. 562.

13 Walsh to O'Connell, 6 Nov. 1919, Walsh Papers, DDA, box 391, folder 386/4.

14 See Hagan to unidentified bishop, 13 Dec. 1920, Hagan Papers, AICR, no. 142 (1920).

15 Morrissey, *William Walsh*, p. 327.

16 Townshend, *British Campaign*, pp. 48–9.

17 Curran Memoirs, Ó Ceallaigh Papers, NLI, MS 27712(2), p. 586.

18 Letter to the Archdiocese, 20 Dec. 1920, Walsh Papers, DDA, box 391, folder 386/4.

19 *ICD*, 1921, p. 499.

20 *Irish Catholic*, 10 Jan. 1920.

21 *ICD*, 1921, pp. 548–9.

22 O'Doherty to Hagan, 30 Jan. 1920, Hagan Papers, AICR, no. 135 (1920).

23 Keogh, *The Vatican, the Bishops and Irish Politics*, p. 38.

24 *ICD*, 1921, p. 506.

25 *Ibid.*, pp. 506–7.

26 Hagan to O'Donnell, 12 June 1914, O'Donnell Papers, ADA, box 6, folder 1, 'Irish College.'

27 Logue to Walsh, 30 Oct. 1917, Walsh Papers, DDA, box 389, folder 385/5.

28 Keogh, *The Vatican, the Bishops and Irish Politics*, pp. 40–1.

29 Curran Memoirs, Ó Ceallaigh Papers, NLI, MS 27712(3), p. 620.

30 *Ibid.*, p. 615.

31 *Ibid.*, p. 616.
32 *ICD*, 1921, p. 519.
33 *Ibid.*, p. 550.
34 *Ibid*, p. 522.
35 *The Times*, 28 Feb. 1920.
36 Logue to O'Donnell, 1 Mar. 1920, O'Donnell Papers, box 9, folder 3, 'Patrick Cardinal O'Donnell'.
37 *The Times*, 27 Feb. 1920.
38 Miller, *Church, State and Nation*, p. 453.
39 *ICD*, 1921, p. 525.
40 Miller, *Church, State and Nation*, p. 453.
41 Greenwood to Logue, 30 Sept. 1920, Logue Papers, ADA, box 4, folder 1, 'Government'.
42 Logue to Greenwood, undated, Logue Papers, ADA, box 4, folder 1, 'Government'.
43 Hopkinson, ed., *Sturgis Diaries*, 2 Aug. 1920, p. 16.
44 *ICD*, 1921, p. 532.
45 *Ibid.*, p. 533.
46 Townshend, *British Campaign*, pp. 195–6.
47 *ICD*, 1921, pp. 558–9.
48 Bishops' pastoral, 10 Oct. 1920, Logue Papers, ADA, box 7, folder 1, 'Political'.
49 Costello, *Enduring the Most*, p. 141.
50 *Ibid.*, p. 210.
51 Morrissey, *William Walsh*, p. 337.
52 Hopkinson, ed., *Sturgis Diaries*, 30 Aug. 1920, p. 30.
53 *ICD*, 1921, pp. 556–9.
54 Morrissey, *William Walsh*, p. 338.
55 Keogh, *The Vatican, the Bishops and Irish Politics*, p. 56.
56 *ICD*, 1921, pp. 545–6.
57 *Ibid.*
58 Ó Ceallaigh to MacRory, 9 Dec. 1920, MacRory Papers, ADA, box 5, folder 3.
59 Ó Ceallaigh to Hagan, 9 Dec. 1920, Hagan Papers, AICR, no. 132 (1920).
60 Logue to Hagan, 10 Dec. 1920, Hagan Papers, AICR, no. 134 (1920).
61 O'Doherty to Hagan, 1 Feb. 1921, O'Donnell Papers, ADA, box 6, folder 1, 'Irish College'.
62 Hagan to Walsh, 23 Jan. 1921, Walsh Papers, DDA, box 393, folder 380/6.
63 Curran to O'Donnell, 29 Jan. 1921, O'Donnell Papers, ADA, box 6, folder 1, 'Irish College'.
64 Townshend, *British Campaign*, p. 113.
65 *Ibid.*, p. 138.
66 *ICD*, 1922, p. 504.
67 *Ibid.*
68 Keogh, *The Vatican, the Bishops and Irish Politics*, p. 60.

69 Ó Ceallaigh to Hagan, 23 Dec. 1920, Hagan Papers, AICR, no. 164 (1920).
70 Barry, *Guerrilla Days*, pp. 39, 57.
71 Hopkinson, ed., *Sturgis Diaries*, 13 Dec. 1920, p. 90.
72 Curran Memoirs, Ó Ceallaigh Papers, NLI, MS 27728(3), p. 501.
73 Hopkinson, ed., *Sturgis Diaries*, 15 Dec. 1920, p. 99.
74 *ICD*, 1922, p. 517.
75 *ICD*, 1921, p. 238.
76 *ICD*, 1922, p. 509.
77 *Ibid.*, pp. 517–18.
78 Curran to Walsh, 17 Jan. 1921, Walsh Papers, DDA, box 393, folder 380/6.
79 O'Connor to Byrne, 27 and 31 Jan. 1921, Byrne Papers, DDA, 'Government 1921–39'.
80 Hopkinson, ed., *Sturgis Diaries*, pp. 153–9.
81 Hopkinson, *War of Independence*, p. 189.
82 Miller, *Church, State and Nation*, p. 480.
83 Pakenham, *Peace by Ordeal*, p. 66.
84 Miller, *Church, State and Nation*, p. 481.
85 Curran Memoirs, Ó Ceallaigh Papers, NLI, MS 27728(3), p. 539.
86 *ICD*, 1922, p. 589.
87 Keogh, *The Vatican, the Bishops and Irish Politics*, p. 70.
88 *ICD*, 1922, p. 553.
89 *Ibid.*, p. 595.
90 *Ibid.*, p. 557.
91 *Ibid.*, p. 557.
92 Townshend, *British Campaign*, p. 197.
93 Keogh, *The Vatican, the Bishops and Irish Politics*, p. 73.
94 *ICD*, 1922, p. 514.
95 *Ibid.*, p. 563.
96 *Ibid.*, pp. 600–1.
97 Keogh, *The Vatican, the Bishops and Irish Politics*, p. 79.
98 Brownrigg to Byrne, 19 Oct. 1921, Byrne Papers, DDA, 'Ossory'.
99 Keogh, *The Vatican, the Bishops and Irish Politics*, p. 79.
100 Logue to Byrne, 9 Dec. 1921, Byrne Papers, DDA, 'Armagh'.
101 *Freeman's Journal*, 8 Dec. 1921.
102 Miller, *Church, State and Nation*, p. 490.
103 *Freeman's Journal*, 8 Dec. 1921.
104 *Ibid.*, 12 Dec. 1921.
105 *ICD*, 1923, p. 538.
106 *Ibid.*, p. 542.
107 *Ibid.*, p. 543.
108 *Ibid.*, p. 545.
109 Logue to Byrne, 21 Jan. 1922, Byrne Papers, DDA, 'Armagh'.
110 De Valera to Hagan, 13 Jan. 1922, Hagan Papers, AICR, no. 42 (1922).

111 Hagan to O'Donnell, 7 Feb. 1922, O'Donnell Papers, ADA, box 6, folder 1, 'Irish College'.
112 *ICD*, 1923, pp. 551–2.
113 Logue to Byrne, 5 Apr. 1922, Byrne Papers, DDA, 'Armagh'.
114 Logue to Byrne, 15 Apr. 1922, Byrne Papers, DDA, 'Armagh'.
115 Minute book, undated Apr. 1922, Byrne Papers, DDA, 'Office of the Executive Council'.
116 Logue to Mulhern, 22 Mar. 1922, Logue Papers, ADA, box 3, folder 8, 'Irish dioceses'.
117 McKenna to Logue, 24 Mar. 1922, Logue Papers, ADA, box 3, folder 8, 'Irish dioceses'.
118 Logue to O'Donnell, 8 Apr. 1922, O'Donnell Papers, ADA, box 9, folder 3, 'Patrick Cardinal O'Donnell'.
119 *ICD*, 1923, pp. 598–600.
120 Harty to Byrne, 8 Apr. 1922, Byrne Papers, DDA, 'Cashel'.
121 Curran, *Irish Free State*, p. 184.
122 *ICD*, 1923, p. 607.
123 Hopkinson, *Green Against Green*, pp. 109–10.

9

Two Irelands

Civil war

The attack on the Four Courts confirmed the outbreak of a conflict which had been simmering since February. From the outset, the bishops moved quickly to use all the moral pressure and theological weapons at their disposal to uphold the authority of the Free State. On 16 July 1922 Logue condemned IRA units operating around Carlingford. He told a congregation that the country had never dreamt of liberties such as were afforded by the Treaty. He denounced republicans as a mere faction who were flouting the Government nominated by themselves and the democratically expressed will of the people. As the IRA fell back on the tried and tested tactics of the Anglo-Irish War, Logue decried the recurrence of guerrilla warfare in Ireland as mere brigandage. Anyone guilty of raiding, looting or abetting such actions in the Carlingford area, he said, 'would by that very fact be excommunicated'.[1] While some of his colleagues merely appealed for peace, there was no mistaking the fact that the bishops were now morally and politically committed to the survival of the Irish Free State.[2]

This commitment was evident in the reaction among the episcopate to the deaths of Griffith and Collins in August. Logue was particularly saddened. On receiving the news of Griffith's death on 12 August he sent a telegram to the Dáil stating that 'it is a great blow to Ireland when she most needs a sane president's temperate guidance'. The cardinal was stunned ten days later on receiving word of the death in an ambush of Michael Collins. 'This second blow to the hopes of Ireland', he said, 'should awaken the consciences even of those misguided men who show their love of country by drenching its soil with blood and leaving behind them a trail of hideous ruin and destruction'.[3] Logue's comments showed a remarkable change in attitude from the previous conflict. Leading figures in the Anglo-Irish War were now rehabilitated, not by their actions, but through the righteousness of their cause in defending the Free State. The architect of what the cardinal had described as 'cold-blooded murder' on Bloody Sunday 1921 was now 'the young patriot, brave and wise' and the chief hope for a peaceful and prosperous Ireland.

The deaths of Collins and Griffith robbed the Provisional Government of an irreplaceable reservoir of talent and intellect at a time of great crisis.[4] The reins of the Provisional Government were taken up by the Local Government Minister in the first Dáil, William Cosgrave. The new President lacked the charisma of Collins and, perhaps, the intellectual gravitas of Griffith but he brought with him the utter conviction that the Free State had to be preserved. Because of the precarious security situation in Dublin, the Dáil had not met since before the assault on the Four Courts. Following the ambush on Michael Collins, the Dáil passed a Public Safety Bill on 22 September 1922 which was intended to arm the State with sufficient powers to defeat the insurrection. The measures contained in the bill were remarkably similar to those of the Restoration of Order in Ireland Act of 1920. Military tribunals replaced the system of Dáil courts and the death penalty was instituted for a range of offences, including possession of firearms. Sweeping powers of arrest were introduced and a concerted campaign of internment was put into effect. Prior to the Government offensive, republicans were offered an amnesty wherein they could surrender their weapons and take an oath recognising the legitimacy of the Irish Free State.[5]

Along with strengthening the apparatus necessary for a successful counter-insurgency campaign, the Provisional Government used the close relationship with the bishops to ask that they pronounce on the condition of the country. This request found the hierarchy as anxious as Cosgrave for the preservation of the new State.[6] The result was a statement issued from the bishops' meeting in October which was every bit as powerful as the condemnation of the British Government in 1920. The bishops accused republicans of attacking their country as if it were a foreign power. They declared that they had no legitimate authority for their campaign and, more significantly, branded the republican movement as being inherently opposed to Catholic doctrine. 'In spite of their obvious sin and the fact of their unlawful rebellion', they went on, 'they still play the role of good Catholics and demand the Sacraments'.

Consequently, the bishops moved to cut republicans off from the Church. All those who participated in the insurrection were guilty of the gravest sin and would not be absolved in confession nor admitted to holy communion. It was a stunning counter-blow which was aimed at removing any sense of moral sanction from republicans and their campaign. The bishops had effectively politicised the sacraments by placing the faculties of the Church at the sole disposal of disinterested parties and those loyal to the Provisional Government. Moreover, the hierarchy declared that any priests who aided the 'irregulars' were 'false to their sacred duty and are guilty of the greatest scandal and will not be allowed to retain the faculties they hold from us'.[7]

Hopkinson has argued that the bishops' decree was divisive and difficult to enforce.[8] It was certainly true that the strictures laid down traded heavily on the oaths of obedience sworn by the clergy to their ordinaries. There is evidence, however, that a sizeable portion of the junior clergy obeyed the directive and refused holy communion to republicans in churches and to internees.[9] Nevertheless, republicans could count on the support of at least some of the clergy. In March 1923, for example, the Free State's Commander-in-Chief, Richard Mulcahy, complained to Byrne over a letter sent to an internee from a priest. Father John Costello had written to the prisoner Bernard Fagan declaring that 'the honour of Ireland will not be washed clean till a few of these FS government members are set dancing on air. May the Lord have mercy on their souls then!'[10] In February, Mulcahy had informed Byrne of the arrest by CID in Dublin of Father P. Brown of Maynooth. In his possession was a list of twenty-five priests sympathetic to the republican cause.[11]

For their part, republicans reacted angrily to the attempt to ostracise them from their Church. On 31 October 1922 de Valera issued a protest to the Vatican denouncing the bishops for 'presuming to pronounce an authoritative judgement upon the question of constitutional and political fact now in Ireland'. He accused the hierarchy of using the sanction of religion to enforce their political views and 'compel acquiescence on the part of Irish republicans'.[12] If repentance was required before the sacraments could be administered, the Church now had a political measure for that repentance in the form of a pledge of allegiance to the Irish Free State. The bishops' pastoral had little discernible effect on the level of violence save that, in seeking to make pariahs out of republicans, it embittered the conflict still further.[13]

Clergy who were close to the republican movement reacted badly to the position adopted by the hierarchy. John Hagan in Rome viewed developments with considerable anxiety. He and his Vice-Rector, Michael Curran, had opposed the Treaty from the outset and were horrified to find their closest political contacts on the receiving end of an all-out offensive by the Government under episcopal sanction. The Rector met with Byrne in

Dublin on 8 October 1922 and was relieved to find the archbishop sharing his concerns over the political positioning of the hierarchy. 'I am glad', Hagan told Curran, 'he is opposed to Armagh's tactic of nagging and is inclined to the principle that having expressed their mind they ought to leave it at that'.[14] If Hagan had any illusions, however, that Byrne could end the policy of episcopal 'nagging' of republicans, they were shattered by the October pastoral. He was supremely conscious of the fact that the uncompromising stance taken by the bishops had made his own position and that of the Irish College, with its republican tendencies, extremely precarious. Hagan found the pastoral embarrassing and believed it would do religion no good at all. He told Curran of an occasion after its publication when a crowd gathered on the steps of the Mansion House to boo and hiss the bishops.[15] However, he had grossly underestimated the determination of Logue and his colleagues to give their utmost support to the Government.

Despite their support for the State, some of the bishops reacted badly to the Government's unflinching determination to crush republicans. In November 1922, the Bishop of Raphoe, Patrick O'Donnell, appealed for clemency for Erskine Childers who faced execution for possession of a small pistol which had been given to him by Michael Collins.[16] The execution, however, was carried out regardless. Cosgrave was committed to the policy of executions. 'Although I have always objected to the death penalty', he told the Dáil, 'there is no way that I know of in which ordered conditions can be restored in this country'. He was primarily concerned with the safety of Government troops, he said, and believed that this onerous responsibility on the Government, to preserve the State at all costs, had to be undertaken.[17] In response to the murder in Dublin of Seán McHales TD, the Government ordered the execution in reprisal of four leading republicans, Rory O'Connor, Liam Mellows, Joe McKelvey and Dick Barret.

There was no episcopal protest at the harsh treatment meted out to republicans. Hagan was particularly concerned by the silence of the hierarchy. In March 1923 he told O'Donnell that the executions would never have been possible had the bishops not given their corporate sanction by the October pastoral.[18] The extent to which the Government drew moral licence from the bishops was shown in a letter from William Cosgrave to Byrne in November 1922. The Archbishop of Dublin had asked for clemency for several women prisoners who had commenced a hunger-strike in Mountjoy. Cosgrave refused to extend any concession on this matter or on the policy of executions. 'Before God and man', he told Byrne, 'we must take responsibility for all these actions, believing firmly that in doing so we are acting in the spirit of the solemn teaching of our highest moral authority'. Taking an exert from the October pastoral, he told the archbishop 'that in all this there is no question of mere politics but of what is morally right or wrong according to the divine law'.[19]

Despite Cosgrave's convictions concerning his own and the Government's righteousness, the reprisals carried out on 7 December horrified Byrne. Of all the bishops, he maintained the closest contact with the Executive. Although the hierarchy maintained its policy of absolute support for the Government, the Archbishop of Dublin continued to take a more conciliatory and measured approach. Byrne was unimpressed with Cosgrave's attempts to presume approbation from the bishops for his every act and protested against the December reprisals in the strongest terms. He told the president he had heard the news of the killings with dismay. Such an act, he said, was completely unjust and could only serve to alienate whatever friends the Government had.[20] Byrne's protests succeeded in curbing the Government's inclination to match murder with murder and the policy of reprisals was abandoned. Prisoners were still executed but they were granted the formality of a trial first.[21]

The intensity and growing bitterness of the war in Ireland caused much anxiety and alarm in Rome. On 12 December 1922 Michael Curran told O'Donnell that the executions had left him feeling humiliated and ashamed. 'Séan McHales' murder was shocking', he said, 'but the falling back by the government on reprisals opens up the most horrible possibilities and reveals how normal reason has fled the country'.[22] Nevertheless, both Curran and Hagan continued to place the Irish College at the disposal of republicans. In October de Valera had been installed as President of a republican government in Ireland and, two months later, Hagan facilitated a meeting between representatives of that republic and the Pope.[23] Logue was incensed by the visit. In January 1923 he received a letter from Cardinal Gasparri, the Vatican Secretary of State, containing an appeal against the bishops. Writing to Byrne he impatiently dismissed republican explanations of their position and the history of the first and second Dáil. 'The only charge they can bring against us is that we commented on the state of the country', he told the archbishop. The real complaint was that the bishops had deprived republicans of the sacraments, which was untrue. 'We made no reserve case', he went on, 'but merely stated that those who persisted in committing crimes which we enumerated were not fit for the sacraments which is the plain doctrine of the Church. Unrepentant sinners are not fit for the sacraments.'[24]

This same dismissive attitude towards republicans was very much in evidence in Logue's Lenten pastoral published in February 1923. He accused them of wreaking war on the country over a formulation of words and oaths. 'The storm has long since burst', he said, 'and never before in the world's history did such a wild and disruptive hurricane spring from such a thin, intangible, unsubstantial vapour'. The Irish Free State provided all the freedoms a republic could promise and he denounced republicans for leading the young and impressionable astray and putting rifles in the hands of boys.[25] Unlike Byrne, Logue saw no reason for compromise or conciliation. While the other archbishops appealed for peace in their own pastorals, his remained full of the language of condemnation and contempt. He resented republican rejectionism, their resorting to what he viewed as needless insurrection and the terrible waste of life. The cause of much of Logue's resentment, however, was the fact that republicans had flouted and questioned the authority of the bishops.

Even before word reached him of the republican delegation to Rome, Logue had favoured some kind of papal intervention in the conflict. This was not quite a reversal of the Irish Church's long-held aversion to Roman intervention in Irish politics. He wanted the Vatican to uphold the authority of the Irish episcopate and thereby help end republican opposition to the Free State. In November 1922, he shared his thoughts with Byrne. 'The authority of the bishops is impeached, vilified and condemned', he told the archbishop, 'and it is the part of the Holy See to support and maintain the authority of the bishops'. He had written to Gasparri arguing just that point. Logue's idea rather ignored the fact that the Irish had a poor record of listening to political remonstrations from Rome.[26]

The appointment of Salvatore Luzio as papal legate, despite rumours circulating in the Holy See, caught Hagan and Curran by surprise. On 8 March, Hagan told O'Donnell that the appointment had been made but that he knew nothing of the brief given to the legate or the scope of his mission.[27] Curran set out immediately to undermine the peace effort. He told O'Donnell that Luzio, a former professor of canon law at Maynooth, was merely a precursor for some kind of permanent papal presence in Ireland.[28] In the end, the mission dissolved into confusion and farce. Luzio arrived in Armagh in March 1923 and alienated Logue by suggesting he meet with republicans. He further angered Byrne by not consulting the archbishop before taking meetings in Dublin. The Government was not interested in the legate as, by now, the army had the upper hand in the conflict, and Cosgrave requested his recall at the end of April.[29]

By the spring of 1923, the war was effectively over. Since February, IRA activity had dropped sharply. Over ten thousand republicans were now in internment camps and the eight thousand still at large were faced by over forty thousand Government troops.[30] On 24 April Logue reported the turning of the tide in a letter to Hagan. Things were going quiet, he said, the greater part of republican forces and nearly all the leadership had either been killed or were in prison. Despite his abhorrence of the insurrection, the cardinal viewed the imminent end of the conflict with a deep sense of sadness rather than satisfaction. 'The misery is', he told Hagan, 'that so many young lives on both sides have been sacrificed'.[31] Despite the subsequent unconditional surrender of the IRA, the Free State Government maintained its war footing and continued to hold twelve thousand republicans in internment camps.[32]

By October, Cosgrave's reluctance to release political prisoners precipitated a mass hunger-strike among the internees. The sympathy with which the bishops had treated prison fasts during the Anglo-Irish War, however, was never extended to republicans in this conflict. Throughout 1923 there had been intermittent hunger-strikes in Dublin prisons. There was no formal episcopal pronouncement but Edward Byrne mounted what was in effect a lone campaign to secure clemency. In November 1922, for example, he had attempted to secure the release of Mary MacSwiney who, like her brother, Terence, had gone on hunger-strike. The archbishop told Cosgrave that MacSwiney's 'voluntary abstention from food will have a more harmful effect than her continued internment'. The President refused, arguing that women had played a prominent and most destructive part in the present revolt.[33] By April 1923 Cosgrave's attitude and that of the Government had hardened on the issue. He told Byrne that he believed each minister would rather resign than release these prisoners.[34]

The fact of hunger-strikes presented the Church with a new dilemma. Theologically they remained anathema and were now doubly in error following the October pastoral with its doctrinal condemnation of republicans and their cause. However, the morality of denying the sacraments to sick and dying prisoners was also of concern. Byrne chose to act with compassion. He had told Mary MacSwiney in February 1923 that 'danger of death is not in itself any reason for administering the Sacraments to a person indisposed for them'.[35] In April, however, in response to an appeal from three women on hunger-strike, Byrne rescinded the restrictions of the October pastoral and allowed the women to receive holy communion daily.[36]

Logue was reluctant to extend the same charity. The cardinal told Byrne on 27 October that he would likely have trouble. 'I have had two women from this town already', he said, 'and one of them was very wild and I am sorry to say that I lost my temper with her'. The women had gone to *Ara Coeli* to plead for Logue's intervention on behalf of their husbands who had joined the hunger-strike but found the cardinal unsympathetic. He told Byrne regarding one of the women, 'this same husband of hers was a troublesome character here'.[37] The archbishop was more sympathetic and on 28 October he appealed to Cosgrave to take action to end the hunger-strikes. 'No government, however strong', he said, 'could afford to allow thousands of men to die. It would arouse here such a revulsion of feeling that would shake the very foundation of the Free State.'[38] The divergence among some of the bishops in their handling of the strikes was illustrated in the reaction of the Bishop of Cork, Daniel Cohalan, to the death on hunger-strike of Dennis Barry. Where Byrne was prepared to bend the strictures of the October pastoral, Cohalan, the bishop who had buried Terence MacSwiney with such honour, refused to give Barry the burial rites of the Church. 'Anyone who deliberately takes his own life', he explained, 'is deprived of a Christian burial and I shall interpret that law of the Church and refuse a Christian burial. I feel bound to do so.'[39]

Logue's patience, already wearing thin, snapped in November and he issued a curt letter aimed at both republicans and the Free State Government. He called the prison fasts 'foolish and ineffective and of very dubious morality' and demanded that republicans abandon this 'dangerous and unlawful expedient'. He also saw no reason for the Government to continue to detain republicans if they were not guilty of specific crimes and called for their immediate release.[40] It is impossible to say how much effect Logue's intervention had, but the strike was called off at the end of November and releases commenced soon after. The cardinal's letter had been published in the *Osservatore Romano* and Hagan noted with incredulity that Logue was being credited with not only ending the hunger-strikes but also securing the release of eight thousand prisoners. He had told Pius XI that the reports had been exaggerated.[41]

The State that emerged following the steadfast and unflinching support of Logue and the hierarchy was not quite a theocracy. But as Miller has pointed out, 'the Church had a role in the new state as would be the envy of any Churchman throughout the world'. As an interest group, it certainly had more influence than any other.[42] Keogh has argued that, in private, the bishops acknowledged the debt of gratitude owed to William Cosgrave for his role in preserving the Free State.[43] The debt, however, was a mutual one. In return for their unflagging support the hierarchy expected, and received, action to protect Catholic principles. Thus, for example, when an amendment on divorce was introduced in the Irish Senate, the Government moved quickly to have it quashed at the request of the bishops.[44] In one of the new Irish states, at least, Logue had been instrumental in reversing the Catholic grievances which had caused him so much angst throughout his career. The Irish Free State at last offered him the prospect of that longed-for union between politics and religion.

Northern Ireland

It had been Logue's expressed fear that the Irish bishops would go down to posterity as the 'destroyers of the country'.[45] It is difficult to see, however, what more he and the episcopate could have done in the face of the British Government's unflagging commitment to the cause of Ulster Unionism. Logue had signed petitions, issued denunciations of partition and, along with his colleagues, had battled since 1916 to avoid the dismemberment of the country. He had done his utmost to deliver a united nationalist protest vote in the form of the 1918 electoral pact. In the end the bishops simply had no response that would reverse Lloyd George's determination on partition. As the Prime Minister told the Cabinet in 1920, 'we will not break the pledges which successive governments have given to the six counties of Ulster. They must not be coerced into any form of government they do not desire.'[46] The introduction of the Government of Ireland Bill in 1920 presented the Irish bishops with partition as a *fait accompli*.

Before the structures of the new state were established the north was convulsed by violence. In May 1920 Derry experienced prolonged engagements between IRA units and elements of the UVF. Tensions were further heightened as anti-partition candidates polled well in local government elections under proportional representation. Nationalists won a majority on Derry Corporation and promptly declared the city's allegiance to the Dáil.[47] In the summer of 1920 the sectarian tension which had been simmering since the beginning of the year erupted into violence in Belfast. In July a series of prolonged attacks against Catholics in the city followed the assassination of Lieutenant-Colonel F. Smyth, an RIC District Commissioner, in Cork. Smyth had been born in Ulster and, in retaliation for the refusal of southern railway workers to ship the body to Belfast, Protestant mobs rampaged through the shipyards on Queen's Island driving Catholics from work. The action spread beyond the city with attacks on Catholic businesses and the expulsion of Catholic workers from engineering works and mills across the north.[48]

The activity of IRA units contributed to the air of crisis which engulfed the new state. Attacks on the police were met with reprisals against Catholics. The Provisional Government in Belfast, which had been established to oversee the implementation of the Government of Ireland Bill, responded to the violence with the creation of the Ulster Special Constabulary. Ostensibly a paramilitary force, the A, B and C Specials were primarily intended not to restore order but to defend the new state against the perceived threat from republicans and nationalists. Catholic politicians viewed the new body with suspicion and fear. Joe Devlin condemned the Provisional Government for its creation of the new force. 'Their pogrom is to be made less difficult', he said, 'instead of paving stones and sticks they are to have rifles'.[49]

The new police followed the policy of reprisal and counter-terror which characterised the efforts of Crown forces against republicans in the south. Acts of revenge were utterly indiscriminate and, often, there was scant difference between the police and the Protestant mobs that attacked Catholic homes and businesses.[50] On 10 June 1920 three Catholics were murdered in reprisal for a gun attack on police in Belfast. On 12 June two more were shot dead following an attack on a special constable. Meanwhile the campaigns of intimidation and arson continued. At the end of August the Dáil moved to take action in response to the continuing pogroms in Belfast by instituting a boycott of goods from the city.

The Catholic bishops of northern dioceses were subject to the same threats to their safety faced by some of their southern colleagues. On 26 June the *Catholic Times* reported that the home of the Bishop of Derry, Charles McHugh, had been attacked by gunmen.[51] In the same month, Logue revealed that he had received death threats. Speaking in Maynooth, he made light of the matter, joking that, like Oliver Plunkett, he had his own chance of martyrdom if he ever came within range of those 'Orange rifles that were causing so much depredation in the north'. The following day, however, while addressing the Maynooth Union, he treated the threats more seriously. He told his audience that a time had been set for him but he was grateful to the one who had sent the warning as it gave him time to prepare. He did not know for sure if the threat on his life was serious or not but he was unafraid. 'From the day I came to Armagh', he said, 'and from the day I was bishop and was ordained a priest, I never consciously said one word to offend any man'.[52]

The outrage among the bishops at what they perceived as the inability of the British Government to rein in the worst excesses in Northern Ireland, and the abject failure of the Provisional Government there to defend Catholics, was given full vent in their pastoral issued on 10 October 1920. The bishops stated the number of expelled workers had now reached 23,000. They prayed that the eyes of England would be opened to the iniquity of furnishing Ulster bigotry with its own Government and Special Constabulary. Such actions, they said, served only to 'enable it all the more readily to trample underfoot the victims of its intolerance'. The bishops bitterly condemned the British Government's commitment which demanded that Ulster 'must not suffer the contamination of a Dublin parliament. But all Ireland must be coerced for the sake of the north-east'.[53] The problem for Logue and his colleagues was that on the question of Ulster few people were listening.

The October pastoral reflected much of Logue's current thinking on the situation in Ireland. In his letter to the Chief Secretary in September 1920 he had condemned the pogroms and the administration's tolerance of the UVF. 'It is hard to believe', he told Greenwood, 'that any responsible government with the examples of Derry, Belfast, Lisburn and other towns before their eyes . . . would arm and cast them loose among their Catholic neighbours'.[54] Despite the impassioned pleas and harsh words in the October pastoral, the Ulster question remained a source of confusion for the Church's potential allies in Europe. Their condemnation of the actions of British forces was quite understandable, as Michael Curran informed William Walsh. The October pastoral had been well received in Rome but 'many foreigners naturally get lost in the "Ulster" sections of that long statement'.[55]

As the Government of Ireland Bill passed into law at the end of 1920 Logue condemned the lack of safeguards provided for Catholics in the new state. In previous Home Rule Bills, he said, much had made of the need to protect the interests of the Protestant minority in southern Ireland. 'Now', he said in an interview with the press, 'there is not a word about protecting the interests, especially the spiritual interests, of the large Catholic minority'.[56] The enactment of the partition bill paved the way for elections to the new northern Parliament in 1921. Logue, however, had no need to intervene as he had been forced to do on previous occasions.[57] As the election approached, a deal was brokered in Dublin by Séan McEntee, TD for South Monaghan, which entailed an electoral pact similar to that reached in 1918. Nationalists, however, agreed to abstain from taking up seats in accordance with the wishes of Sinn Féin.[58] On the eve of the election, de Valera met with the Ulster Unionist leader, Sir James Craig, in Dublin but the conference failed to produce any substantial agreement. Amid an upsurge in political and sectarian violence the general election went ahead in May 1921. The turnout was around ninety per cent and the Irish Party and Sinn Féin managed to win twelve seats between them. Unionists, with a massive turnout, secured the remaining forty seats. The total Unionist vote stood at 343,355 to the Nationalist total of 169,751. The Provisional Government did not fail to note that Sinn Féin polled the lion's share of the nationalist vote, which stood at 102,698.[59]

On 8 June the Irish civil servant Mark Sturgis wrote in his diary, 'Ireland has a new parliament for the first time since the Act of Union and who, ten years ago, would have dreamed that Ireland's first parliament would have been in Belfast?'[60] The establishment of what would be called Northern Ireland caused only dismay among nationalists. Logue was invited to the state opening but refused to attend, causing Unionist politicians to decry this 'insult to Ulster'.[61] The Irish episcopate could not and would not acknowledge the legitimacy of the new Parliament. This was evident in their refusal even to call the new state 'Northern Ireland'. It was consistently referred to as the 'Six Counties', 'North-East Ulster', or simply the 'the North'. The *Catholic Times* later derided the new entity as 'Carsonia'.[62] The bishops viewed the new state with a mixture of foreboding and fear. They regarded the pogroms as only the beginning of a concerted offensive against Catholicism, particularly Catholic education. On 14 June Logue told an audience in Cookstown, 'I cannot lose sight of the fact that before the people of these northern counties there lies a future which is doubtful and which fills me with anxiety'. Judging by the public utterances of those soon to be in authority there, he went on, 'we have a time of persecution before us'.[63]

Logue refused to recognise or participate in the new state. At the end of August 1921, Northern Ireland's Education Minister, Lord Londonderry, contacted the cardinal to invite him to participate in a Government education commission. 'I should be glad', he told Logue, 'if your Eminence would be good enough to give me the names of four Catholic representatives whom I should ask to serve on the committee. One of which might represent Catholic interests.'[64] Logue was in no mood to aid the Government in any way. He viewed the new commission as the first step in the long dreaded assault on Catholic education. In a terse reply, he told Londonderry that normally he would be glad to cooperate in any collaboration for the betterment of education. But, 'judging from the public utterances of some members of the Belfast Parliament and their sympathisers,

I have little doubt that an attack is being organised against our Catholic schools'. Logue told him he believed that the commission was no more than a pretext for this attack.[65]

Londonderry was rather taken aback and somewhat hurt by the vehemence of the cardinal's refusal. He complained to Ireland's Lord Lieutenant, Lord FitzAlan, who was himself Catholic, that Logue simply could not have understood what was being proposed. He further protested that he would do his utmost to lift the commission above political and sectarian prejudices. 'I cannot feel', he concluded, 'that there is any justice to Cardinal Logue's accusation'.[66] Londonderry was sufficiently stung by Logue's reaction to bring the matter to the attention of the Northern Ireland Cabinet on 9 September 1921. He suggested that a collective letter be sent to *Ara Coeli* castigating the cardinal for his accusations.[67] He personally wrote to Logue the following day to emphatically reject the accusation that the state was preparing to undermine Catholic schools.[68]

Buckland has argued that Logue's failure to participate in what became the Lynn Commission on education represented a lost opportunity and that this failure somehow made the Church complicit in the climate of discrimination which followed.[69] It is difficult to see, however, how Logue and the northern episcopate could have cooperated with a Government that they routinely accused of complicity in a wholesale campaign of murder and intimidation against Catholics. Logue could not countenance bestowing even the modicum of legitimacy on the Belfast regime that his cooperation might entail. The bishops preferred to put their faith in the Dáil as the only acceptable government in Ireland.

Such belief seemed vindicated in January 1922 when Sir James Craig and Michael Collins reached agreement at a summit meeting in London. The conference resulted in the ending of the Belfast boycott and an apparent resolution of the crisis over the expelled workers. Developments caused some alarm among northern nationalists but Collins managed to placate dissent by referring the partition question to the future working of the boundary commission established under the Treaty.[70] Despite this détente, the level of violence in Belfast and elsewhere showed no signs of diminishing. The following month a hand grenade was thrown into a group of children playing in Weaver Street in Belfast, killing six. In a country already numbed by a cavalcade of outrage, events in Weaver Street represented a shocking low. The coroner, James Graham, recorded that 'this was a most dastardly outrage. Poor innocent children have been attacked and killed. It was a shocking crime, fit to horrify the whole world.'[71] Churchill later told Collins that the incident was 'the worst thing which has happened in Ireland in the last three years'. Attacks such as this one, he said, had unquestionably cost Unionists some support in England.[72]

At the end of February a united appeal for peace was issued by Catholic, Church of Ireland and Methodist clergy in Belfast. 'We condemn in the strongest terms', they said, 'the murders and other forms of lawless violence that have taken place and which are a disgrace to any civilised community'.[73] In March two women were injured in a hand grenade attack on St Matthew's chapel in the Markets area of Belfast. At the end of the month eight members of the McMahon family were shot in their home in north Belfast. Six men died immediately and one later in hospital. Parkinson has described the shootings as an attempt to 'systematically eliminate the whole male line of the family'.[74] The murders sent a new frisson of horror throughout Ireland.

At the end of March Craig and Collins met again in London to try to effect some settlement to curb the violence. Although deeply disturbed by events in the north, the British Government was reluctant to intervene as the new administration resisted the introduction of martial law. The Northern Ireland Government had recently enacted special powers legislation giving it, in effect, its own version of the Restoration of Order in Ireland Act with sweeping powers of internment and summary justice. Collins was concerned that the act would provide new means to persecute Catholics. The conference in London resulted in another pact. The agreement bound both northern and southern governments to the restoration of peace. Craig agreed to a change in the make-up of the Special Constabulary to allow Catholics to join and take part in patrolling interface areas. Northern police were to be given new guidelines to curb excesses and improve discipline. Collins agreed to order the cessation of all IRA activities in the north. Arrangements were also made to provide for the return of expelled workers to their jobs. The border question was placed in the hands of the boundary commission.[75]

The northern bishops greeted the new deal with relief. Logue believed that if the pact was honestly and fairly carried out it was likely to lead to a satisfactory settlement and to peace.[76] The Bishop of Down and Connor also welcomed the respite offered by the agreement. In a statement to the press MacRory declared that it was only through reconciliation that peace could be established. He viewed the London settlement as a means to ending the systematic discrimination and attacks against Catholics in Belfast. 'Thank God the agreement now entered into', he said, 'seems to have been conceived in a new spirit which does them credit and which seems to promise recognition of our rights'.[77] Such was the level of optimism among the northern bishops that at a meeting in April they considered formal recognition of Northern Ireland through the framework of the Craig-Collins pact. Seán T. Ó Ceallaigh told John Hagan that the bishops had discussed the possibility of Catholics joining the Special Constabulary and the difficulty presented by swearing an oath of allegiance to the new state. It was Ó Ceallaigh's opinion that the bishops now realised that the Provisional Government in the south had 'thrown up the sponge' as far as fighting partition was concerned.[78]

By the time the bishops' Standing Committee met on 26 April, the initial optimism regarding the pact had evaporated. The agreement collapsed amid renewed violence. Sectarian attacks on Catholics in the north were now greeted with reprisals against Protestants living in the south. Beginning on 26 April 1922, Protestant homes and businesses in west Cork came under attack from republicans. By the following evening, ten had been shot dead. More attacks followed and the ensuing climate of fear caused many Protestant families to flee their homes.[79] There was genuine shock at the killings in Ireland and in Britain. On 30 April 1922, the Bishop of Cork, Daniel Cohalan condemned the attacks as a 'vicious circle of crime'.[80] At their meeting in June, the bishops denounced the attacks in the strongest terms as contrary to the teaching of the Catholic Church. 'No plea of reprisals', they went on, 'for treatment meted out with impunity to the Catholics in the Six Counties can justify these immoral attacks on life and property'.[81] Although events in the north provided some of the impetus for the attacks, Hart has argued that the actual spark was the shooting dead of IRA officer Michael O'Neill in Cork on 26 April.[82]

The bishops also renewed their condemnation of the Northern Government at their June meeting. 'The deadly fact of partition has been to ruin Ireland', they said, 'in the north-east there is no government, or if there be, it is not for Catholics any more than the Turk has government for the Armenians'. The British Government had been warned of the effect of putting power in the hands of people remarkable for their intolerance. 'Now they are backing their Turkey in Ireland with an army', they said, 'and are paying a sectarian police, not to uphold justice, but to follow the bent of unbridled bigotry'.[83]

In the summer months of 1922, Logue found himself in direct confrontation with Craig's administration. On the night of 25 May the car he was travelling in was stopped and searched at Lisnadill in County Armagh. The cardinal complained of his treatment in a letter to the press on 8 June.

Logue stated that he had not mentioned the matter previously for fear of causing irritation but that reports in the newspapers had played down the severity of the incident. He had remonstrated with police when they began to search his belongings but the order had been given to 'cover that man with a rifle'. Logue related that 'immediately a rifle was thrust under my nose and I was covered with a revolver'. Seeing the nervousness of the 'young lad' holding him at gunpoint, Logue asked that the gun be pointed away from him but was refused. 'So I sat there', he said, 'under the rifle and revolver while the search was going on'. The cardinal was returning to *Ara Coeli* from confirmations and he told how the box containing holy oils was also searched. When he protested, Logue was told that there were 'no ecclesiastical functions in this government; or something to that effect'.[84]

In their June statement the bishops denounced what they saw as harassment. 'For such maltreatment of an old man of such exalted station', they declared, 'there is scarcely a parallel in the annals of the most savage tribe'. They deemed it their solemn duty, they went on, 'to lay before the Holy Father and the whole civilised world a faint outline of the barbarities heaped upon him, who is the beloved head of the Irish Church'.[85] On 15 June 1922, however, Logue was again stopped and searched on his way to Newry. The outcry caused by this occasion forced the Colonial Office to intervene. On 17 June the Northern Ireland Cabinet Secretary, Wilfrid Spender, fielded the first of a series of enquiries from the Colonial Under-Secretary, Lionel Curtis, on the actions of police. Spender was annoyed that with all that was going on in the north Whitehall could bother him over what he saw as the trivial matter of Cardinal Logue. 'We are trying to stamp out murder', he told Curtis, 'and no citizen need object to being a little inconvenienced'. He had no time for this now as he had just heard of the murder of five Unionists in Armagh.[86] Despite his reluctance, Spender acceded to Curtis' request for a report from the Special police on the incidents. The RUC Area Commander, G. S. Maxwell, told Spender that the car carrying the cardinal had indeed been stopped but that Logue had not been manhandled in any way. Instructions had been given to patrols of B Specials in the area to refrain from stopping cars carrying church dignitaries of all religions.[87]

Curtis seemed somewhat mollified by Spender's response but reminded him that criticism of the police in Northern Ireland reflected badly on the Colonial Office and it was the Minister, Winston Churchill, who ultimately had to deal with it. It was of paramount importance that opportunities should not be handed to Sinn Féin – 'people whose genius for propaganda is almost incredible'. Curtis concluded with a vague admonishment that it was 'important not to antagonise Catholics as such'.[88] Spender blamed Logue for the trouble with the police. 'It is only right that you should be told', he informed Curtis, 'that the cardinal apparently did not use the road which had been agreed upon [with the police] and on which the Special Constabulary had been warned he would travel'.[89] However, the controversy refused to go away. On 26 June 1922 Craig was questioned on the matter during an interview with the *Irish Independent*. 'You would think', he replied testily, 'the old man had been injured. Our account of it is that he did not give his name until it was all over.' All cars were stopped as a matter of policy, he went on, and 'if he had been anxious for peace in the north he would have been pleased to find the net so fine'.[90] Such remarks did not play well in England, though Sir Samuel Watt, the Northern Ireland Parliamentary Secretary, told Spender that the words attributed to Craig did not seem like something the Prime Minister would say.[91]

Despite the furore and the warnings from London, Logue was again stopped by the police at the funeral of the Reverend Dr Loughran near Jonesborough in July. The press reported that the cortege was stopped by the RUC who proceeded in a search of the clergy there which was 'needlessly insulting'. One priest who was rather slow in complying with an order to put up his hands was told that 'if he did not put up his hands damned quickly there would be another priest's funeral there'. Several priests were poked with rifles and told, 'we are sick of you people'. Logue himself was removed from his car and physically searched.[92] The *Catholic Herald* condemned this latest episode in what they called a campaign of persecution against the cardinal. 'Craig's lambs', the editorial declared, 'possibly believing that best way to bait a Catholic is to insult his clergy, have never lost an opportunity of carrying out their blackguardly designs'.[93]

If anything, the July incident caused more controversy than the others. On 5 August FitzAlan wrote to Craig regarding the police action. 'I find it difficult, if not impossible', he said, 'to imagine what real necessity there could be for such conduct'. He honestly believed, however, that no one would condemn such harassment more than the Prime Minister.[94] On 10 August the Colonial Office communicated its displeasure at being embroiled in another controversy regarding Logue. Mark Sturgis, who had transferred to London from Dublin Castle, sent Craig part of a letter of protest from the Catholic Federation of Salford which had been sent to Churchill. The Federation denounced the treatment of the cardinal and the threat to bayonet the eighty-year-old Canon O'Donnell from Dundalk.[95]

In response to the criticism Craig told the Lord Lieutenant that he would personally request a report on the incident from the Minister for Home Affairs and the Security Commander for Northern Ireland, General Solly-Flood.[96] He later informed Sturgis that the 'cardinal is very difficult to deal with'. He consistently refused to reveal his identity when stopped and he 'refused the accommodation we have offered him in the form of a regular member of the RUC to accompany him on motor journeys'. The Prime Minister agreed to request a full report on the matter but he had already been assured that the police were not involved in the Jonesborough searches and it was the army who had, in fact, stopped the cortege.[97]

The police report confirming Craig's statement to Sturgis duly arrived from W. W. B Topping at the Ministry for Home Affairs on 31 August. Writing on behalf of the Inspector-General of the RUC, Chief Inspector J. Lenthall reported that no police had been in the Jonesborough area on the day in question. This was confirmed in an account given to the RUC County Inspector for Armagh, W. S. Moore, from District Inspector McFarland. Lenthall also reported that in July Logue had been given a pass signed by the County Inspector and the police had been ordered not to interfere with the cardinal on his travels.[98]

There was, perhaps, some truth in Craig's exasperated comment that Logue was simply being difficult. If so, this was not the first small act of defiance he had undertaken in the face of emergency legislation and what was deemed an oppressive Government. During the Anglo-Irish War he flouted Government-imposed travel restrictions on motor cars by journeying in a horse and carriage.[99] If Logue had indeed embarked upon a campaign to irritate and embarrass the Government through a game of cat and mouse with the police, he certainly succeeded. He again clashed with the authorities in Belfast in December 1920 over a curfew in Armagh which threatened midnight mass at Christmas. Although initially willing to defy the ban, Logue cancelled the mass amid the threat of wholesale arrests and violence.[100]

There had been a marked decrease in violence in the north throughout the summer of 1922. IRA units were paralysed by the civil war in the south and ceased activity. The conflict also lessened the siege mentality of the Government, which began, following pressure from Westminster, to rein in the activities of Loyalists and to curb the excesses of the police. There was a realisation in London that, as Lloyd George described it, 'our Ulster case is not a very good one'.[101] For Catholics, however, and the Church in particular, the ending of the pogrom brought only temporary relief.

Violence was replaced by what many interpreted as a systematic campaign of discrimination and marginalisation. In April 1922 the Northern Ireland Parliament abolished proportional representation and set about the redrawing of electoral boundaries to ensure the largest Unionist majorities possible on local councils and other public bodies. All local officials, including teachers and clergy in the employ of the state, had to swear an oath of allegiance to the Northern Ireland Government in order to remain in their jobs. In March 1923, the long dreaded Education Bill was unveiled by Londonderry. Schools were placed under the control of local education authorities and funding was withheld from those who retained their denominational status. The system of clerical managers for Catholic schools was abolished. Hennessy has argued that the Lynn Commission had tried to institute a truly non-denominational approach to primary and secondary education. Protestants, too, were unhappy with the lack of provision for religious instruction but it was Catholic schools which bore the brunt of financial penalties.[102]

The political reality of partition forced the northern bishops to meet independently of their southern colleagues to address the peculiar problems of the Catholic population in Northern Ireland. On 12 October 1923 they delivered a damning indictment of conditions faced by Catholics in the new state. 'It is doubtful whether in modern times', they said, 'any parallel can be found in the way in which the Catholic minority in the north of Ireland is being systematically wronged under the laws of the northern parliament'. The bishops denounced the Government's gerrymandering, the provisions regarding Catholic education and the discrimination inherent in the rigid application of the oath of allegiance. 'We consider the time has come', they concluded, 'for our people to organise openly, on constitutional lines , and resolve to lie down no longer under this degrading thraldom'.[103]

However, this was not a call for Catholics to participate politically in the new state. It was instead a rallying cry for political protest. In no sense did the statement offer recognition for the Government in Belfast. Logue had no desire to rush the bishops headlong into sanctioning the 'Six Counties' as he had done with the Irish Free State. What occurred was an effort to galvanise the nationalist vote against partition. In every parish, especially in border areas, committees under local clergy were formed to highlight political and social grievances and maximise the electoral turnout.[104] Alongside this political realignment, the bishops played a leading role in a campaign to secure the release of political prisoners and internees in the north.

On 6 January 1924 Logue wrote to a public meeting in Armagh apolo-
gising for being unable to attend in person. He told those assembled, 'I
deeply sympathise with the object for which it has been called; to protest
against the state of things which has caused so much suffering and to
appeal to the northern government to bring it to an end'. He was particularly pained to learn of conditions aboard the prison ship *Argenta*
anchored in Belfast Lough. 'Conditions which are unsanitary', he said,
'ruinous to health, brimful of suffering and which fall little short of those
inflicted on galley slaves in the past'. He also denounced the terms of
release for nationalist prisoners as inhumane. 'Exile from home and
family, or conferment to a distance of two miles with frequent reports to
the police', he said, were 'drastic and degrading punishment inflicted on
prisoners who had committed no crime'.[105]

A chance to test the mettle of the new political alliance arose with elections in Fermanagh and Tyrone at the end of 1923. The clergy were heavily
involved in canvassing and turning out the vote. On the eve of polling, the
Bishop of Derry, Charles McHugh, told the electors of Tyrone that this was
probably their last chance to register their vote for inclusion in the Irish
Free State before the boundary commission sat.[106] In terms of political
goals, the election of December 1923 was very much a plebiscite on the
border question. The nationalist candidate, Cahir Healy from Sinn Féin,
was returned and duly refused to take up his seat. The result was viewed
by nationalists as a 'resounding blow on behalf of the unity of our
country'.[107] However, political euphoria at the success was short lived. In
April 1924 Tyrone nationalists withdrew from local government elections
in protest against Government gerrymandering of electoral wards. At a
meeting in Omagh Father Philip Doherty, in the chair, declared, 'we seem
to be utterly forgotten and all our efforts ignored and now we find ourselves in pre-emancipation days'. He told the electors that what they now
faced was a war of extermination.[108]

Despite the electoral success of December 1923 and the re-emergence
of cohesive nationalist politics encouraged by the Church, political
progress was hampered by the air of general expectancy surrounding the
boundary commission. There was a conviction that the political and geo-
graphical boundaries of Northern Ireland were not yet settled. The commission represented the hope of deliverance for the large Catholic
populations of Derry, South Down, Fermanagh and Tyrone. Until it sat,
the thorny questions of recognition of and participation in the northern
state remained unanswered. In what would be his last Lenten pastoral,
Logue remained remarkably optimistic. 'Men are now engaged in a

laudable effort to restore peace', he said, 'to repair the wreck and ruin of the past, to build up the country materially and restore prosperity'. Such efforts were worthy of praise, he said, 'in which every man of good will should earnestly cooperate'.[109]

Efforts at cooperation, however, did not extend to the Government of Northern Ireland. Nevertheless, Logue's pastoral contained the implied hope that at some future date a settlement could be negotiated. In many ways, the cardinal's attitude of non-recognition and non-cooperation, and, it must be said, confrontation, typified the nationalist response to the creation of the northern state. There remained the hope that a boundary commission would act as a panacea for Catholic political and social desperation. Until it began, nationalist politics would remain in a state of paralysis. Logue, however, did not see the commission start and ultimately fail. He died at *Ara Coeli* at six o'clock, on the morning of 19 November 1924.

Watershed

Despite his advanced years, Logue's death caused shock and grief throughout Catholic Ireland and beyond. The day before his death he had appeared in good health, saying mass as usual and visiting the cathedral in Armagh that evening.[110] Logue's last words held little of import, except, perhaps, for him. He told his physician, 'is it not a great blessing, Doctor, that I have the use of all my faculties?'[111] His funeral on 25 November 1924 was attended by the archbishops of Ireland, twenty bishops and six hundred priests. Representatives attended from the Irish Free State and the King was represented by Ireland's Governor-General, Tim Healy. Telegrams of sympathy arrived from Rome and the hierarchies and governments of many countries.[112] A sour note, perhaps unsurprisingly, was sounded by John Hagan from the Irish College. He told Patrick O'Donnell, Logue's coadjutor, on 22 November that no members of the Curia or Sacred Congregations had attended the cardinal's requiem mass in his titular church of Santa Maria della Pace. Little notice had been taken, he said, 'of the passing away of one who certainly did not err on the side of want of reverence for the Holy See'.[113] Subsequently, Father J. Downey wrote O'Donnell from Rome to tell him that Pius XI had personally ordered that the *Cappella Papale* be sung in the Sistine Chapel in Logue's honour. 'To show', Downey said, 'his great affection for the late cardinal and sympathy with the bishops, priests and people of Ireland and the great loss they had sustained'.[114]

Nationalist newspapers eulogised the passing of the cardinal. The *Irish News* extolled his simplicity and piety and stated that, like many popes, Logue had been a 'child of the common people' and had exercised a 'comprehensive moral influence' over Ireland.[115] The *Freeman's Journal* told how Logue had 'loved all Irishmen and longed for the peace and union that it was denied him to see. But his prayers will be even more powerful in death than in life.'[116] A more measured evaluation was provided by *The Times* which noted that the passing of Cardinal Logue was 'the most considerable break between the old and the new Ireland. It is the fall of the oldest tree in the forest, the grand old man of Irish life and the patriarch of Irish Catholicism.'[117]

Logue's death, however, was only a watershed in some respects. The hierarchy had already begun the process of necessary adaptation to life in the two Irelands. Before his death, Logue acknowledged the depth of division within the Irish Free State. His support for the Government had remained constant after the end of the civil war and on the eve of the general election at the end of 1923 he told the electors of Dundalk to 'go forward as a body in support of the Ministry'. They may have made mistakes but had 'done wonders to reorganise the country'.[118] In spite of the unflagging support of the bishops for the Government, some 290,000 people in the Free State sided with the excommunicated and voted for republican candidates.[119]

The realisation that such a significant number remained alienated within the State which the bishops had done so much to shape contributed to a process of clerical disengagement from politics. In his Lenten pastoral of February 1924 Logue deemed reconciliation more important than material reparation in Ireland. Efforts should be undertaken, he said, 'to bring back our people to a sense of peace, charity, honesty and obedience in all things to God's law. Upon this reparation depends eternity.'[120] He also saw that this alienation was not confined to politics. The politicisation of the sacraments during the civil war had separated a large section of the population from the Church. In June 1924 Logue told the Maynooth Union that the younger clergy should stay out of politics altogether until they had gained more experience. They would have to meet a divided people and 'people who had lost much of their reverence for religion and the Church'. It was, he said, 'their duty to endeavour to bring men back to a sense of their religious duty'.[121] Regan has argued that, in this way, Logue set the parameters for the post-conflict relationship between the Church and the Irish Free State.[122]

In some respects, Logue's death marked a turning point in the relationship between nationalists and the state of Northern Ireland. With his passing, the policy of non-recognition lost one of its most distinguished and consistent proponents. Logue's successor, Patrick O'Donnell, was much less confrontational regarding the Northern Ireland Government. Speaking at his confirmation as primate in February 1925, O'Donnell abandoned the language of rejection and called on both the northern and southern governments to protect the minorities in their respective countries.[123] However, the political orientation of northern nationalists, like the abject position of northern Catholics, was not of Logue's making. He, along with other northern nationalists, still retained the hope that Dáil Éireann and the boundary commission could provide respite and a more favourable settlement. Despite a willingness on the part of the Free State Government to participate in the commission, the stumbling block remained the attitude of Ulster Unionists. Craig consistently refused to appoint a Northern Ireland representative and threatened to resign when one was foisted upon him by London.

The commission sat in 1925 amid a general election on the border issue. There was a dawning realisation among nationalists, however, that the commission would merely confirm the boundaries of Northern Ireland and not redraw them.[124] For the bishops, crushing grievances remained which could never be redressed by the policies of non-recognition and non-participation. The 1925 election saw an increase in the nationalist vote with the addition of six new MPs. The abstentionist vote collapsed and Joe Devlin, MP for West Belfast, led a gradual procession of nationalists taking their seats in the Belfast Parliament.

Notes

1 *ICD*, 1923, p. 578
2 *Ibid.*, p. 580.
3 *Freeman's Journal*, 13 and 22 Aug. 1922.
4 Regan, *Irish Counter-Revolution*, p. 79.
5 Hopkinson, *Green Against Green*, p. 181.
6 Keogh, *The Vatican, the Bishops and Irish Politics*, p. 95.
7 *ICD*, 1923, pp. 608–11.
8 Hopkinson, *Green Against Green*, p. 182.
9 See Byrne to Mary MacSwiney, 24 Feb. 1923, Byrne Papers, DDA, 'Department of Justice', and to Anne O'Rahilly, 15 and 30 Dec. 1922, Byrne Papers, DDA, 'Government 1921–39'.
10 Mulcahy to Byrne, 13 Mar. 1923, Byrne Papers, DDA, no. A/8402, 'Department of Defence'.
11 Mulcahy to Byrne, 16 Feb. 1923, Byrne Papers, DDA, no. A/8402, 'Department of Defence'.

12 *ICD*, 1923, p. 593.
13 Keogh, *The Vatican, the Bishops and Irish Politics*, p. 106.
14 Hagan to Curran, 8 Oct. 1922, Curran Political Papers, DDA, 1919–23.
15 Hagan to Curran, 13 Dec. 1922, Curran Political Papers, DDA, 1919–23.
16 Hopkinson, *Green Against Green*, p. 188.
17 *Ibid.*, p. 181.
18 Hagan to O'Donnell, 26 Mar. 1923, O'Donnell Papers, ADA, box 6, folder 1, 'Irish College'.
19 Cosgrave to Byrne, 18 Nov. 1922, Byrne Papers, DDA, 'Executive Council'.
20 Byrne to Cosgrave, 10 Dec 1922, Byrne Papers, DDA, 'Executive Council'.
21 Keogh, *The Vatican, the Bishops and Irish Politics*, p. 98.
22 Curran to O'Donnell, 12 Dec. 1922, O'Donnell Papers, ADA, box 6, folder 1, 'Irish College'.
23 Keogh, *Ireland and the Vatican*, pp. 25–6.
24 Logue to Byrne, 17 Jan. 1923, Byrne Papers, DDA, 'Armagh'.
25 Lenten pastoral, 1 Feb. 1923, Logue Papers, ADA, box 9, folder 6, 'Sermons and Pastorals'.
26 Logue to Byrne, 22 Nov. 1922, Byrne Papers, DDA, 'Armagh'.
27 Hagan to O'Donnell, 8 Mar. 1923, O'Donnell Papers, ADA, box 6, folder 1, 'Irish College'.
28 Curran to O'Donnell, 14 Mar. 1923, O'Donnell Papers, ADA, box 6, folder 1, 'Irish College'.
29 Keogh, *The Vatican, the Bishops and Irish Politics*, p. 113.
30 Curran, *Irish Free State*, p. 271.
31 Keogh, *The Vatican, the Bishops and Irish Politics*, p. 116.
32 Hopkinson, *Green against Green*, p. 268.
33 Cosgrave to Byrne, 18 Nov. 1922, Byrne Papers, DDA, 'Executive Council'.
34 Cosgrave to Byrne, 28 Apr. 1923, Byrne Papers, DDA, 'Executive Council'.
35 Byrne to MacSwiney, 24 Feb. 1923, Byrne Papers, DDA, 'Department of Justice'.
36 Walsh (Byrne's secretary) to Kathleen Costello, Nelly O'Ryan and Annie O'Neill, 21 Apr. 1923, Byrne Papers, DDA, 'Department of Justice'.
37 Logue to Byrne, 17 Oct. 1923, Byrne Papers, DDA, 'Armagh'.
38 Byrne to Cosgrave, 28 Oct. 1923, Byrne Papers, DDA, 'Executive Council'.
39 *ICD*, 1924, p. 600.
40 *Ibid.*
41 Hagan to O'Donnell, 23 Dec. 1923, O'Donnell Papers, ADA, box 6, folder 1, 'Irish College'.
42 Miller, *Church, State and Nation*, pp. 492–3.
43 Keogh, *The Vatican, the Bishops and Irish Politics*, p. 128.
44 *Ibid.*, p. 129.
45 Logue to O'Donnell, 7 June 1916, O'Donnell Papers, ADA, box 9, folder 3, 'Patrick Cardinal O'Donnell'.
46 Cabinet Conclusions, 13 Aug. 1920, TNA, CAB 23/22 (48).

47 Farrell, *Orange State*, p. 26.
48 Hennessy, *Northern Ireland*, p. 13.
49 *Ibid.*, p. 35.
50 See Parkinson, *Belfast*, pp. 152–4. For a government or Unionist interpretation of events in 1920–24, however, see Follis, *State Under Siege*, ch. 5.
51 *Catholic Times*, 26 June 1920.
52 *ICD*, 1921, p. 522.
53 *Ibid.*, pp. 556–9.
54 Logue to Greenwood, undated Sept. 1920, Logue Papers, ADA, box 4, folder 1, 'Chief Secretary'.
55 Curran to Walsh, 17 Jan. 1920, Walsh Papers, DDA, box 393, folder 380/6.
56 *The Times*, 15 Dec. 1920.
57 Laffan, *Resurrection*, p. 336.
58 Hennessy, *Northern Ireland*, p. 16.
59 Northern Ireland Cabinet Conclusions, undated May 1921, PRONI, CAB 6/62.
60 Hopkinson, ed., *Sturgis Diaries*, 8 June 1921, p. 186.
61 *The Times*, 15 Jun. 1921.
62 *Catholic Times*, 18 Feb. 1922. It is worth noting, however, that throughout his speech at the opening of the Northern Ireland Parliament, King George V referred constantly to Northern Ireland as 'the Six Counties'. See Jeffery, ed., *An Irish Empire?* p. 7.
63 *ICD*, 1922, p. 533.
64 Londonderry to Logue, 29 Aug. 1921, PRONI, CAB 4/1(18).
65 Logue to Londonderry, 2 Sept. 1921, PRONI, CAB 4/7(18).
66 Londonderry to FitzAlan, 4 Sept. 1921, PRONI, CAB 4/13(18).
67 Northern Ireland Cabinet Conclusions, 9 Sept. 1921, PRONI, CAB 4/21 (18).
68 Londonderry to Logue, 10 Sept. 1921, PRONI, CAB 4/19 (18).
69 Buckland, *Northern Ireland*, p. 52.
70 Curran, *Irish Free State*, p. 165.
71 *Catholic Times*, 11 Mar. 1922.
72 Parkinson, *Belfast*, p. 215.
73 *ICD*, 1923, p. 551.
74 Parkinson, *Belfast*, p. 231.
75 Curran, *Irish Free State*, pp. 177–8.
76 *ICD*, 1923, p. 560.
77 *Ibid.*, p. 561.
78 Ó Ceallaigh to Hagan, 11 April 1922, Hagan Papers, AICR, no. 86 (1922).
79 Hart, *The IRA and its Enemies*, pp. 276–9.
80 *Freeman's Journal*, 30 Apr. 1922.
81 *ICD*, 1923, pp. 605–6.
82 Hart, *The IRA and its Enemies*, p. 279.
83 *ICD*, 1923, p. 606.
84 *Ibid.*, p. 574.

85 *Freeman's Journal*, 22 June 1923.
86 Spender to Curtis, 17 June 1922, PRONI, CAB 6/48, H1491. The murders of John and Robert Heslip, William Lockhart, Thomas Crozier and his wife occurred near Newry on 18 June.
87 Maxwell to Spender, 17 June 1922, PRONI, CAB 6/48, H1491.
88 Curtis to Spender, 22 June 1922, PRONI, CAB 6/48, H1491.
89 Spender to Curtis, 24 June 1922, PRONI, CAB 6/48, H1491.
90 *Irish Independent*, 26 June 1922.
91 Watt to Spender, undated June 1922, PRONI, CAB 6/48, H1491.
92 *ICD*, 1923, p. 578.
93 *Catholic Herald*, 29 July 1922.
94 FitzAlan to Craig, 5 Aug. 1922, PRONI, CAB 6/48, H1491.
95 Sturgis to Craig, 10 Aug. 1922, PRONI, CAB 6/48, H1491.
96 Craig to FitzAlan, 10 Aug. 1922, PRONI, CAB 6/48, H1491.
97 Craig to Sturgis, 12 Aug. 1922, PRONI, CAB 6/48, H1491.
98 Topping to Craig, 31 Aug. 1922, PRONI, CAB 6/48, H1491.
99 Laffan, *Resurrection of Ireland*, p. 286.
100 *Freeman's Journal*, 20 and 24 Dec. 1920.
101 Parkinson, *Belfast*, pp. 286–7.
102 Hennessy, *Northern Ireland*, pp. 41–2.
103 *Freeman's Journal*, 13 Oct. 1923.
104 Harris, *Catholic Church*, pp. 158–9.
105 *ICD*, 1925, p. 553.
106 *Ibid.*, p. 546.
107 Harris, *Catholic Church*, p. 160.
108 *ICD*, 1925, p. 567.
109 *Ibid.*, p. 560.
110 *Irish News*, 20 Nov. 1924,
111 *Cardinal Logue: Primate of All Ireland*, p. 4.
112 *ICD*, 1925, p. 607.
113 Hagan to O'Donnell, 22 Nov. 1924, O'Donnell Papers, ADA, box 6, folder 1, 'Irish College'.
114 Downey to O'Donnell, 1 Dec. 1924, O'Donnell Papers, box. 6, folder 2.
115 *Irish News*, 20 Nov. 1924.
116 *Freeman's Journal*, 20 Nov. 1924.
117 *The Times*, 24 Nov. 1924.
118 *ICD*, 1924, p. 586.
119 Regan, *Irish Counter-Revolution*, p. 285.
120 *ICD*, 1925, p. 561.
121 *Ibid.*, p. 582.
122 Regan, *Irish Counter-Revolution*, p. 285.
123 *ICD*, 1926, p. 555.
124 Hennessy, *Northern Ireland*, pp. 38–40.

10

Legacy

Despite his prominence as a historical figure and the length of his career, Michael Logue has suffered to a surprising degree in the historiography of the period. When not ignored by historians, he has often been dismissed as a known quantity, a one-dimensional character lacking nuance and depth. Most often, historians have questioned his nationalist credentials. Miller's description of the cardinal has remained rather typical. 'He enjoyed waiting upon royalty', he has stated, and 'delighted in entertaining visiting British dignitaries with champagne and oysters'.[1] Keogh has also picked up the notion that Logue was a royalist, declaring that the cardinal had 'caused general annoyance when he dined with Queen Victoria at the Vice-Regal Lodge in 1900 and received King Edward in 1903 and 1911'.[2] But these remain accusations which do not stand up to scrutiny. True, Logue did entertain Richard Haldane with champagne and oysters but once does not constitute a habit. It must be remembered that Haldane's visit offered the bishops their first opportunity in over a decade to discuss the University Question with a representative, even an unofficial one, of the British Government.

On the issue of British royalty, Logue remained respectful of the monarchy but no more or less enamoured with it than other constitutional nationalists of the Home Rule period. He did respect Queen Victoria but attended the reception for her at the Vice-Regal Lodge in 1900 out of a sense of duty befitting his station. One of the Queen's party, Lord Denbigh, told Logue's biographer, Father Patrick Toner, that the cardinal was very nervous and uncomfortable during the visit. He and the Queen had actually had very little contact, though both were present at the dinner. Victoria had asked Logue how they in Ireland were getting along to which he replied that they were fine except for 'two or three little things'.

The Queen was anxious to find out what these things were and despatched Denbigh the following morning to meet the cardinal. Over lunch, Logue told Denbigh the first thing was the small matter of a university for Catholics. The second was the way in which the Irish remained at the political whim of Westminster and whichever party was in power. He confessed that he remained a conservative at heart who was forced to countenance the Liberal Party because 'English Radicals' were the only ones from whom the Irish could expect concessions. 'The Conservative Party', he told Denbigh, 'were always associated with the Orange Party so that it felt they were governed by the Orangemen from the north'.[3]

Keogh's point regarding the royal visits in 1903 and 1911 is slightly misleading. It was Walsh who feted the King and Queen in 1903, as Logue was in Rome for the conclave to elect Pius X. In 1911 both men shared the duties, though neither was particularly comfortable looking after their royal guests.[4] To dismiss Logue, therefore, as a royalist or to question his nationalism on these grounds is remarkably unfair. Logue, after all, had used Victoria's visit to raise Catholic grievances. It was the Archbishop of Dublin who undertook the reception of King Edward in 1903, and was photographed showing Queen Mary around Maynooth in 1911.[5] Such encounters with English royalty, however, have not detracted from Walsh's historical status as the ecclesiastical doyen of Irish nationalism.

Indeed, as a nationalist, the whole issue of English royalty and their relationship to Ireland remained difficult for Logue. In 1902, for example, the Holy See decreed a dispensation from the normal Friday fasting in honour of King Edward's coronation. The cardinal was not enthusiastic. 'In the present circumstances', he told Walsh, 'the patriots would be in revolt. I thought that, as there is no obligation to use a privilege, I might let the matter rest.' He thought it unlikely that the dispensation would be necessary as no one in Ireland would be having a banquet.[6] In 1910 Logue took the *Tablet* to task over the clauses in the coronation oath binding the monarch to foreswear the Catholic faith and to uphold the Anglican tradition. He condemned the 'wanton insult which the declaration in question heaps upon Catholics' and asked why Catholics alone of the King's subjects should be singled out for 'indignities and insults'.[7]

Logue was consistent in his attitude towards the monarchy, even resisting pressure from the Holy See to attend Queen Victoria's jubilee celebrations in 1897. Leo XIII, ever-solicitous of the good will of the British Government, sent a representative and urged the Irish bishops to do the same.[8] Logue informed Michael Kelly, Rector of the Irish College, that the jubilee was not so much a personal homage to the Queen as it was a celebration of the prosperity which England had enjoyed during the past sixty years. 'As you well know', he said, 'Ireland has had no share in this progress and prosperity'. To send a representative from the clergy, he went on, would be viewed as a declaration that the Irish remained content under English rule.[9] Kelly translated Logue's points into a memorial which he presented to the Cardinal Secretary of State. No further mention of an Irish delegation was made.

Logue's style of ecclesiastical management has also proved problematic for historians. Miller has stated that he 'possessed none of the political sensitivity which enabled Walsh to lead the hierarchy in such a creative fashion'.[10] However, Logue did not assume the primacy with a clearly defined political vision for the hierarchy which he could proceed to foist upon his colleagues. His predecessor and great friend in Armagh, Daniel McGettigan, had pursued a fairly placid and pious tenure as archbishop and there was every indication that Logue would follow suit. The bishops had long been led from Dublin and he had no inclination to usurp the influence of Walsh. Besides, apart from some anxiety over clerical partic-ipation in the Plan of Campaign, Logue was satisfied with the political direction of the bishops and the terms of the clerical-nationalist alliance. He was content to follow the lead provided by Walsh and the Archbishop of Cashel, Thomas William Croke, venturing his support when called upon and generally not getting in the way. He had, however, enough polit-ical acumen to stand clear when Walsh's creative leadership rather blew up in the bishops' faces in 1888.

Logue recognised his own weaknesses. He was keenly aware that in the eyes of many he had been appointed cardinal over the head of the Archbishop of Dublin. He was genuinely appalled that he had been chosen, not least because of the deep respect and admiration he had for William Walsh. Logue's trust in Walsh was implicit and he valued the arch-bishop's advice above all others. The ecclesiastical historian, Father Miles V. Rogan, observed that at the bishops' meetings Logue allowed free dis-cussion of any issue. After a certain amount of time had elapsed, however, he would say, 'my Lords, I think you have discussed long enough. But what has his Grace of Dublin to say?' Walsh would put his case to which Logue replied, 'well, my Lords, you have heard what his Grace of Dublin has said'. With that, the discussion was over and the archbishop was asked to put his ideas in writing.[11]

The close relationship between the two men undoubtedly frustrated bishops who had their own ideas on the direction of the hierarchy. Thomas O'Dwyer in Limerick and the Archbishop of Tuam, John Healy, for example, developed their own proposals on the university issue at the turn of the century, only to be thwarted by the collaboration between

Armagh and Dublin. Logue may have been content for Walsh to be the political face of the bishops but that is not to say he was incapable of independent action. It was his foot-dragging and eventual hostility over the St Patrick's proposals, when Walsh seemed on the verge of accepting them which contributed to the scheme's collapse. Despite some exasperation at Logue's propensity for dithering, the cardinal and the archbishop enjoyed a close personal friendship as well as a working relationship which dominated the direction of the hierarchy for over twenty years.

If the political orientation of the hierarchy and the direction of the university campaign were entrusted to Walsh, ecclesiastical discipline remained Logue's responsibility. This is not to say, however, that the collaborative management of the hierarchy undertaken by Armagh and Dublin was any more successful in maintaining unity than previous leaderships. Thomas O'Dwyer, for example, remained as rebellious over the education question under Logue as he had been on the Plan of Campaign under Walsh's direction. The hierarchy was subject, at times, to the same factionalism and divisions no matter who was nominally in control. Logue, however, was a stern enforcer of doctrinal orthodoxy as laid down by Rome. He viewed clerical dalliances with evolution and the new science with incomprehension. He simply could not understand the desire among certain priests to seek to deviate from the Catholic doctrine handed down by the Holy See. Logue's commitment to orthodoxy stemmed from a deep respect and reverence for the person and the office of the supreme pontiff. His beliefs on society and religion were steeped in the traditions of Leo XIII. On matters of faith, therefore, the opinion of the Pope was sacrosanct and should necessarily form the basis for the attitude of the clergy. Evolution and science represented a threat to that simplicity of faith and docility of mind in Catholics that Logue prized so highly.

To find that Maynooth, then, had the potential to become of a 'nest of heresy' came as a shock. Logue's handling of Walter McDonald and the *Motion* controversy at once demonstrated his devotion to orthodoxy and his deftness of touch when dealing with ecclesiastical politics. The issue had the potential for great embarrassment but Logue succeeded in having *Motion* withdrawn and McDonald censured without scandal or opprobrium. His general mistrust of science and progressive theology caused him to object to and attempt to block the publication of the *Irish Theological Quarterly*. It also heightened his determination that any scientific teaching in the new National University should be strictly supervised.

Logue was instrumental in implementing the strictures laid down by Pius X to combat Modernism in 1908. He championed the cause of the

Vigilance Committees as they transformed from watchtowers against Modernism to moral censors of literature and culture. His patronage of propaganda organisations such as the Catholic Truth Society encouraged the dissemination of the orthodox message to ordinary Catholics through the medium of publications such as the *Catholic Bulletin*. Throughout the turbulent years after their inauguration, the Vigilance Committees remained active. They campaigned steadily against immoral literature, films and plays and their influence grew steadily under the approving glances and words of encouragement from *Ara Coeli*.

Although such historians as Miller and Keogh are dismissive of Logue's political acumen, he remained a committed nationalist through-out his career. He retained an unshakeable belief that the Irish should govern themselves and resented what he saw as the daily injustices on land, education, employment and in politics faced by Irish Catholics. His nationalism was streaked with a large measure of sectarianism and bit-terness against what he viewed as the British-maintained Protestant Ascendancy. Logue found his political voice during the Parnell crisis. His vehement repudiation of Parnell was motivated as much by the disinte-gration of the clerical-nationalist alliance as it was by the 'sin' of divorce. For Logue, there could be no division between religion and politics. The clerical-nationalist alliance represented the ideal format for political endeavour in Ireland. He was enough of a political pragmatist to recog-nise that Home Rule was desirable as a distant goal but that, in the mean-time, Irish Catholics had plenty of other grievances which needed redressing. Having deposed Parnell, Logue (and Walsh), played little part in nudging the factions of the Irish Party towards unity by refusing to back a successor.

The whole episode and anticlerical atmosphere thereafter poisoned Logue's attitude towards the party. He could not view Home Rule as the panacea for Ireland's ills if the ruling elite would encompass such figures as John Redmond and William O'Brien. Logue's disillusionment pushed him towards Tim Healy, who was unafraid to take a Catholic agenda into the House of Commons. Despite confessing a lack of knowledge about political matters, the cardinal had a remarkable propensity to interfere in elections on the side of his only political ally. Walsh shared Logue's sense of disaffection and became a convert to the cause of Healy in North Louth. Along with Logue's loss of faith in the Irish Party, he became extremely jaded on the issue of Home Rule itself. None of the bills proffered by London offered the opportunity for the kind of reform he deemed essential on the rights and privileges of Irish Catholics.

Despite Logue's disaffection, however, he simply could not embrace republicanism in the way that Walsh did and this was ultimately the cause of the political divergence between Armagh and Dublin. Where Walsh saw a new and vibrant political moment and had hope in the idea of separation, Logue saw only the potential for disaster and bloodshed. Throughout his career, Logue found violence deeply disturbing. The petty viciousness of the boycott in the Land War and during the Plan of Campaign filled him with revulsion. War was a source of suffering and misery in which could be found no glory and filled him only with horror. He did not 'support' the Allies in the First World War, though he condemned German tactics. He refrained from making any definitive moral pronouncement on the conflict, including the participation of Irishmen. What he retained was an abiding concern for the spiritual welfare of Catholic soldiers and sailors, and he did his best to ensure it was provided for. Historians, especially Aan de Wiel, have made much of Logue's willingness to participate in the Hay plan in 1918. This, however, is problematic. The whole episode was completely out of character for the cardinal and he discussed it with no one: the scheme, if it existed at all, remains something of an enigma.

For Logue, there was nothing glorious, then, in the events of Easter Week in 1916. The Rising was a bloody and disastrous failure. It was the prospect of another failed insurrection which blighted his attitude towards Sinn Féin and caused his bitter personal antipathy towards Eamon de Valera. The Rising held no mystique or romanticism for Logue. He simply could not conceive of any circumstances in which the Irish could prevail against the might of the British army and empire. In many respects, Logue's disapproval of the republican cause led him to dismiss the sacrifices of Irish volunteers who gave their lives on the streets of Dublin. It was only through the intervention and persuasion of William Walsh that he entered into the last of the clerical-nationalist collaborations under the threat of conscription. While, in 1917, Walsh could embrace the new movement regardless of consequences, Logue felt the need to warn the people against the impending disaster of another rebellion. It was this fear which led him to put so much hope in the Irish Convention and was at the root of his reticence to engage with Sinn Féin.

Nevertheless, Logue was enough of a political pragmatist to recognise the new political order in Ireland after the 1918 general election and do business with the republican movement on the issue of partition. He remained dubious about Dáil Éireann and could not extend moral sanction to the new body in the way that Walsh did. The estrangement between

Armagh and Dublin was symptomatic of a wider division among the bishops on republicanism. For Logue, the moral dilemma inherent in physical force nationalism precluded any show of public support or association with the Dáil. The outbreak of the Anglo-Irish War accentuated divisions within the hierarchy. Unity was evident in the condemnations of Britain and the actions of Crown forces but the episcopate as a body never extended their moral or theological approval to the republican government or the IRA campaign. They were only able to recognise the Dáil when the element of violent confrontation had diminished.

In many respects, Walsh's death enabled Logue to dictate the political direction of the bishops. Both had enjoyed a long collaboration and friendship which had resulted in the notable triumph of finally securing a university for Catholics in Ireland. Politically, however, the two men had grown increasingly distant following the outbreak of the First World War and the emergence and eventual dominance of physical force nationalism. Walsh's death robbed the republican movement of one of its most powerful advocates, even if the archbishop was morally opposed to the IRA campaign. Logue finally forged a degree of political unity among the bishops around the pressure on both sides for a truce. In the absence of violence and with the prospect of a negotiated settlement to the Irish Question, the cardinal finally extended the moral sanction of the episcopate to the Dáil.

It is in this period that the nature of Logue's legacy can be found. His uncompromising and unflinching support for the Treaty contributed to the survival of the Irish Free State. In addition to legitimising the Provisional Government with the blessing of the Irish episcopate, Logue positioned the full theological power of the Catholic Church in Ireland, including the sacraments, at the political disposal of Cosgrave's administration. The policy of blanket excommunications was divisive and not without controversy, but Logue remained adamant and quite ruthless in his determination to oppose the republican insurrection. The result was a Government indebted to the Church and dependent on the approbation given it. Logue ensured that not only was the Irish Free State founded on principles commensurate with Catholicism, but that the state would be constitutionally bound to defend those principles and punish those who traduced them.

Logue finessed a Catholic agenda upon a needy Government and created a state in which the Church was the largest and most influential interest group. The Free State represented the fulfilment of his conviction that religion and politics could not be separate. The power of the Church and the willingness of the Government to bow to ecclesiastical pressure were evident in the campaign against immoral literature. The Vigilance Committees now had influence beyond their size and began lobbying for the Government to underwrite their campaign of censorship. In February 1922, Father J. S. Sheehan of Blackrock College told a meeting of the Irish Vigilance Association that the Free State should have a central bureau to censor the moral content of films, plays and publications. All films alien to Catholic and Irish ideals should be banned along with films bearing on the 'eugenic' – featuring unmarried mothers, birth control and 'other movements which in Pagan countries like England are tolerated and encouraged'.[12] Such sentiments underpinned and provided the yardstick for the Free State's Censorship Act in 1923.

Logue had spent most of his ecclesiastical career willingly in the shadow of the Archbishop of Dublin. He remained supremely aware of his own shortcomings and retained a remarkable conviction that he was not worthy of the office of primate, let alone cardinal. Augustine Birrell called him 'the simplest and most devout Christian man I think I have ever met'.[13] Logue remained his own fiercest critic. In reply to an address from Patrick O'Donnell on the occasion of his sacerdotal jubilee in 1916 he told an audience that he had 'found himself placed in a position of serious responsibility for which he had no ambition whatever'. He would have been content to remain a simple priest his whole life but he found that 'Providence, in its wise designs, seemed to determine otherwise'. The prospect of giving an account of his deeds and his use of the opportunities for good provided by God filled him with 'fear and anxiety'.[14]

Personally, Michael Logue was a simple man. He enjoyed sailing and the sea. He was, perhaps surprisingly, an expert shot and enjoyed fishing. He possessed a self-deprecating and dry wit and, despite a lack of published work, he had a quick and keen mind. He was prone to bouts of indecision and dithering and in his early years as primate, displayed a remarkable lack of self-confidence. He was capable of utter ruthlessness as well as acts of great kindness and compassion. He had a simple faith which permeated almost every action. In times of trouble or political strife he preferred to place his trust in the Almighty rather than politicians.

In terms of ecclesiastical history, Logue appears to have been forgotten. There are no monuments to him in Ireland. In the grounds of Saint Eunan's Cathedral in Letterkenny, the episcopate of Patrick O'Donnell is commemorated with a statue. Neither has Ireland's longest-serving primate been remembered in his titular church in Rome. The seventeenth-century Santa Maria della Pace, situated just off the Piazza Novono, bears no mention of him, nor of any of his successors to which the church was ceded. Perhaps the cathedral in Armagh represents a memorial of sorts. Logue completed it in 1904 having raised most of the funding himself and supervised the refurbishment. One of the few portraits of the cardinal hangs in the Ulster Museum but it is a most unflattering and intimidating rendering in oils by Sir John Lavery.

Historians have long been dazzled with the erudition of William Walsh and his readily accessible body of political and social study. Walsh was the great link figure who had 'met O'Connell as a child, corresponded with Davitt and Parnell and supported Sinn Féin'.[15] The political dimensions of Logue's career contained none of this pleasing historical symmetry. In 1892 the Duke of Norfolk described Logue as a bishop and not a politician and this was essentially correct. He was most comfortable when dealing with religion and ecclesiastical affairs. Logue's influence may, at times, have been obscured during his collaboration with the Archbishop of Dublin, but the legacy he bequeathed is clear. William Walsh may have taken the plaudits for the foundation of a university for Catholics but it was Michael Logue who emerged to shape the constitution of a state.

Notes

1 Miller, *Church, State and Nation*, pp. 11–12.
2 Keogh, *The Vatican, the Bishops and Irish Politics*, p. 12.
3 Denbigh to Toner, undated, 1927, Logue Papers, ADA, box 10, folder 8, 'Biography – letters'.
4 Walsh to Logue, 21 May 1911, Logue Papers, ADA, box 3, 'Dublin Archdiocese 1905–16'.
5 See photograph in Morrissey, *William Walsh*.
6 Logue to Walsh, 8 May 1902, Walsh Papers, DDA, box 374, folder 358/2.
7 The *Tablet*, 4 June 1910.
8 Kelly to Logue, 11 June 1897, Kelly Papers, AICR, no. 392 (1897).
9 Logue to Kelly, 14 June 1897, Kelly Papers, AICR, no. 395 (1897).
10 Miller, *Church, State and Nation*, p. 11.
11 Morrissey, *William Walsh*, p. 161.
12 *ICD*, 1923, p. 546.
13 *The Times*, 20 Nov. 1924.
14 *ICD*, 1917, pp. 501–2.
15 Morrissey, *William Walsh*, p. 352.

Bibliography

Manuscript sources

Armagh Diocesan Archive, Ó Fiaich Library
Michael Cardinal Logue Papers
Archbishop Daniel McGettigan Papers
Joseph Cardinal MacRory Papers
Patrick Cardinal O'Donnell Papers

British Library
Arthur J. Balfour Papers

Dublin Diocesan Archive
Archbishop Edward Byrne Papers
Michael Curran Political Papers
Edward Cardinal McCabe Papers
Archbishop William Walsh Papers

Irish College, Rome
Hagan Papers
Kelly Papers
Kirby Papers
O'Riordan Papers

Limerick Archives
Thomas Edward O'Dwyer Papers

National Archive
CAB 23. Cabinet Conclusions and Memoranda
CAB 37. Cabinet Conclusions and Memoranda

National Library of Ireland
Archbishop Thomas William Croke Papers
Séan T. Ó Ceallaigh Papers (Michael Curran's Memoirs)

National Library of Scotland
Richard Haldane Papers
Viscount Elibank (Arthur C. Murray) Papers

Public Records Office Northern Ireland
CAB 4. Cabinet Conclusions and Memoranda
CAB 6. Cabinet Conclusions and Memoranda

Raphoe Diocesan Archive
Michael Logue Papers
Patrick O'Donnell Papers

Printed primary sources

Belfast Naturalists Field Club Reports, 2nd ser., (1874)
Cardinal Logue: Primate of All Ireland (Dublin, 1927)
De Christiana Doctrina Tradenda (Dublin, 1905)
Dublin Mansion House Relief Committee Proceedings and Reports (Dublin, 1880)
Pascendi Dominici Gregis (Dublin, 1907)
Report and Proceedings of the Irish Convention, Cd 9019 (Dublin, 1918)
Royal Commission on Education (Ireland), Reports and Appendices, Cd 826–1483
    (Dublin, 1902–3)

Other contemporary publications

Balfour, Arthur J. (ed.), *Against Home Rule* (London, 1912)
Drysdale, A. M., *Canada to Ireland: the Visit of the Duchess of Connaught's Own*
    (London, 1917)
Gladstone, William E., *The Vatican Decrees and their Bearing on Civil Allegiance*
    (London, 1874)
J. K. C., *Tyndall and Materialism* (London, 1875)
McDonald, Walter, *Motion: Its Origin and Conservation* (Dublin, 1898)
William, Walsh, *The Irish University Question: the Catholic Case* (Dublin, 1897)

Contemporary periodicals

Catholic Bulletin
Irish Catholic Directory
Irish Ecclesiastical Record
Irish Theological Quarterly
The Tablet

Newspapers

An Claidheamh Soluis
Catholic Herald
Catholic Times
Derry Journal
Drogheda Argus
Freeman's Journal
Irish Catholic
Irish Independent
Irish News
Irish Times
Le Monde
The Leader
National Press
Northern Whig
The Times

Secondary sources

Aan de Wiel, Jerome, *The Catholic Church in Ireland, 1914–18: War and Politics* (Dublin, 2000)

Appleby, R. Scott, 'Exposing Darwin's "Hidden Agenda": Roman Catholic Responses to Evolution, 1875–1925', in R. L. Numbers and J. Stenhouse (eds), *Disseminating Darwinism: the Role of Place, Race, Religion and Gender* (Cambridge, 1999), pp. 173–207

Barry, Tom, *Guerrilla Days in Ireland* (Dublin, 1949)

Bew, Paul, *Land and the National Question 1858–82* (Dublin, 1978)

Bowen, Desmond, *Paul Cardinal Cullen and the Shaping of Modern Irish Society* (Dublin, 1992)

Bowler, Peter, *The Eclipse of Darwinism: Anti-Darwinian Evolution Theories in the Decades around 1900* (Baltimore, 1993)

——, *Evolution: the History of an Idea* (Berkeley, 1983)

Boyce, D. George, *Nineteenth-Century Ireland: the Search for Stability* (Dublin, 1993)

——, *Englishmen and Irish Troubles: British Public Opinion and the Making of Irish Policy, 1918–22* (Cambridge, 1972)

Briody, Michael, 'From Carrickbeg to Rome: the Story of Father Michael O'Hickey', *Decies*, lvii (2000), pp. 143–66

Brooke, J.H., 'Darwin and Victorian Christianity', in J. Hodge and G. Radick (ed.), *The Cambridge Companion to Darwin* (Cambridge, 2003), pp. 169–213

Brown, Terence, *Ireland: a Social and Cultural History, 1922–2002* (London, 2004)

Brundell, Barry, 'Catholic Church Politics and Evolution Theory', *British Journal of Historical Studies*, xxxiv (2001), pp. 81–95

Buckland, Patrick, *A History of Northern Ireland* (Dublin, 1992)

Bull, Phillip, 'The Significance of the Nationalist Response to the Land Act of 1903', *Irish Historical Studies*, xxxvii: 111 (May 1993), pp. 283–306

——, 'The United Irish League and the Reunion of the Irish Parliamentary Party', *Irish Historical Studies*, xxvi: 101 (May 1988), pp. 51–78

Callan, Patrick, 'Recruiting for the British Army in Ireland during the First World War', *Irish Sword*, xvii (1987), pp. 42–56

Callanan, Frank, *T. M. Healy* (Cork, 1995)

——, *The Parnell Split, 1890–91* (Cork, 1992)

Canning, Bernard J., *Bishops of Ireland, 1870–1987* (Donegal, 1987)

Chadwick, Owen, *A History of the Popes, 1830–1914* (Oxford, 1998)

——, *The Popes and European Revolution* (Oxford, 1981)

Coogan, Tim Pat, *De Valera: Long Fellow, Long Shadow* (London, 1993)

Costello, Francis J., *Enduring the Most: the Life and Death of Terence MacSwiney*, (Kerry, 1995)

Cullen, L. M., *An Economic History of Ireland Since 1660* (Bristol, 1972)

Curran, Joseph M., *The Birth of the Irish Free State* (Tuscaloosa, Alabama, 1980)

Curtis, L. P., *Coercion and Conciliation in Ireland, 1880–92: a Study in Conservative Unionism* (Princeton, 1963)

Dangerfield, George, *The Damnable Question: a Study in Anglo-Irish Relations* (London, 1977)

D'Arcy, Charles Frederick, *Adventures of a Bishop* (London, 1934)

Denman, Terence, 'The Catholic Irish soldier in the First World War: the racial environment', *Irish Historical Studies*, xvii: 108 (Nov. 1991), pp. 352–65

Duffy, Eamon, *Saints and Sinners: a History of the Popes* (New Haves, Connecticut, 1997)

Elliot, Marianne, *The Catholics of Ulster* (New York, 2002)

Ellis, Ian M., *Vision and Reality: a Survey of Twentieth-Century Irish Inter-Church Relations* (Belfast, 1992)

Farrell, Michael, *Northern Ireland: the Orange State* (London, 1976)

Fitzpatrick, David, 'The Logic of Collective Sacrifice: Ireland and the British Army, 1914–18', *Historical Journal*, xxxviii: 4 (1995), pp. 1017–30

Follis, Bryan A., *A State under Siege: the Establishment of Northern Ireland 1920–25* (Oxford, 1995)

Fowler, W. B., *British-American Relations: the Role of William Wiseman* (New Jersey, 1969)

Fraser, T. G., *Ireland in Conflict, 1922–1998* (London, 2000)

Gailey, Andrew, *Ireland and the Death of Kindness: the Experience of Constructive Unionism* (Cork, 1987)

Gildea, Robert, *Barricades and Borders: Europe, 1800–1914* (Oxford, 1996)

Glick, Thomas F. (ed.), *The Comparative Reception of Darwinism* (Chicago, 1988)

Gwynn, Dennis (ed.), *Walter McDonald: Reminiscences of a Maynooth Professor* (Cork, 1967)

Haldane, Richard B., *An Autobiography* (London, 1929)

Harkness, D. W., *Ireland in the Twentieth Century: Divided Island* (London, 1995)

Harris, Mary, *The Catholic Church and the Foundation of the Northern Irish State* (Cork, 1993)

Hart, Peter, *The IRA and its Enemies* (Oxford, 1998)

Hastings, James (ed.), *The Encyclopaedia of Religion and Ethics* (New York, 1921)

Healy, T. M., *Letters and Leaders of My Day* (London, 1928)

Hennessy, Thomas, *A History of Northern Ireland* (Dublin, 1997)

Hepburn, A. C., *A Past Apart: Studies in the History of Catholic Belfast, 1850–1950* (Belfast 1996)

Hobsbawm, Eric, *The Age of Empire, 1875–1914* (London, 2002)

Hodge, J., 'England', in Thomas F. Glick (ed.), *The Comparative Reception of Darwinism* (Chicago, 1988), pp. 3–31

Hopkinson, Michael, *Green Against Green: the Irish Civil War* (Dublin, 2004)

——, *The Irish War of Independence*, (Dublin, 2002)

——, (ed.), *The Last Days of Dublin Castle: the Diaries of Mark Sturgis* (Dublin, 1999)

——, 'The Craig-Collins Pacts of 1922: Two Attempted Reforms of the Northern Ireland Government', *Irish Historical Studies*, xxviii: 105 (May 1990), pp. 145–250

Hull, David L., *Darwin and His Critics: the Reception of Darwin's Theory of Evolution by the Scientific Community* (Cambridge, 1973)

Jackson, Alvin, *Ireland, 1798–1998: Politics and War* (Oxford, 1998)

Jeffery, Keith, *Ireland and the Great War* (Cambridge, 2000)

——, *The British Army and the Crisis of Empire* (Manchester, 1984)

Jeffery, Keith (ed), *An Irish Empire? Aspects of Ireland and the British Empire* (Manchester, 1996)

Jones, Greta, 'Darwinism in Ireland', in David Attis and Charles Mollan (eds), *Science and Irish Culture*, vol 1, Royal Dublin Society (Dublin, 2004), pp. 115–37

——, 'Scientists against Home Rule', in D. Boyce and A. O'Day, *Defenders of the Union* (London, 2001), pp. 188–205

——, 'Catholicism, Nationalism and Science', *Irish Review*, (Winter/Spring 1997), pp. 47–61

——, 'Eugenics in Ireland: the Belfast Eugenics Society, 1911–15', *Irish Historical Studie*, xxviii: 109 (May 1992), pp. 81–96

——, *Social Darwinism and English Thought: the Interaction Between Biological and Social Theory* (Brighton, 1980)

Kennedy, Liam, *Colonialism, Religion and Nationalism in Ireland* (Belfast, 1996)

Keogh, Dermot, *Ireland and the Vatican: The Politics and Diplomacy of Church-State Relations, 1922–60* (Cork, 1995)

——, *Twentieth-Century Ireland: Nation and State* (Dublin, 1994)

——, *The Vatican, the Bishops and Irish Politics, 1919–1939* (Cambridge, 1986)

Kissane, Bill, *The Politics of the Irish Civil War* (Oxford, 2005)

Laffan, Michael, *The Resurrection of Ireland: the Sinn Féin Party, 1916–23* (Cambridge, 1999)

Lane, Fintan, *The Origins of Modern Irish Socialism, 1881–96* (Cork, 1997)

Larkin, Emmett, *The Historical Dimensions of Irish Catholicism* (Washington, 1984)

——, *The Roman Catholic Church and the Fall of Parnell, 1888–91* (Liverpool, 1979)

——, *The Roman Catholic Church and the Plan of Campaign, 1886–88* (Cork, 1978)

——, *The Roman Catholic Church and the Creation of the Modern Irish State, 1878–86* (Dublin, 1975)

Lee, J. J., *Ireland 1912–85: Politics and Society* (Cambridge, 1989)

——, *The Modernisation of Irish Society, 1848–1918* (London, 1973)

Leonard, Jane, 'The Catholic Chaplaincy', in David Fitzpatrick (ed.), *Ireland and the First World War* (Dublin, 1986), pp. 1–14

Luce, J.V., *Trinity College Dublin: The First 400 Years* (Dublin, 1992)

Lyons. F. S. L., *Charles Stewart Parnell* (London, 1977)

——, *Ireland since the Famine* (London, 1972)

Macaulay, Ambrose, *The Holy See, British Policy and the Plan of Campaign in Ireland, 1885–93* (Dublin, 2002)

Maume, Patrick, *The Long Gestation: Irish Nationalist Life, 1891–1918* (Dublin, 1999)

McBride, Lawrence, W., *The Greening of Dublin Castle: the Transformation of Bureaucratic and Judicial Personnel in Ireland, 1892–1922* (Washington, 1991)

McDowell, R. B., *Trinity College Dublin 1592–1952: an Academic History* (Cambridge, 1982)

——, *The Irish Convention, 1917–18* (London, 1972)

Miller, David W., *Church, State and Nation in Ireland, 1898–1921* (Dublin, 1973)

Morrissey, Thomas J. (SJ), *William Walsh, Archbishop of Dublin, 1841–1921* (Dublin, 2000)

Norman, E. R., *A History of Modern Ireland* (London, 1971)

——, *Anti-Catholicism in Victorian England* (London, 1968)

——, *The Catholic Church in the Age of Rebellion* (London, 1965)

O'Callaghan, Edward, 'Letters and Papers of Archbishop Ignatio Persico, Papal Commissary to Ireland', *Collectanea Hibernica*, xxxiv/xxxv (1992–93), pp. 160–89; xxxvi/xxxvii (1994–95), pp. 271–303; xxxviii (1996), pp. 120–41

O'Connor, Emmet, *A Labour History of Ireland, 1824–1960* (Dublin, 1992)

O'Day, Alan, *Irish Home Rule, 1867–1921* (Manchester, 1998)

O'Donnell, E. E., *Father Browne: a Life in Pictures* (Dublin, 1994)

Pakenham, Frank (ed.), *Lord Longford: Peace by Ordeal* (London, 1972)

Parkes, Susan M., 'Higher Education, 1793 – 1908', in W. E. Vaughan (ed.), *A New History of Ireland* (Oxford, 1996), pp. 540–70

Parkinson, Alan F., *Belfast's Unholy War* (Dublin, 2004)

Paul, Harry W., 'Religion and Darwinism: Varieties of Catholic Reaction', in Thomas F. Glick (ed.), *The Comparative Reception of Darwinism*' (Chicago, 1988), pp. 403–37

——, *The Edge of Contingency: French Catholic Reaction to Scientific Change from Darwin to Duhan* (Gainsville, Florida, 1979)

Phoenix, Eamon, *Northern Nationalism: Nationalist Politics, Partition and the Catholic Minority in Northern Ireland, 1890–1940* (Belfast, 1994)

Rafferty, Oliver, *Catholicism in Ulster, 1603–1983: an Interpretive History* (London, 1994)

Ranchetti, Michelle, *The Catholic Modernists* (London, 1969)

Regan, John M., *The Irish Counter-Revolution, 1921–36: Treatyite Politics and Settlement in Independent Ireland* (Dublin, 2002)

Thomson, David, *Europe since Napoleon* (London, 1966)

Townshend, Charles, *Ireland: the Twentieth Century* (London, 1999)

——, *Political Violence in Ireland: Government and Resistance since 1848* (Oxford, 1983)

——, *The British Campaign in Ireland, 1919–21: the Development of Political and Military Policies* (Oxford, 1975)

Vaughan, W. E., *Landlords and Tenants in Mid-Victorian Ireland*, (Oxford, 1994)

——, (ed.), *Irish Historical Statistics, 1821–1971* (Dublin, 1978)

Walsh, Aisling, 'Michael Cardinal Logue, 1840–1924', *Seanchas Ard Macha*, xvii (1996–7) 1, pp. 108–115; 2, pp. 163–95

Walsh, Patrick, J., *William Walsh, Archbishop of Dublin* (Dublin, 1928)

Whyte, John, H., *Church and State in Modern Ireland, 1923–79* (Dublin, 1980)

Yeates, Padraig, *Lockout: Dublin, 1913* (Dublin, 2000)

Index